What readers are saying about
The Definitive ANTLR Reference

Over the past few years ANTLR has proven itself as a solid parser generator. This book is a fine guide to making the best use of it.

► **Martin Fowler**
Chief Scientist, ThoughtWorks

The Definitive ANTLR Reference deserves a place in the bookshelf of anyone who ever has to parse or translate text. ANTLR is not just for language designers anymore.

► **Bob McWhirter**
Founder of the JBoss Rules Project (a.k.a. Drools), JBoss.org

Over the course of a career, developers move through a few stages of sophistication: becoming effective with a single programming language, learning which of several programming languages to use, and finally learning to tailor the language to the task at hand. This approach was previously reserved for those with an education in compiler development. Now, *The Definitive ANTLR Reference* reveals that it doesn't take a PhD to develop your own domain-specific languages, and you would be surprised how often it is worth doing. Take the next step in your career, and buy this book.

► **Neal Gafter**
Java Evangelist and Compiler Guru, Google (formerly at Sun Microsystems)

This book, especially the first section, really gave me a much better understanding of the principles of language recognition as a whole. I recommend this book to anyone without a background in language recognition looking to start using ANTLR or trying to understand the concept of language recognition.

► **Steve Ebersole**
Hibernate Lead Developer, Hibernate.org

Eclipse IDE users have become accustomed to cool features such as single-click navigation between symbol references and declarations, not to mention intelligent content assist. ANTLR v3 with its *LL(*)* parsing algorithm will help you immensely in building highly complex parsers to support these features. This book is a critical resource for Eclipse developers and others who want to take full advantage of the power of the new features in ANTLR.

▶ **Doug Schaefer**
Eclipse CDT Project Lead, Tools PMC Member, QNX Software Systems

Terence's new book is an excellent guide to ANTLR v3. It is very well written, with both the student and the developer in mind. The book does not assume compiler design experience. It provides the necessary background, from a pragmatic rather than a theoretical perspective, and it then eases the new user, whether someone with previous compiler design experience or not, into the use of the ANTLR tools. I recommend this book highly for anyone who needs to incorporate language capabilities into their software design.

▶ **Jesse Grodnik**
Software Development Manager, Sun Microsystems, Inc.

ANTLR v3 and *The Definitive ANTLR Reference* present a compelling package: an intuitive tool that handles complex recognition and translation tasks with ease and a clear book detailing how to get the most from it. The book provides an in-depth account of language translation utilizing the new powerful *LL(*)* parsing strategy. If you're developing translators, you can't afford to ignore this book!

▶ **Dermot O'Neill**
Senior Developer, Oracle Corporation

Whether you are a compiler newbie itching to write your own language or a jaded YACC veteran tired of shift-reduce conflicts, keep this book by your side. It is at once a tutorial, a reference, and an insider's viewpoint.

▶ **Sriram Srinivasan**
Formerly Principal Engineer, BEA/WebLogic

The Definitive ANTLR Reference

Building Domain-Specific Languages

The Definitive ANTLR Reference
Building Domain-Specific Languages

Terence Parr

The Pragmatic Bookshelf
Raleigh, North Carolina   Dallas, Texas

Our Pragmatic courses, workshops, and other products can help you and your team create better software and have more fun. For more information, as well as the latest Pragmatic titles, please visit us at

http://www.pragmaticprogrammer.com

ISBN-10: 0-9787392-5-6

ISBN-13: 978-09787392-5-6

Printed on acid-free paper with 85% recycled, 30% post-consumer content.

P2.0 printing, August 2007

Version: 2007-7-29

This is Tom's fault.

Contents

Acknowledgments

A researcher once told me after a talk I had given that "It was clear there was a single mind behind these tools." In reality, there are many minds behind the ideas in my language tools and research, though I'm a benevolent dictator with specific opinions about how ANTLR should work. At the least, dozens of people let me bounce ideas off them, and I get a lot of great ideas from the people on the ANTLR interest list.[1]

Concerning the ANTLR v3 tool, I want to acknowledge the following contributors for helping with the design and functional requirements: Sriram Srinivasan (Sriram had a knack for finding holes in my *LL(*)* algorithm), Loring Craymer, Monty Zukowski, John Mitchell, Ric Klaren, Jean Bovet, and Kay Roepke. Matt Benson converted all my unit tests to use JUnit and is a big help with Ant files and other goodies. Juergen Pfundt contributed the ANTLR v3 task for Ant. I sing Jean Bovet's praises every day for his wonderful ANTLRWorks grammar development environment. Next comes the troop of hardworking ANTLR language target authors, most of whom contribute ideas regularly to ANTLR:[2] Jim Idle, Michael Jordan (no not that one), Ric Klaren, Benjamin Niemann, Kunle Odutola, Kay Roepke, and Martin Traverso.

I also want to thank (then Purdue) professors Hank Dietz and Russell Quong for their support early in my career. Russell also played a key role in designing the semantic and syntactic predicates mechanism.

The following humans provided technical reviews: Mark Bednarczyk, John Mitchell, Dermot O'Neill, Karl Pfalzer, Kay Roepke, Sriram Srinivasan, Bill Venners, and Oliver Ziegermann. John Snyders, Jeff Wilcox, and Kevin Ruland deserve special attention for their amazingly detailed feedback. Finally, I want to mention my excellent development editor Susannah Davidson Pfalzer. She made this a much better book.

---

1. See http://www.antlr.org:8080/pipermail/antlr-interest/.
2. See http://www.antlr.org/wiki/display/ANTLR3/Code+Generation+Targets.

Preface

In August 1993, I finished school and drove my overloaded moving van to Minnesota to start working. My office mate was a curmudgeonly astrophysicist named Kevin, who has since become a good friend. Kevin has told me on multiple occasions that only physicists do real work and that programmers merely support physicists. Because all I do is build language tools to support programmers, I am at least two levels of indirection away from doing anything useful.[3] Now, Kevin also claims that Fortran 77 is a good enough language for anybody and, for that matter, that Fortran 66 is probably sufficient, so one might question his judgment. But, concerning my usefulness, he was right—I am fundamentally lazy and would much rather work on something that made other people productive than actually do anything useful myself. This attitude has led to my guiding principle:[4]

Why program by hand in five days what you can spend five years of your life automating?

Here's the point: The first time you encounter a problem, writing a formal, general, and automatic mechanism is expensive and is usually overkill. From then on, though, you are much faster and better at solving similar problems because of your automated tool. Building tools can also be much more fun than your real job. Now that I'm a professor, I have the luxury of avoiding real work for a living.

---

3. The irony is that, as Kevin will proudly tell you, he actually played solitaire for at least a decade instead of doing research for his boss—well, when he wasn't scowling at the other researchers, at least. He claimed to have a winning streak stretching into the many thousands, but one day Kevin was caught overwriting the game log file to erase a loss (apparently per his usual habit). A holiday was called, and much revelry ensued.

4. Even as a young boy, I was fascinated with automation. I can remember endlessly building model ships and then trying to motorize them so that they would move around automatically. Naturally, I proceeded to blow them out of the water with firecrackers and rockets, but that's a separate issue.

My passion for the last two decades has been ANTLR, ANother Tool for Language Recognition. ANTLR is a parser generator that automates the construction of language recognizers. It is a program that writes other programs.

From a formal language description, ANTLR generates a program that determines whether sentences conform to that language. By adding code snippets to the grammar, the recognizer becomes a translator. The code snippets compute output phrases based upon computations on input phrases. ANTLR is suitable for the simplest and the most complicated language recognition and translation problems. With each new release, ANTLR becomes more sophisticated and easier to use. ANTLR is extremely popular with 5,000 downloads a month and is included on all Linux and OS X distributions. It is widely used because it:

- Generates human-readable code that is easy to fold into other applications
- Generates powerful recursive-descent recognizers using *LL(*)*, an extension to *LL(k)* that uses arbitrary lookahead to make decisions
- Tightly integrates StringTemplate,[5] a template engine specifically designed to generate structured text such as source code
- Has a graphical grammar development environment called ANTLRWorks[6] that can debug parsers generated in any ANTLR target language
- Is actively supported with a good project website and a high-traffic mailing list[7]
- Comes with complete source under the BSD license
- Is extremely flexible and automates or formalizes many common tasks
- Supports multiple target languages such as Java, C#, Python, Ruby, Objective-C, C, and C++

Perhaps most importantly, ANTLR is much easier to understand and use than many other parser generators. It generates essentially what you would write by hand when building a recognizer and uses technology that mimics how your brain generates and recognizes language (see Chapter 2, *The Nature of Computer Languages*, on page 17).

---

5. See http://www.stringtemplate.org.
6. See http://www.antlr.org/works.
7. See http://www.antlr.org:8080/pipermail/antlr-interest/.

You generate and recognize sentences by walking their implicit tree structure, from the most abstract concept at the root to the vocabulary symbols at the leaves. Each subtree represents a phrase of a sentence and maps directly to a rule in your grammar. ANTLR's grammars and resulting top-down recursive-descent recognizers thus feel very natural. ANTLR's fundamental approach dovetails your innate language process.

Why a Completely New Version of ANTLR?

For the past four years, I have been working feverishly to design and build ANTLR v3, the subject of this book. ANTLR v3 is a completely rewritten version and represents the culmination of twenty years of language research. Most ANTLR users will instantly find it familiar, but many of the details are different. ANTLR retains its strong mojo in this new version while correcting a number of deficiencies, quirks, and weaknesses of ANTLR v2 (I felt free to break backward compatibility in order to achieve this). Specifically, I didn't like the following about v2:[8]

- The v2 lexers were very slow albeit powerful.
- There were no unit tests for v2.
- The v2 code base was impenetrable. The code was never refactored to clean it up, partially for fear of breaking it without unit tests.
- The linear approximate *LL(k)* parsing strategy was a bit weak.
- Building a new language target duplicated vast swaths of logic and print statements.
- The AST construction mechanism was too informal.
- A number of common tasks were not easy (such as obtaining the text matched by a parser rule).
- It lacked the semantic predicates hoisting of ANTLR v1 (PCCTS).
- The v2 license/contributor trail was loose and made big companies afraid to use it.

ANTLR v3 is my answer to the issues in v2. ANTLR v3 has a very clean and well-organized code base with lots of unit tests. ANTLR generates extremely powerful *LL(*)* recognizers that are fast and easy to read.

---

8. See http://www.antlr.org/blog/antlr3/antlr2.bashing.tml for notes on what people did not like about v2. ANTLR v2 also suffered because it was designed and built while I was under the workload and stress of a new start-up (jGuru.com).

Many common tasks are now easy by default. For example, reading in some input, tweaking it, and writing it back out while preserving whitespace is easy. ANTLR v3 also reintroduces semantic predicates hoisting. ANTLR's license is now BSD, and all contributors must sign a "certificate of origin."[9] ANTLR v3 provides significant functionality beyond v2 as well:

- Powerful *LL(*)* parsing strategy that supports more natural grammars and makes it easier to build them

- Auto-backtracking mode that shuts off all grammar analysis warnings, forcing the generated parser to simply figure things out at runtime

- Partial parsing result memoization to guarantee linear time complexity during backtracking at the cost of some memory

- Jean Bovet's ANTLRWorks GUI grammar development environment

- StringTemplate template engine integration that makes generating structured text such as source code easy

- Formal AST construction rules that map input grammar alternatives to tree grammar fragments, making actions that manually construct ASTs no longer necessary

- Dynamically scoped attributes that allow distant rules to communicate

- Improved error reporting and recovery for generated recognizers

- Truly retargetable code generator; building a new target is a matter of defining StringTemplate templates that tell ANTLR how to generate grammar elements such as rule and token references

This book also provides a serious advantage to v3 over v2. Professionally edited and complete documentation is a big deal to developers. You can find more information about the history of ANTLR and its contributions to parsing theory on the ANTLR website.[10,11]

Look for *Improved in v3* and *New in v3* notes in the margin that highlight improvements or additions to v2.

---

9. See http://www.antlr.org/license.html.
10. See http://www.antlr.org/history.html.
11. See http://www.antlr.org/contributions.html.

Who Is This Book For?

The primary audience for this book is the practicing software developer, though it is suitable for junior and senior computer science under-graduates. This book is specifically targeted at any programmer interested in learning to use ANTLR to build interpreters and translators for domain-specific languages. Beginners and experts alike will need this book to use ANTLR v3 effectively. For the most part, the level of discussion is accessible to the average programmer. Portions of Part III, however, require some language experience to fully appreciate. Although the examples in this book are written in Java, their substance applies equally well to the other language targets such as C, C++, Objective-C, Python, C#, and so on. Readers should know Java to get the most out of the book.

What's in This Book?

This book is the best, most complete source of information on ANTLR v3 that you'll find anywhere. The free, online documentation provides enough to learn the basic grammar syntax and semantics but doesn't explain ANTLR concepts in detail. This book helps you get the most out of ANTLR and is required reading to become an advanced user. In particular, Part III provides the only thorough explanation available anywhere of ANTLR's *LL(*)* parsing strategy.

This book is organized as follows. Part I introduces ANTLR, describes how the nature of computer languages dictates the nature of language recognizers, and provides a complete calculator example. Part II is the main reference section and provides all the details you'll need to build large and complex grammars and translators. Part III treks through ANTLR's predicated-*LL(*)* parsing strategy and explains the grammar analysis errors you might encounter. Predicated-*LL(*)* is a totally new parsing strategy, and Part III is essentially the only written documentation you'll find for it. You'll need to be familiar with the contents in order to build complicated translators.

Readers who are totally new to grammars and language tools should follow the chapter sequence in Part I as is. Chapter 1, *Getting Started with ANTLR*, on page 3 will familiarize you with ANTLR's basic idea; Chapter 2, *The Nature of Computer Languages*, on page 17 gets you ready to study grammars more formally in Part II; and Chapter 3, *A Quick Tour for the Impatient*, on page 43 gives your brain something concrete to consider. Familiarize yourself with the ANTLR details in Part II, but I suggest trying to modify an existing grammar as soon as you can. After you become comfortable with ANTLR's functionality, you can attempt your own translator from scratch. When you get grammar analysis errors from ANTLR that you don't understand, then you need to dive into Part III to learn more about *LL(*)*.

Those readers familiar with ANTLR v2 should probably skip directly to Chapter 3, *A Quick Tour for the Impatient*, on page 43 to figure out how v3 differs. Chapter 4, *ANTLR Grammars*, on page 71 is also a good place to look for features that v3 changes or improves on.

If you are familiar with an older tool, such as YACC [Joh79], I recommend starting from the beginning of the book as if you were totally new to grammars and language tools. If you're used to JavaCC[12] or another top-down parser generator, you can probably skip Chapter 2, *The Nature of Computer Languages*, on page 17, though it is one of my favorite chapters.

I hope you enjoy this book and ANTLR v3 as much as I have enjoyed writing them!

Terence Parr
March 2007
University of San Francisco

---

12. See https://javacc.dev.java.net.

Part I

Introducing ANTLR and Computer Language Translation

Chapter 1

Getting Started with ANTLR

This is a reference guide for ANTLR: a sophisticated parser generator you can use to implement language interpreters, compilers, and other translators. This is not a compiler book, and it is not a language theory textbook. Although you can find many good books about compilers and their theoretical foundations, the vast majority of language applications are not compilers. This book is more directly useful and practical for building common, everyday language applications. It is densely packed with examples, explanations, and reference material focused on a single language tool and methodology.

Programmers most often use ANTLR to build translators and interpreters for *domain-specific languages* (DSLs). DSLs are generally very high-level languages tailored to specific tasks. They are designed to make their users particularly effective in a specific domain. DSLs include a wide range of applications, many of which you might not consider languages. DSLs include data formats, configuration file formats, network protocols, text-processing languages, protein patterns, gene sequences, space probe control languages, and domain-specific programming languages.

DSLs are particularly important to software development because they represent a more natural, high-fidelity, robust, and maintainable means of encoding a problem than simply writing software in a general-purpose language. For example, NASA uses domain-specific command languages for space missions to improve reliability, reduce risk, reduce cost, and increase the speed of development. Even the first Apollo guidance control computer from the 1960s used a DSL that supported vector computations.[1]

---

1. See http://www.ibiblio.org/apollo/assembly_language_manual.html.

This chapter introduces the main ANTLR components and explains how they all fit together. You'll see how the overall DSL translation problem easily factors into multiple, smaller problems. These smaller problems map to well-defined translation phases (lexing, parsing, and tree parsing) that communicate using well-defined data types and structures (characters, tokens, trees, and ancillary structures such as symbol tables). After this chapter, you'll be broadly familiar with all translator components and will be ready to tackle the detailed discussions in subsequent chapters. Let's start with the big picture.

1.1 The Big Picture

A translator maps each input sentence of a language to an output sentence. To perform the mapping, the translator executes some code you provide that operates on the input symbols and emits some output. A translator must perform different actions for different sentences, which means it must be able to recognize the various sentences.

Recognition is much easier if you break it into two similar but distinct tasks or phases. The separate phases mirror how your brain reads English text. You don't read a sentence character by character. Instead, you perceive a sentence as a stream of words. The human brain subconsciously groups character sequences into words and looks them up in a dictionary before recognizing grammatical structure. The first translation phase is called *lexical analysis* and operates on the incoming character stream. The second phase is called *parsing* and operates on a stream of vocabulary symbols, called *tokens*, emanating from the lexical analyzer. ANTLR automatically generates the lexical analyzer and parser for you by analyzing the grammar you provide.

Performing a translation often means just embedding *actions* (code) within the grammar. ANTLR executes an action according to its position within the grammar. In this way, you can execute different code for different phrases (sentence fragments). For example, an action within, say, an expression rule is executed only when the parser is recognizing an expression.

Some translations should be broken down into even more phases. Often the translation requires multiple passes, and in other cases, the translation is just a heck of a lot easier to code in multiple phases. Rather than reparse the input characters for each phase, it is more convenient to construct an intermediate form to pass between phases.

Language Translation Can Help You Avoid Work

In 1988, I worked in Paris for a robotics company. At the time, the company had a fairly demanding coding standard that required very formal and structured comments on each C function and file.

After finishing my compiler project, I was ready to head back to the United States and continue with my graduate studies. Unfortunately, the company was withholding my bonus until I followed its coding standard. The standard required all sorts of tedious information such as which functions were called in each function, the list of parameters, list of local variables, which functions existed in this file, and so on. As the company dangled the bonus check in front me, I blurted out, "All of that can be automatically generated!" Something clicked in my mind. Of course. Build a quick C parser that is capable of reading all my source code and generating the appropriate comments. I would have to go back and enter the written descriptions, but my translator would do the rest.

I built a parser by hand (this was right before I started working on ANTLR) and created template files for the various documentation standards. There were holes that my parser could fill in with parameters, variable lists, and so on. It took me two days to build the translator. I started it up, went to lunch, and came back to commented source code. I quickly entered the necessary descriptions, collected my bonus, and flew back to Purdue University with a smirk on my face.

The point is that knowing about computer languages and language technology such as ANTLR will make your coding life much easier. Don't be afraid to build a human-readable configuration file (I implore everyone to please stop using XML as a human interface!) or to build domain-specific languages to make yourself more efficient. Designing new languages and building translators for existing languages, when appropriate, is the hallmark of a sophisticated developer.

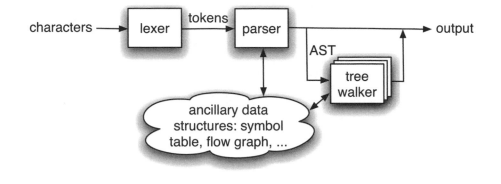

Figure 1.1: OVERALL TRANSLATION DATA FLOW; EDGES REPRESENT DATA STRUCTURE FLOW, AND SQUARES REPRESENT TRANSLATION PHASES

This intermediate form is usually a tree data structure, called an *abstract syntax tree* (AST), and is a highly processed, condensed version of the input. Each phase collects more information or performs more computations. A final phase, called the *emitter*, ultimately emits output using all the data structures and computations from previous phases.

Figure 1.1 illustrates the basic data flow of a translator that accepts characters and emits output. The lexical analyzer, or *lexer*, breaks up the input stream into tokens. The parser feeds off this token stream and tries to recognize the sentence structure. The simplest translators execute actions that immediately emit output, bypassing any further phases.

Another kind of simple translator just constructs an internal data structure—it doesn't actually emit output. A configuration file reader is the best example of this kind of translator. More complicated translators use the parser only to construct ASTs. Multiple *tree parsers* (depth-first tree walkers) then scramble over the ASTs, computing other data structures and information needed by future phases. Although it is not shown in this figure, the final emitter phase can use templates to generate structured text output.

A template is just a text document with holes in it that an emitter can fill with values. These holes can also be expressions that operate on the incoming data values. ANTLR formally integrates the StringTemplate engine to make it easier for you to build emitters (see Chapter 9, *Generating Structured Text with Templates and Grammars*, on page 195).

StringTemplate is a domain-specific language for generating structured text from internal data structures that has the flavor of an output grammar. Features include template group inheritance, template polymorphism, lazy evaluation, recursion, output autoindentation, and the new notions of group interfaces and template regions.[2] StringTemplate's feature set is driven by solving real problems encountered in complicated systems. Indeed, ANTLR makes heavy use of StringTemplate to translate grammars to executable recognizers. Each ANTLR language target is purely a set of templates and fed by ANTLR's internal retargetable code generator.

Now, let's take a closer look at the data objects passed between the various phases in Figure 1.1, on the preceding page. Figure 1.2, on the following page, illustrates the relationship between characters, tokens, and ASTs. Lexers feed off characters provided by a CharStream such as ANTLRStringStream or ANTLRFileStream. These predefined streams assume that the entire input will fit into memory and, consequently, buffer up all characters. Rather than creating a separate string object per token, tokens can more efficiently track indexes into the character buffer.

Similarly, rather than copying data from tokens into tree nodes, ANTLR AST nodes can simply point at the token from which they were created. CommonTree, for example, is a predefined node containing a Token *payload*. The type of an ANTLR AST node is treated as an Object so that there are no restrictions whatsoever on your tree data types. In fact, you can even make your Token objects double as AST nodes to avoid extra object instantiations. The relationship between the data types described in Figure 1.2, on the next page, is very efficient and flexible.

The tokens in the figure with checkboxes reside on a hidden *channel* that the parser does not see. The parser *tunes* to a single channel and, hence, ignores tokens on any other channel. With a simple action in the lexer, you can send different tokens to the parser on different channels. For example, you might want whitespace and regular comments on one channel and Javadoc comments on another when parsing Java. The token buffer preserves the relative token order regardless of the token channel numbers. The token channel mechanism is an elegant solution to the problem of ignoring but not throwing away whitespace and comments (some translators need to preserve formatting and comments).

---

2. Please see http://www.stringtemplate.org for more details. I mention these terms to entice readers to learn more about StringTemplate.

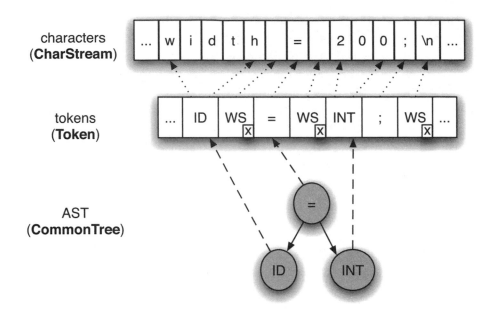

Figure 1.2: RELATIONSHIP BETWEEN CHARACTERS, TOKENS, AND ASTS; CHARSTREAM, TOKEN, AND COMMONTREE ARE ANTLR RUNTIME TYPES

As you work through the examples and discussions later in this book, it may help to keep in mind the analogy described in the next section.

1.2 An A-mazing Analogy

This book focuses primarily on two topics: the discovery of the implicit tree structure behind input sentences and the generation of structured text. At first glance, some of the language terminology and technology in this book will be unfamiliar. Don't worry. I'll define and explain everything, but it helps to keep in mind a simple analogy as you read.

Imagine a maze with a single entrance and single exit that has words written on the floor. Every path from entrance to exit generates a sentence by "saying" the words in sequence. In a sense, the maze is analogous to a grammar that defines a language.

You can also think of a maze as a sentence recognizer. Given a sentence, you can match its words in sequence with the words along the floor. Any sentence that successfully guides you to the exit is a valid sentence (a *passphrase*) in the language defined by the maze.

Language recognizers must discover a sentence's implicit tree structure piecemeal, one word at a time. At almost every word, the recognizer must make a decision about the interpretation of a phrase or subphrase. Sometimes these decisions are very complicated. For example, some decisions require information about previous decision choices or even future choices. Most of the time, however, decisions need just a little bit of *lookahead* information. Lookahead information is analogous to the first word or words down each path that you can see from a given fork in the maze. At a fork, the next words in your input sentence will tell you which path to take because the words along each path are different. Chapter 2, *The Nature of Computer Languages*, on page 17 describes the nature of computer languages in more detail using this analogy. You can either read that chapter first or move immediately to the quick ANTLR tour in Chapter 3, *A Quick Tour for the Impatient*, on page 43.

In the next two sections, you'll see how to map the big picture diagram in Figure 1.1, on page 6, into Java code and also learn how to execute ANTLR.

1.3 Installing ANTLR

ANTLR is written in Java, so you must have Java installed on your machine even if you are going to use ANTLR with, say, Python. ANTLR requires a Java version of 1.4 or higher. Before you can run ANTLR on your grammar, you must install ANTLR by downloading it[3] and extracting it into an appropriate directory. You do not need to run a configuration script or alter an ANTLR configuration file to properly install ANTLR. If you want to install ANTLR in /usr/local/antlr-3.0, do the following:

```
$ cd /usr/local
$ tar xvfz antlr-3.0.tar.gz
antlr-3.0/
antlr-3.0/build/
antlr-3.0/build.properties
antlr-3.0/build.xml
antlr-3.0/lib/
antlr-3.0/lib/antlr-3.0.jar
...
$
```

---

3. See http://www.antlr.org/download.html.

As of 3.0, ANTLR v3 is still written in the previous version of ANTLR, 2.7.7, and with StringTemplate 3.0. This means you need both of those libraries to run the ANTLR v3 tool. You do not need the ANTLR 2.7.7 JAR to run your generated parser, and you do not need the StringTemplate JAR to run your parser unless you use template construction rules. (See Chapter 9, *Generating Structured Text with Templates and Grammars*, on page 195.) Java scans the CLASSPATH environment variable looking for JAR files and directories containing Java .class files. You must update your CLASSPATH to include the antlr-2.7.7.jar, stringtemplate-3.0.jar, and antlr-3.0.jar libraries.

Just about the only thing that can go wrong with installation is setting your CLASSPATH improperly or having another version of ANTLR in the CLASSPATH. Note that some of your other Java libraries might use ANTLR (such as BEA's WebLogic) without your knowledge.

To set the CLASSPATH on Mac OS X or any other Unix-flavored box with the **bash** shell, you can do the following:

```
$ export CLASSPATH="$CLASSPATH:/usr/local/antlr-3.0/lib/antlr-3.0.jar:\
/usr/local/antlr-3.0/lib/stringtemplate-3.0.jar:\
/usr/local/antlr-3.0/lib/antlr-2.7.7.jar"
$
```

Don't forget the export. Without this, subprocesses you launch such as Java will not see the environment variable.

To set the CLASSPATH on Microsoft Windows XP, you'll have to set the environment variable using the System control panel in the Advanced subpanel. Click Environment Variables, and then click New in the top variable list. Also note that the path separator is a semicolon (;), not a colon (:), for Windows.

At this point, ANTLR should be ready to run. The next section provides a simple grammar you can use to check whether you have installed ANTLR properly.

1.4 Executing ANTLR and Invoking Recognizers

Once you have installed ANTLR, you can use it to translate grammars to executable Java code. Here is a sample grammar:

Introduction/T.g

```
grammar T;
/** Match things like "call foo;" */
r : 'call' ID ';' {System.out.println("invoke "+$ID.text);} ;
ID: 'a'..'z'+ ;
WS: (' '|'\n'|'\r')+    {$channel=HIDDEN;} ; // ignore whitespace
```

Java class Tool in package org.antlr contains the main program, so you execute ANTLR on grammar file T.g as follows:

```
$ java org.antlr.Tool T.g
ANTLR Parser Generator   Version 3.0   1989-2007
$ ls
T.g             TLexer.java     T__.g
T.tokens        TParser.java
$
```

As you can see, ANTLR generates a number of support files as well as the lexer, TLexer.java, and the parser, TParser.java, in the current directory.

To test the grammar, you'll need a main program that invokes start rule **r** from the grammar and reads from standard input. Here is program Test.java that embodies part of the data flow shown in Figure 1.1, on page 6:

Introduction/Test.java

```
import org.antlr.runtime.*;

public class Test {
    public static void main(String[] args) throws Exception {
        // create a CharStream that reads from standard input
        ANTLRInputStream input = new ANTLRInputStream(System.in);

        // create a lexer that feeds off of input CharStream
        TLexer lexer = new TLexer(input);

        // create a buffer of tokens pulled from the lexer
        CommonTokenStream tokens = new CommonTokenStream(lexer);

        // create a parser that feeds off the tokens buffer
        TParser parser = new TParser(tokens);
        // begin parsing at rule r
        parser.r();
    }
}
```

> ### What's Available at the ANTLR Website?
>
> At the http://www.antlr.org website, you will find a great deal of information and support for ANTLR. The site contains the ANTLR download, the ANTLRWorks graphical user interface (GUI) development environment, the ANTLR documentation, prebuilt grammars, examples, articles, a file-sharing area, the tech support mailing list, the wiki, and much more.

To compile everything and run the test rig, do the following (don't type the $ symbol—that's the command prompt):

```
⇐   $ javac TLexer.java TParser.java Test.java
⇐   $ java Test
⇐   call foo;
⇐   EOF
⇒   invoke foo
    $
```

In response to input call foo; followed by the newline, the translator emits invoke foo followed by the newline. Note that you must type the end-of-file character to terminate reading from standard input; otherwise, the program will stare at you for eternity.

This simple example does not include any ancillary data structures or intermediate-form trees. The embedded grammar action directly emits output invoke foo. See Chapter 7, *Tree Construction*, on page 149 and Chapter 8, *Tree Grammars*, on page 179 for a number of test rig examples that instantiate and launch tree walkers.

Before you begin developing a grammar, you should become familiar with ANTLRWorks, the subject of the next section. This ANTLR GUI will make your life much easier when building or debugging grammars.

1.5 ANTLRWorks Grammar Development Environment

ANTLRWorks is a GUI development environment written by Jean Bovet[4] that sits on top of ANTLR and helps you edit, navigate, and debug

---

4. See http://www.antlr.org/works. Bovet is the developer of ANTLRWorks, with some functional requirements from me. He began development during his master's degree at the University of San Francisco but is continuing to develop the tool.

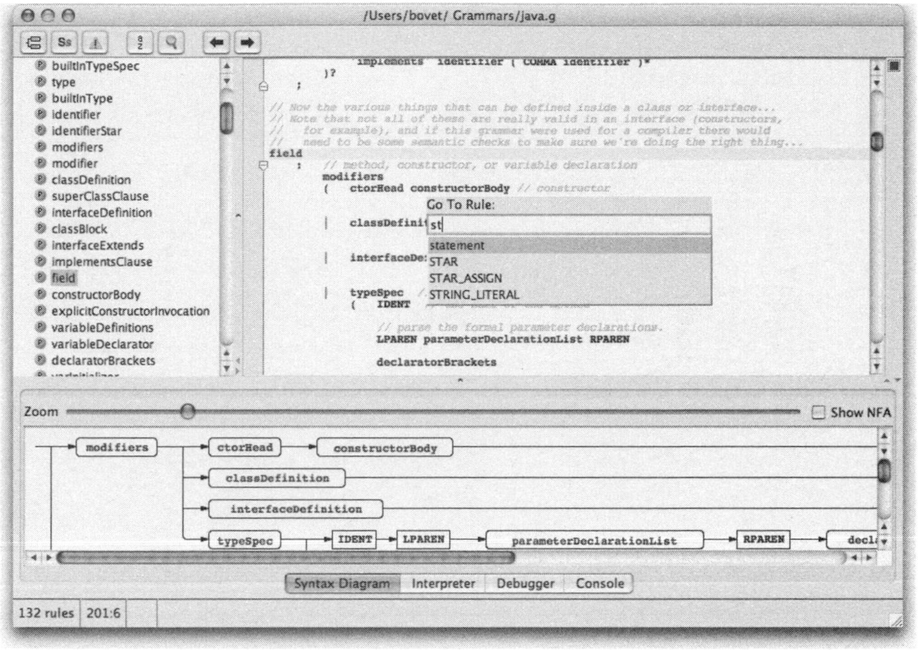

Figure 1.3: ANTLRWORKS GRAMMAR DEVELOPMENT ENVIRONMENT; GRAMMAR EDITOR VIEW

grammars. Perhaps most important, ANTLRWorks helps you resolve grammar analysis errors, which can be tricky to figure out manually. ANTLRWorks currently has the following main features:

- Grammar-aware editor

- Syntax diagram grammar view

- Interpreter for rapid prototyping

- Language-agnostic debugger for isolating grammar errors

- Nondeterministic path highlighter for the syntax diagram view

- Decision lookahead (DFA) visualization

- Refactoring patterns for many common operations such as "remove left-recursion" and "in-line rule"

- Dynamic parse tree view

- Dynamic AST view

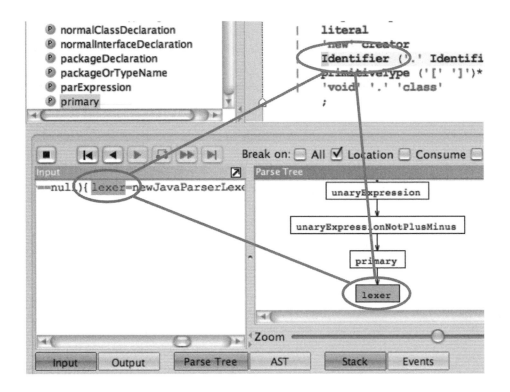

Figure 1.4: ANTLRWORKS DEBUGGER WHILE PARSING JAVA CODE; THE INPUT, PARSE TREE, AND GRAMMAR ARE SYNCHED AT ALL TIMES

ANTLRWorks is written entirely in highly portable Java (using Swing) and is available as open source under the BSD license. Because ANTLR-Works communicates with running parsers via sockets, the ANTLR-Works debugger works with any ANTLR language target (assuming that the target runtime library has the necessary support code). At this point, ANTLRWorks has a prototype plug-in for IntelliJ[5] but nothing yet for Eclipse.

Figure 1.3, on the previous page, shows ANTLRWorks' editor in action with the Go To Rule pop-up dialog box. As you would expect, ANTLR-Works has the usual rule and token name autocompletion as well as syntax highlighting. The lower pane shows the syntax diagram for rule **field** from a Java grammar. When you have ambiguities in other non-

---

5. See http://plugins.intellij.net/plugin/?id=953.

determinisms in your grammar, the syntax diagram shows the multiple paths that can recognize the same input. From this visualization, you will find it straightforward to resolve the nondeterminisms. Part III of this book discusses ANTLR's $LL(*)$ parsing strategy in detail and makes extensive use of the ambiguous path displays provided by ANTLRWorks.

Figure 1.4, on the facing page, illustrates ANTLRWorks' debugger. The debugger provides a wealth of information and, as you can see, always keeps the various views in sync. In this case, the grammar matches input identifier lexer with grammar element **Identifier**; the parse tree pane shows the implicit tree structure of the input. For more information about ANTLRWorks, please see the user guide.[6]

This introduction gave you an overall view of what ANTLR does and how to use it. The next chapter illustrates how the nature of language leads to the use of grammars for language specification. The final chapter in Part I—Chapter 3, *A Quick Tour for the Impatient*, on page 43—demonstrates more of ANTLR's features by showing you how to build a calculator.

---

6. See http://www.antlr.org/works/help/index.html.

Chapter 2

The Nature of
Computer Languages

This book is about building translators with ANTLR rather than resorting to informal, arbitrary code. Building translators with ANTLR requires you to use a formal language specification called a *grammar*. To understand grammars and to understand their capabilities and limitations, you need to learn about the nature of computer languages. As you might expect, the nature of computer languages dictates the way you specify languages with grammars.

The whole point of writing a grammar is so ANTLR can automatically build a program for you that recognizes sentences in that language. Unfortunately, starting the learning process with grammars and language recognition is difficult (from my own experience and from the questions I get from ANTLR users). The purpose of this chapter is to teach you first about language generation and then, at the very end, to describe language recognition. Your brain understands language generation very well, and recognition is the dual of generation. Once you understand language generation, learning about grammars and language recognition is straightforward.

Here is the central question you must address concerning generation: how can you write a stream of words that transmits information beyond a simple list of items? In English, for example, how can a stream of words convey ideas about time, geometry, and why people don't use turn signals? It all boils down to the fact that sentences are not just clever sequences of words, as Steven Pinker points out in *The Language Instinct* [Pin94]. The implicit structure of the sentence, not just

> **Example Demonstrating That Structure Imparts Meaning**
>
> Humans are hardwired to recognize the implicit structure within a sentence (a linear sequence of words). Consider this English sentence:
>
> "Terence says Sriram likes chicken tikka."
>
> The sentence's subject is "Terence," and the verb is "says." Now, interpret the sentence differently using "likes" as the verb:
>
> "Terence, says Sriram, likes chicken tikka."
>
> The commas alter the sentence structure in the same way that parentheses alter operator precedence in expressions. The key observation is that the same sequence of words means two different things depending on the structure you assume.

the words and the sequence, imparts the meaning. What exactly is sentence structure? Unfortunately, the answer requires some background to answer properly. On the bright side, the search for a precise definition unveils some important concepts, terminology, and language technology along the way. In this chapter, we'll cover the following topics:

- State machines (DFAs)
- Sentence word order and dependencies that govern complex language generation
- Sentence tree structure
- Pushdown machines (syntax diagrams)
- Language ambiguities
- Lexical phrase structure
- What we mean by "recognizing a sentence"

Let's begin by demonstrating that generating sentences is not as simple as picking appropriate words in a sequence.

2.1 Generating Sentences with State Machines

When I was a suffering undergraduate student at Purdue University (back before GUIs), I ran across a sophisticated documentation generator that automatically produced verbose, formal-sounding manuals. You could read about half a paragraph before your mind said, "Whoa!

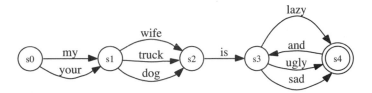

Figure 2.1: A STATE MACHINE THAT GENERATES BLUES LYRICS

That doesn't make sense." Still, it was amazing that a program could produce a document that, at first glance, was human-generated. How could that program generate English sentences? Believe it or not, even a simple "machine" can generate a large number of proper sentences. Consider the blues lyrics machine in Figure 2.1 that generates such valid sentences as "My wife is sad" and "My dog is ugly and lazy."[1,2]

The *state machine* has states (circles) and transitions (arrows) labeled with vocabulary symbols. The transitions are directed (one-way) connections that govern navigation among the states. Machine execution begins in state s0, the *start state*, and stops in s4, the *accept state*. Transitioning from one state to another emits the label on the transition. At each state, pick a transition, "say" the label, and move to the target state. The full name for this machine is *deterministic finite automaton* (DFA). You'll see the acronym DFA used extensively in Chapter 11, *LL(*) Parsing*, on page 253.

DFAs are relatively easy to understand and seem to generate some sophisticated sentences, but they aren't powerful enough to generate all programming language constructs. The next section points out why DFAs are underpowered.

---

1. Pinker's book has greatly influenced my thinking about languages. This state machine and related discussion were inspired by the machines in *The Language Instinct*.
2. What happens if you run the blues machine backward? As the old joke goes, "You get your dog back, your wife back. . . ."

The Maze as a Language Generator

A state machine is analogous to a maze with words written on the floor. The words along each path through the maze from the entrance to the exit represent a sentence. The set of all paths through the maze represents the set of all sentences and, hence, defines the language.

Imagine that at least one loopback exists along some path in the maze. You could walk around forever, generating an infinitely long sentence. The maze can, therefore, simulate a finite or infinite language generator just like a state machine.

Finite State Machines

The blues lyrics state machine is called a *finite state automaton*. An *automaton* is another word for machine, and *finite* implies the machine has a fixed number of states. Note that even though there are only five states, the machine can generate an infinite number of sentences because of the "and" loop transition from s4 to s3. Because of that transition, the machine is considered *cyclic*. All cyclic machines generate an infinite number of sentences, and all acyclic machines generate a finite set of sentences. ANTLR's *LL(*)* parsing strategy, described in detail in Part III, is stronger than traditional *LL(k)* because *LL(*)* uses cyclic prediction machines whereas *LL(k)* uses acyclic machines.

One of the most common acronyms you'll see in Part III of this book is DFA, which stands for *deterministic finite automaton*. A deterministic automaton (state machine) is an automaton where all transition labels emanating from any single state are unique. In other words, every state transitions to exactly one other state for a given label.

A final note about state machines. They do not have a memory. States do not know which states, if any, the machine has visited previously. This weakness is central to why state machines generate some invalid sentences. Analogously, state machines are too weak to recognize many common language constructs.

2.2 The Requirements for Generating Complex Language

Is the lyrics state machine correct in the sense it generates valid blues sentences and only valid sentences? Unfortunately, no. The machine can also generate invalid sentences, such as "Your truck is sad and sad." Rather than choose words (transitions) at random in each state, you could use known probabilities for how often words follow one another. That would help, but no matter how good your statistics were, the machine could still generate an invalid sentence. Apparently, human brains do something more sophisticated than this simple state machine approach to generate sentences.

State machines generate invalid sentences for the following reasons:[3]

- Grammatical does not imply sensible. For example, "Dogs revert vacuum bags" is grammatically OK but doesn't make any sense. In English, this is self-evident. In a computer program, you also know that a syntactically valid assignment such as employeeName= milesPerGallon; might make no sense. The variable types and meaning could be a problem. The meaning of a sentence is referred to as the *semantics*. The next two characteristics are related to syntax.

- There are dependencies between the words of a sentence. When confronted with a], every programmer in the World has an involuntary response to look for the opening [.

- There are order requirements between the words of a sentence. You immediately see "(a[i+3)]" as invalid because you expect the] and) to be in a particular order (I even found it hard to type).

So, walking the states of a state machine is too simple an approach for the generation of complex language. There are word dependencies and order requirements among the output words that it cannot satisfy. Formally, we say that state machines can generate only the class of *regular languages*. As this section points out, programming languages fall into a more complicated, demanding class, the *context-free languages*. The difference between the regular and context-free languages is the difference between a state machine and the more sophisticated machines in the next section. The essential weakness of a state machine is that it has no memory of what it generated in the past. What do we need to remember in order to generate complex language?

---

3. These are Pinker's reasons from pp. 93–97 in *The Language Instinct* but rephrased in a computer language context.

2.3 The Tree Structure of Sentences

To reveal the memory system necessary to generate complex language, consider how you would write a book. You don't start by typing "the" or whatever the first word of the book is. You start with the concept of a book and then write an outline, which becomes the chapter list. Then you work on the sections within each chapter and finally start writing the sentences of your paragraphs. The phrase that best describes the organization of a book is not "sequence of words." Yes, you can read a book one word at a time, but the book is *structured*: chapters nested within the book, sections nested with the chapters, and paragraphs nested within the sections. Moreover, the substructures are ordered: chapter i must appear before chapter $i+1$. "Nested and ordered" screams tree structure. The components of a book are tree structured with "book" at the root, chapters at the second level, and so on.

Interestingly, even individual sentences are tree structured. To demonstrate this, think about the way you write software. You start with a concept and then work your way down to words, albeit very quickly and unconsciously using a top-down approach. For example, how do you get your fingers to type statement x=0; into an editor? Your first thought is not to type x. You think "I need to reset x to 0" and then decide you need an assignment with x on the left and 0 on the right. You finally add the ; because you know all statements in Java end with ;. The image in Figure 2.2, on the facing page, represents the implicit tree structure of the assignment statement. Such trees are called *derivation trees* when generating sentences and *parse trees* when recognizing sentences. So, instead of directly emitting x=0;, your brain does something akin to the following Java code:

```java
void statement() {
  assignment();
  System.out.println(";");
}

void assignment() {
  System.out.println("x");
  System.out.println("=");
  expr();
}

void expr() {
  System.out.println("0");
}
```

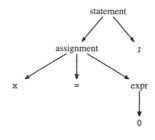

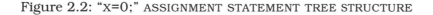

Figure 2.2: "x=0;" ASSIGNMENT STATEMENT TREE STRUCTURE

Each method represents a level in the sentence tree structure, and the print statements represent leaf nodes. The leaves are the vocabulary symbols of the sentence.

Each subtree in a sentence tree represents a *phrase* of a sentence. In other words, sentences decompose into phrases, subphrases, subsubphrases, and so on. For example, the statements in a Java method are phrases of the method, which is itself a phrase of the overall class definition sentence.

This section exposed the tree-structured nature of sentences. The next section shows how a simple addition to a state machine creates a much more powerful machine. This more powerful machine is able to generate complex valid sentences and only valid sentences.

2.4 Enforcing Sentence Tree Structure with Pushdown Machines

The method call chain for the code fragment in Section 2.3, *The Tree Structure of Sentences*, on the preceding page gives a big hint about the memory system we need to enforce sentence structure. Compare the tree structure in Figure 2.2 with the method call graph in Figure 2.3, on the next page, for this code snippet. The trees match up perfectly. Yep, adding a method call and return mechanism to a state machine turns it into a sophisticated language generator.

It turns out that the humble stack is the perfect memory structure to solve both word dependency and order problems.[4] Adding a stack to a

---

4. Method call mechanisms use a stack to save and restore return addresses.

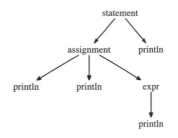

Figure 2.3: METHOD CALL GRAPH FOR "X=0;" ASSIGNMENT STATEMENT GENERATION

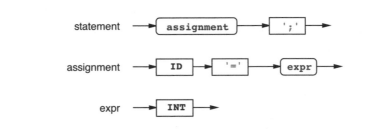

Figure 2.4: SYNTAX DIAGRAM FOR ASSIGNMENT STATEMENT SENTENCE STRUCTURE

state machine turns it into a *pushdown machine* (pushdown automaton). A state machine is analogous to a stream of instructions trapped within a single method, unable to make method calls. A pushdown machine, on the other hand, is free to invoke other parts of the machine and return just like a method call. The stack allows you to partition a machine into submachines. These submachines map directly to the rules in a grammar.

Representing pushdown machines requires a different visualization called a *syntax diagram*, which looks like a flowchart. There is a flowchart-like submachine per phrase (tree structure subtree). Figure 2.4, illustrates the syntax diagram for the assignment statement sentence structure. The rectangular elements generate vocabulary symbols, and the rounded elements invoke the indicated submachine. Like a method call, the pushdown machine returns from a submachine invocation upon reaching the end of that submachine.

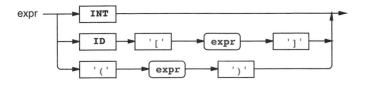

Figure 2.5: SYNTAX DIAGRAM FOR RECURSIVE EXPRESSION GENERATION

Let's take a look at how a syntax diagram enforces word dependencies and word order. Consider the problem of pairing up square brackets and parentheses with the proper nesting. For example, you must close a bracketed subexpression and do so before the closing outer parenthesized expression. Figure 2.5, shows the syntax diagram for an expression generation pushdown machine. The pushdown machine can generate expressions like 29342, a[12], (89), a[(1)], and (a[a[1]]).

The pushdown machine satisfies bracket symbol dependencies because for every [the machine has no choice but to generate a] later. The same is true for parentheses. But what about enforcing the proper word order for nested expressions?

Look at the second alternative of the machine. The machine must generate the] after the index expression. Any structure that the nested index expression generates must terminate before the]. Similarly, the third alternative guarantees that the) occurs after the structure generated by the enclosed expression. That is, the pushdown machine ensures that grouping symbols are properly nested.

Nested phrases can be *recursive*—they can refer to themselves as the expression syntax diagram does. For example, the pushdown machine generates the nested (1) phrase within a[(1)] using recursion because it invokes itself. Figure 2.6, on the following page shows the derivation tree. The nested **expr** invocations represent recursive submachine invocations. Do not let recursion bother you. Languages are highly recursive by their nature—you cannot generate arbitrarily nested code blocks, for example, without recursion. Besides, as L. Peter Deutsch says, "To iterate is human, to recurse divine."[5]

---

5. I've also seen another play on the same phrase, "To err is human, to moo bovine."

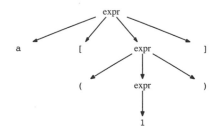

Figure 2.6: RECURSIVE TREE STRUCTURE FOR EXPRESSION A[(1)]

This section demonstrated that pushdown machines generate syntactically valid sentences. In other words, each sentence that the pushdown machine generates has a valid interpretation. The next section demonstrates that, unfortunately, some valid sentences have more than one interpretation.

2.5 Ambiguous Languages

As we all know, English and other natural languages can be delightfully *ambiguous*. Any language with an ambiguous sentence is considered ambiguous, and any sentence with more than a single meaning is ambiguous. Sentences are ambiguous if at least one of its phrases is ambiguous. Here is an ambiguous faux newspaper headline: "Bush appeals to democrats." In this case, the verb *appeals* has two meanings: "is attractive to" and "requests help from." This is analogous to operator overloading in computer languages, which makes programs hard to understand just like overloaded words do in English.[6]

Ambiguity is a source of humor in English but the bane of computing. Computers must always know exactly how to interpret every phrase. At the lowest level, computers must always make decisions *deterministically*—they must know exactly which path to take. A classic example of an ambiguous computer phrase relates to arithmetic expressions.

---

6. A friend put the following dedication into his PhD thesis referring to the advisor he disliked: "To my advisor, for whom no thanks is too much." *The Language Instinct* cites a marvelously ambiguous statement by Groucho Marx: "I once shot an elephant in my pajamas. How he got into my pajamas I'll never know."

The expression 3+4*5 is not ambiguous to an adult human. It means multiply 4 by 5 and add 3, yielding 23. An elementary school student doing the operations from left to right might ask, "Why is the result not 35?" Indeed, why not? Because mathematicians have decreed it so. In fact, German mathematician Leopold Kronecker went so far as to say, "God made the natural numbers; all else is the work of man." So, the language is ambiguous, but syntax and some precedence rules make it unambiguous.

Within a syntax diagram, an ambiguous sentence or phase is one that the diagram can generate following more than one path. For example, a syntax diagram for C can generate statement i*j; following the path for both a multiplicative expression and a variable definition (in other words, j is a pointer to type i). To learn more about the relationship of ambiguous languages to ANTLR grammars, see Section 11.5, *Ambiguities and Nondeterminisms*, on page 264. For example, Section 11.5, *Arithmetic Expression Grammars*, on page 266 has an in-depth discussion of the arithmetic expression ambiguity.

Although syntax is sometimes insufficient to interpret sentences, the informal language definition usually has some extra rules such as precedence that disambiguate the sentences. Chapter 13, *Semantic Predicates*, on page 309 illustrates how to use semantic predicates to enforce these nonsyntactic rules. Semantic predicates are boolean expressions, evaluated at runtime, that guide recognition.

Before turning to the last subject of this chapter, sentence recognition, let's examine the structure of vocabulary symbols themselves. Recognizing sentences is actually a two-level problem: breaking up the input character stream into vocabulary symbols and then applying syntactic structure to the vocabulary symbol sequence.

2.6 Vocabulary Symbols Are Structured Too

Just as sentences consist of phrases, vocabulary symbols have structure. In English, for example, a linguist sees the word *destabilize* as "de.stabil.ize."[7] Similarly, the real number 92.5 is two integers separated by a dot. Humans unconsciously scan sentences with these characters and group them into words.

---

7. See http://en.wikipedia.org/wiki/Stem_(linguistics).

Sentences are actually sequences of characters, but your brain sees them as sequences of words as if they were complete symbols like Chinese characters. This happens no matter how long the words are. For example, the word for the Hawaiian state fish (Humuhumunukunukuapua'a) is pretty long, but you read it as one symbol (pronouncing it is a lot harder). Your brain somehow implicitly forms words from the characters and looks them up in a dictionary of sorts.

Reading Morse code makes this process even more obvious because it is clear you are combining dots and dashes, representing letters, into words before reading the sentence. For example, what does the following say (using international Morse code)?

._ _. _ ._.. ._. .. ... _._. __ __ ._..

If you guessed "ANTLR is cool," you'd be right (and are either an obsequious ANTLR fan or a ham radio operator). Here is the character-by-character translation:[8]

```
.\_ \_. \_ .\_.. .\_. .. ... \_.\_. \_\_ \_\_ .\_..
 A   N T   L    R   I  S   C    O   O    L
```

To mimic the technique your brain uses to recognize sentences, you need to separate the language-level processing from the vocabulary-level processing into two complete recognizers. The language-level recognizer is usually called the *parser*, and the vocabulary recognizer is usually called the *scanner*, *lexical analyzer*, or *lexer*. Lexers create *tokens*[9] (vocabulary symbols) and pass them to the parser. The only difference between the two recognizers is that the parser recognizes grammatical structure in a stream of tokens while the lexer recognizes structure in a stream of characters. Both perform essentially the same task, and ANTLR implements both using the same strategy.

As an example, consider the following simple Java statement:

```
width=200;
```

The lexer scans the individual characters, grouping the letters into an **ID** token type and grouping the digits into an **INT** token type. The punctua-

---

8. Amazingly, experienced operators can receive and decode Morse code without the help of pen and paper and can generate twenty or thirty words per minute!

9. In practice, tokens consist of at least two pieces of information: the token type (which lexical structure) and the text matched by the lexer. You can put anything you want into the token structure. ANTLR's default CommonToken objects include start/stop indexes into the character buffer, the line number, and the token's character position within that line, among other things.

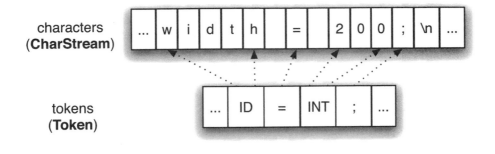

Figure 2.7: Tokens and character buffer. Tokens use character indexes to mark start/stop of tokens in buffer. The lexer does not create tokens for whitespace characters. CharStream and Token are ANTLR runtime types

tion symbols exist as their own token types (that is, no other characters map to that token type). The lexer sees the newline character following the semicolon but throws it out instead of passing it to the parser. The parser therefore sees a sequence of four tokens: **ID**, '=', **INT**, and ';', as illustrated in Figure 2.7. The dotted lines represent the character indexes stored in the tokens that refer to the start and stop character positions (single-character tokens are represented with a single dotted line for clarity).

Separating the parser and lexer might seem like an unnecessary complication if you're used to building recognizers by hand; however, the separation reduces what you have to worry about at each language level. You also get several implementation advantages:

- The parser can treat arbitrarily long character sequences as single tokens. Further, the lexer can group related tokens into token "classes" or *token types* such as **INT** (integers), **ID** (identifiers), **FLOAT** (floating-point numbers), and so on. The lexer groups vocabulary symbols into types when the parser doesn't care about the individual symbols, just the type. For example, the parser doesn't care which integer is approaching on the input stream, just that it is an integer. Also, the parser does not have to wonder whether the next vocabulary symbol is an integer or floating-point number. The lexer can figure this out beforehand and send token type **INT** or **FLOAT** accordingly, allowing the parser to be much simpler.

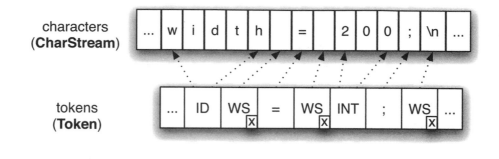

Figure 2.8: TOKEN BUFFER WITH HIDDEN TOKENS. THE LEXER CREATES TOKENS EVEN FOR WHITESPACE, BUT PUTS THEM ON A HIDDEN CHANNEL (TOKENS SHOWN WITH CHECKBOX)

- The parser sees a pipeline of tokens, which isolates it from the token source. The source of the tokens is irrelevant. For efficiency reasons, you want to save the results of lexing a character stream in a number of situations. For example, interpreters walk the same program statements multiple times during a loop. Once your lexer has tokenized the input, the parser can walk the same token buffer over and over. Some compilers (C and C++ come to mind) can even save tokenized header files to avoid repeatedly tokenizing them.

- The lexer can filter the input, sending only tokens of interest to the parser. This feature makes it easy to handle whitespace, comments, and other lexical structures that you want to discard. For example, if comments were passed to the parser, the parser would have to constantly check for comment tokens and filter them out. Instead, the lexer can simply throw them out, as shown in Figure 2.7, on the previous page, or pass them to the parser on a hidden channel, as shown in Figure 2.8. The tokens on the hidden channel are marked with an "x." Note that the channel is an integer and you can put tokens on any channel you want, but the parser listens to only one channel. For more information about token channels, see Section 4.3, *Lexical Rules*, on page 92 and classes Token, CommonToken, and CommonTokenStream in the org.antlr.runtime package.

At this point, you have the entire language generation picture. Sentences are not ingenious word sequences. Complex language generation enforces word dependencies and order requirements. Your brain enforces these constraints by subconsciously creating a tree structure. It does not generate sentences by thinking about the first word, the second word, and so on, like a simple state machine. It starts with the overall sentence concept, the root of the tree structure. From there the brain creates phrases and subphrases until it reaches the leaves of the tree structure. From a computer scientist's point of view, generating a sentence is a matter of performing a depth-first tree walk and "saying" the words represented by the leaves. The implicit tree structure conveys the meaning.

Sentence recognition occurs in reverse. Your eyes see a simple list of words, but your brain subconsciously conjures up the implicit tree structure used by the person who generated the sentence. Now you see why language recognition is the dual of language generation. ANTLR builds recognizers that mimic how your brain recognizes sentences. The next section gives you an intuitive feel for what sentence recognition by computer means. Afterward, you will be in good shape for Chapter 4, *ANTLR Grammars*, on page 71.

2.7 Recognizing Computer Language Sentences

Recognizing a sentence means identifying its implicit tree structure, but how do you do that with a program? Many possible solutions exist, but ANTLR generates recognizers with a method for every grammar rule. The methods match symbols and decide which other methods to invoke based upon what they see on the input stream. This is similar to making decisions in the maze based upon the words in the passphrase. The beauty of this implementation is in its simplicity—the method call graph of the recognizer mirrors the parse tree structure. Recall how the call graph in Figure 2.3, on page 24, overlays the tree structure in Figure 2.2, on page 23, perfectly.

To get the most out of Part II of this book, you'll need a basic understanding of language recognition technology and the definition of a few important terms. This section answers three fundamental questions:

- What is the difference between loading a data file into memory and actually recognizing what's in the file?
- From which grammars can ANTLR generate a valid recognizer?
- Can you define the syntax of every language using grammar rules, and if not, what can you use?

The Difference between Reading and Recognizing Input

To characterize what it means for a computer to recognize input, this section compares two small programs. The first program reads a file full of random characters, and the second reads a file of letters and digits. We'll see that the first program doesn't recognize anything, but the second one does. From there, we'll look at the grammar equivalent of the second program and then morph it into something that ANTLR would generate.

To read the file of random characters into memory, we can use the following Java code:

```
BufferedReader f = new BufferedReader(new FileReader("random.txt"));
int c = f.read(); // get the first char
StringBuffer s = new StringBuffer();
while ( c != -1 ) {
  s.append((char)c);
  c = f.read();
}
```

You could say that the file has no structure or that the structure is simply "one or more characters." Now, consider an input file that contains a series of letters followed by a series of digits such as this:

```
acefbetqd392293
```

We can read in this structured input with something like this:

```
BufferedReader f =
  new BufferedReader(new FileReader("lettersAndDigits.txt"));
int c = f.read(); // get the first char
StringBuffer letters = new StringBuffer();
StringBuffer digits = new StringBuffer();
// read the letters
while ( Character.isLetter((char)c) ) {
  letters.append((char)c);
  c = f.read();
}
// read the digits
while ( Character.isDigit((char)c) ) {
  digits.append((char)c);
  c = f.read();
}
```

On the other hand, the previous simple loop would also read in the letters and digits. The difference lies in the fact that the previous loop would not recognize the structure of the input. Recognizing structure involves comparing the input against a series of constraints dictated by the structure.

In this example, recognition implies that the program verifies that the input consists of letters followed by digits. The previous example verifies no constraints. Another way to think about recognition is that, after recognizing some input, the program can provide the groups of characters associated with the various elements of the structure. In English, this is analogous to being able to identify the subject, verb, and object after reading a sentence. In this case, the second program could provide the letters and digits whereas the first program could not. Simply munching up all the input does not identify the input substructures in any way.

In grammar form, the difference between the two recognizer programs stands out more clearly. The first program, which simply consumes all characters, is equivalent to the following grammar:

```
/** Read this as "a file is defined to be zero-or-more characters." The
 * dot is the wildcard character and the star means zero-or-more.
 */
file : .* ; // consume until EOF
```

The second program that matches a bunch of letters followed by digits is equivalent to the following grammar:

```
file: LETTERS DIGITS ;
LETTERS: 'a'..'z'* ; // zero or more lowercase letters
DIGITS : '0'..'9'* ; // zero or more digits
```

Clearly, the first grammar tells us nothing about the input format, whereas the second grammar explicitly defines the input file language structure.

Now, let's look at the kind of code that ANTLR generates. If we break up the stream of instructions into multiple methods, the second program parallels the second grammar:

```
void file() {
    LETTERS();  // go match the letters
    DIGITS();   // go match the digits
}
void LETTERS() {
    while ( Character.isLetter((char)c) ) {
      c = f.read();
    }
}
void DIGITS() {
    while ( Character.isDigit((char)c) ) {
      c = f.read();
    }
}
```

This is not exactly what ANTLR would generate, but it illustrates the type of recognizer ANTLR generates. Once you get used to seeing grammars, you will find them easier to write and understand than unstructured, hand-built recognizers. Can ANTLR always generate a recognizer from a grammar, though? Unfortunately, the answer is no. The next section describes the different kinds of recognizers, discusses the relationship between grammars and recognizers, and illustrates the kinds of recognizers ANTLR can build.

Categorizing Recognizers

Recognizers that begin the recognition process at the most abstract language level are called *top-down* recognizers. The formal term for a top-down recognizer is *LL*.[10] Within the top-down category, the most common implementation is called a *recursive-descent* recognizer. These recognizers have one (possibly recursive) method per rule and are what programmers build by hand. The method call graph traces out the implicit sentence tree structure (the parse tree). This is how top-down recognizers conjure up tree structure without actually building a tree. You can think of top-down recognizers as walking sentence tree structures in a depth-first manner. The root of the tree for the sentence in the previous section is the **file** level. The root has two children: **LETTERS** and **DIGITS**.

Unfortunately, ANTLR cannot generate a top-down recognizer for every grammar—*LL* recognizers restrict the class of acceptable grammars somewhat. For example, ANTLR cannot accept left-recursive grammars such as the following (see Section 11.5, *Left-Recursive Grammars*, on page 265):

```
/** An expression is defined to be an expression followed by '++' */
expr : expr '++'
     ;
```

ANTLR translates this grammar to a recursive method called expr() that immediately invokes itself:

```
void expr() {
    expr();
    match("++");
}
```

---

10. See http://en.wikipedia.org/wiki/LL_parser. *LL* means "recognize input from left to right using a leftmost derivation." You can interpret "leftmost derivation" as attempting rule references within alternative from left to right. For our purposes, simply consider *LL* a synonym for a top-down recognizer.

Comparing Bottom-Up and Top-Down Recognizers

The other major class of recognizers is called *LR* because these recognizers perform rightmost derivations rather than leftmost (YACC builds *LR*-based recognizers). *LR* recognizers are called *bottom-up* recognizers because they try to match the leaves of the parse tree and then work their way up toward the starting rule at the root. Loosely speaking, *LR* recognizers consume input symbols until they find a matching complete alternative. In contrast, *LL* recognizers are goal-oriented. They start with a rule in mind and then try to match the alternatives. For this reason, *LL* is easier for humans to understand because it mirrors our own innate language recognition mechanism.

Another grammar restriction stems from the fact that the recognition strategy might be too weak to handle a particular grammar. The strength of an *LL*-based recognizer depends on the amount of *lookahead* it has.

Lookahead refers to scanning ahead in the input stream one or more symbols in order to make decisions. In the maze, you match the word under your feet with the next word of lookahead in your passphrase. If you reach a fork where the same word begins both paths, you must use more lookahead to figure out which path to take. Most top-down recognizers use a fixed amount of lookahead, k, and are called *LL(k)* recognizers. *LL(k)* recognizers look up to k words down each path hoping to find a distinguishing word or sequence of words. Here is an example of an *LL(3)* grammar (a grammar for which you can build an *LL(3)* recognizer):

```
/** A decl is 'int' followed by an identifier followed by
 *  an initializer or ';'.
 */
decl : 'int' ID '=' INT ';'  // E.g., "int x = 3;"
     | 'int' ID ';'          // E.g., "int x;"
     ;
```

With less than three lookahead symbols, the recognizer cannot see past the type name and **ID** token to the assignment operator or the semicolon beyond. Depth $k=3$ distinguishes the two alternatives. This grammar is not *LL(1)* or *LL(2)*. Although this grammar needs three symbols of lookahead, that does not mean you can't alter the grammar so that it is *LL(1)*.

To be precise, the syntax is *LL(1)*, but that particular grammar for it is *LL(3)*. Refactoring the grammar is more work and yields a less natural-looking grammar:

```
/** LL(1) version of decl; less lookahead, but less natural */
decl : 'int' ID ('=' INT)? ';' // optionally match initializer
     ;
```

Increasing the lookahead depth from 1 to k significantly increases the decision-making power of a recognizer. With more power comes a larger class of grammars, which means you'll find it easier to write grammars acceptable to ANTLR. Still, some natural grammars are not *LL(k)* for even large values of k.

Extending the previous grammar to allow a sequence of modifiers before the type renders it non-*LL(k)* for any fixed k:

```
decl : // E.g., "int x = 3;", "static int x = 3;"
        modifier* 'int' ID '=' INT ';'

     | // E.g., "int x;", "static int x;", "static register int x;",
       // "static static register int x;" (weird but grammar says legal)
        modifier* 'int' ID ';'
     ;
modifier // match a single 'static' or 'register' keyword
     : 'static'
     | 'register'
     ;
```

Because the grammar allows a prefix of zero or more **modifier** symbols, no fixed amount of lookahead will be able to see past the modifiers. One of ANTLR v3's key features is its powerful extension to *LL(k)* called *LL(*)* that allows lookahead to roam arbitrarily far ahead (see Section 11.2, *Why You Need LL(*)*, on page 255). For rule **decl**, ANTLR generates something similar to the following (assume lookahead() is a method that returns the lookahead at the indicated depth):

```
void decl() {
    // PREDICT EITHER ALT 1 or 2
    int alt;
    int k = 1; // start with k=1
    // scan past all the modifiers; LL(k) for fixed k cannot do this!
    while ( lookahead(k) is a modifier ) { k++; }
    k++; // scan past 'int'
    k++; // scan past ID
    if ( lookahead(k) is '=' ) alt = 1; // predict alternative 1
    else alt = 2;                        // else predict alternative 2
```

```
    // MATCH ONE OF THE ALTS
    switch (alt) {
        case 1 :
            // match modifier* 'int' ID '=' INT ';'
            break;
        case 2 :
            // match modifier* 'int' ID ';'
            break;
    }
}
```

$LL(*)$'s arbitrary lookahead is like bringing a trained monkey along in the maze. The monkey can race ahead of you down the various paths emanating from a fork. It looks for some simple word sequences from your passphrase that distinguish the paths. $LL(*)$ represents a significant step forward in recognizer technology because it dramatically increases the number of acceptable grammars without incurring a large runtime speed penalty. Nonetheless, even $LL(*)$ is not enough to handle some useful grammars. $LL(*)$ cannot see past nested structures because it uses a DFA, not a pushdown machine, to scan ahead. This means it cannot handle some decisions whose alternatives have recursive rule references. In the following grammar, rule **decl** allows C-like declarators instead of simple identifiers:

```
decl : 'int' declarator '=' INT ';' // E.g., "int **x=3;"
     | 'int' declarator ';'         // E.g., "int *x;"
     ;
declarator // E.g., "x", "*x", "**x", "***x"
     : ID
     | '*' declarator
     ;
```

Rule **decl** is not $LL(*)$, but don't worry. ANTLR has an even more powerful strategy that can deal with just about any grammar for a slight reduction in recognition speed.

When ANTLR cannot generate a valid $LL(*)$ recognizer from a grammar, you can tell ANTLR to simply try the alternatives in the order specified (see Section 5.3, *backtrack Option*, on page 107). If the first alternative fails, ANTLR rewinds the input stream and tries the second alternative, and so on, until it finds a match. In the maze, this is analogous to trying the alternative paths until you find one that leads to the exit. Such a mechanism is called *backtracking* and is very powerful, but it comes at an exponential speed complexity in the worst case. The speed penalty arises from having to repeatedly evaluate a rule for the same input position. A decision can have multiple alternatives that begin with the same rule reference, say, **expression**. Backtracking over several of these alternatives means repeatedly invoking rule **expression** at the left edge. Because the input position will always be the same, evaluating **expression** again and again is a waste of time.

Surprisingly, using a technique called *memoization*,[11] ANTLR can completely eliminate such redundant computation at the cost of some memory (see Section 14.5, *Memoization*, on page 335). By recording the result of invoking **expression** while attempting the first alternative, the remaining alternatives can reuse that result. Memoization plus backtracking provides all the power you need with fast recognition speed.

So, ANTLR can usually build a recognizer from a grammar, but can you always define a grammar for a given language? The answer is no. Well, you can't always define one purely with the grammar rules themselves. The next section describes language constructs that are easy to define in English language descriptions, but difficult to express in a straightforward grammar.

Encoding Phrase Context and Precedence

Some languages have phrases that only make sense in the context of other phrases, which is sometimes difficult to encode properly with a grammar. For example, some phrase x of sentence s might make sense only if preceded (or succeeded) by the phrase p; i.e., s="...p...x...". This case abstracts some common programming language recognition problems. Take arithmetic expressions that reference variables. Expressions must have corresponding definitions for those variables, such as s="...int i;...i+1...". In English, this is analogous to x="open it", which only makes sense in the context of another phrase p that defines "it." Is "it" a window or a bottle of German dunkel beer? Here, the meaning of the phrase is clear; you just need to know what to open according to p.

Computer recognizers typically record variable definitions such as i in dictionaries called *symbol tables* that map variable names to their type and scope. Later, user-defined actions embedded within the expression rules can look up i in the symbol table to see whether i has been defined.

---

11. See http://en.wikipedia.org/wiki/Memoization. Bryan Ford applied memoization to parsing, calling it *packrat parsing*.

Some Sentences Force Humans to Backtrack

Sometimes you have to see an entire sentence to get the proper meaning for the initial phrase(s). In some English sentences, you find a word halfway through that is inconsistent with your current understanding. You have to restart from the beginning of the sentence. Trueswell et al in (TTG94) performed experiments that tracked people's eye movements as they read the following sentence:

"The defendant examined by the lawyer turned out to be unreliable."

People paused at *by* because their initial interpretation was that the defendant examined something. The researchers found that people have a strong preference to interpret *examined* as the main verb upon first reading of the sentence. After seeing *by*, people usually backtracked to the beginning of the sentence to begin a new interpretation. Adding commas allows your brain to interpret the sentence properly in one pass:

"The defendant, examined by the lawyer, turned out to be unreliable."

Just like adding commas in an English sentence, adding new symbols to computer language phrases can often reduce the need for backtracking. If you are in control of the language definition, try to make statements as clear as possible. Use extra vocabulary symbols if necessary.

See Section 6.5, *Rule Scopes*, on page 137 for a grammar that looks up variable definitions in a symbol table. For an in-depth discussion, see *Symbol Tables and Scopes*.[12]

What if you can't interpret a phrase at all without examining a previous or future phrase? For example, in C++, expression T(i) is either a function call or a constructor-style typecast (as in (T)i). If T is defined elsewhere as a function, then the expression is a function call. If T is defined as a class or other type, then the expression is a typecast. Such phrases are *context-sensitive*. Without the context information, the phrase is ambiguous. The problem is that grammars, as we've defined them, have

---

12. See http://www.cs.usfca.edu/~parrt/course/652/lectures/symtab.html.

no way to restrict the context in which rules can be applied. The grammars we've examined are called *context-free grammars* (CFGs). Each grammar rule has a name and list of alternatives, and that's it—no context constraints.

To recognize context-sensitive language constructs, ANTLR augments CFGs with *semantic predicates* (see Chapter 13, *Semantic Predicates*, on page 309). Semantic predicates are boolean expressions, evaluated at parse time, that basically turn alternatives on and off. If a semantic predicate evaluates to false, then the associated alternative disappears from the set of viable alternatives. You can use semantic predicates to ask questions about context in order to encode context-sensitivity. In the following rule, both alternatives can match expression T(i), but the predicates turn off the alternative that makes no sense in the current context:

```
expr : {«lookahead(1) is function»}? functionCall
     | {«lookahead(1) is type»}?     ctorTypecast
     ;
```

The predicates are the actions with question marks on the left edge of the alternatives. If T, the first symbol of lookahead, is a function, the recognizer will attempt the first alternative; otherwise, it will attempt the second. This easily resolves the ambiguity.

Even with context information, some phrases are still ambiguous. For example, even if you know that T is a type, you can interpret statement T(i); in two ways: as a constructor-style typecast expression statement and as a variable declaration statement (as in T i;). Multiple alternatives within the statement rule are able to match the same input phrase. The C++ language specification resolves the ambiguity by stating that if a statement can be both a declaration and an expression, interpret it as a declaration. This is not an ambiguity arising from lack of context—it is an ambiguity in the language syntax itself. Consequently, semantic predicates won't help in this situation.

To encode the C++ language specification's resolution of this ambiguity, we need a way to encode the precedence of the alternatives. ANTLR provides *syntactic predicates* that order a rule's alternatives, effectively letting us specify their precedence (see Chapter 14, *Syntactic Predicates*, on page 323). Syntactic predicates are grammar fragments enclosed in parentheses followed by =>.

In the following rule, the first alternative has a syntactic predicate that means, "If the current statement looks like a declaration, it is." Even if both alternatives can match the same input phrase, the first alternative will always take precedence.

```
stat : (declaration)=> declaration
     | expression
     ;
```

By adding semantic and syntactic predicates to an *LL(*)* grammar, you can usually convince ANTLR to build a valid recognizer for even the nastiest computer language.

This chapter demonstrated that a sentence's implicit tree structure conveys much of its meaning—it's not just the words and word sequence. You learned that your brain generates word sequences using an implicit tree structure and that computers can mimic that behavior with a pushdown machine. Pushdown machines use a stack to re-create sentence tree structure—the submachine invocation trace mirrors the sentence tree structure.

Sentence recognition is the dual of sentence generation. Recognition means identifying the phrases and subphrases within a sentence. To do this, a computer must find the implicit tree structure appropriate for the input sentence. Finding the implicit tree structure is a matter of finding subtrees that match the various phrases.

Rather than writing arbitrary code to recognize implicit sentence tree structure, we'll use formal grammars to define languages. Grammars conform to a domain-specific language that is particularly good at specifying sentence structure. The first chapter of Part II will explain why we use grammars and describes ANTLR's specific grammar notation. Before diving into the reference section of this book, we'll look at a complete example to give your brain something concrete to consider. The next chapter illustrates ANTLR's main components by showing how to build a simple calculator.

Chapter 3

A Quick Tour for the Impatient

The best way to learn about ANTLR is to walk through a simple but useful example. In this chapter, we'll build an arithmetic expression evaluator that supports a few operators and variable assignments. In fact, we'll implement the evaluator in two different ways. First, we'll build a parser grammar to recognize the expression language and then add actions to actually evaluate and print the result. Second, we'll modify the parser grammar to build an intermediate-form tree data structure instead of immediately computing the result. We'll then build a tree grammar to walk those trees, adding actions to evaluate and print the result. When you're through with this chapter, you'll have a good overall view of how to build translators with ANTLR. You'll learn about parser grammars, tokens, actions, ASTs, and tree grammars by example, which will make the ensuing chapters easier to understand.

This chapter is not the ideal starting point for programmers who are completely new to languages and language tools. Those programmers should begin by studying this book's introduction.

To keep it simple, we'll restrict the expression language to support the following constructs:

- Operators plus, minus, and multiply with the usual order of operator evaluation, allowing expressions such as this one:
  3+4*5-1

- Parenthesized expressions to alter the order of operator evaluation, allowing expressions such as this one:
  (3+4)*5

- Variable assignments and references, allowing expressions such as these:

  tour/basic/input

  a=3
  b=4
  2+a*b

Here's what we want the translator to do: when it sees 3+4, it should emit 7. When it sees dogs=21, it should map dogs to value 21. If the translator ever sees dogs again, it should pretend we typed 21 instead of dogs. How do we even start to solve this problem? Well, there are two overall tasks:

A parser triggers an embedded action after seeing the element to its left.

1. Build a grammar that describes the overall syntactic structure of expressions and assignments. The result of that effort is a recognizer that answers yes or no as to whether the input was a valid expression or assignment.

2. Embed code among the grammar elements at appropriate positions to evaluate pieces of the expression. For example, given input 3, the translator must execute an action that converts the character to its integer value. For input 3+4, the translator must execute an action that adds the results from two previous action executions, namely, the actions that converted characters 3 and 4 to their integer equivalents.

After completing those two large tasks, we'll have a translator that translates expressions to the usual arithmetic value. In the following sections, we'll walk through those tasks in detail. We'll follow this process:

1. Build the expression grammar.

2. Examine the files generated by ANTLR.

3. Build a test rig and test the recognizer.

4. Add actions to the grammar to evaluate expressions and emit results.

5. Augment the test rig and test the translator.

Now that we've defined the language, let's build an ANTLR grammar that recognizes sentences in that language and computes results.

3.1 Recognizing Language Syntax

We need to build a grammar that completely describes the syntax of our expression language, including the form of identifiers and integers. From the grammar, ANTLR will generate a program that recognizes valid expressions, automatically issuing errors for invalid expressions. Begin by thinking about the overall structure of the input, and then break that structure down into substructures, and so on, until you reach a structure that you can't break down any further. In this case, the overall input consists of a series of expressions and assignments, which we'll break down into more detail as we proceed.

Ok, let's begin your first ANTLR grammar. The most common ANTLR grammar is a combined grammar that specifies both the parser and lexer rules. These rules specify an expression's grammatical structure as well as its lexical structure (the so-called tokens). For example, an assignment is an identifier, followed by an equals sign, followed by an expression, and terminated with a newline; an identifier is a sequence of letters. Define a combined grammar by naming it using the **grammar** keyword:

```
grammar Expr;
«rules»
```

Put this grammar in file Expr.g because the filename must match the grammar name.

A *program* in this language looks like a series of statements followed by the newline character (newline by itself is an empty statement and ignored). More formally, these English *rules* look like the following when written in ANTLR notation where : starts a rule definition and | separates rule alternatives:

tour/basic/Expr.g

```
prog:   stat+ ;

stat:   expr NEWLINE
    |   ID '=' expr NEWLINE
    |   NEWLINE
    ;
```

A grammar rule is a named list of one or more alternatives such as **prog** and **stat**. Read **prog** as follows: a **prog** is a list of **stat** rules. Read rule **stat** as follows: a **stat** is one of the three alternatives:

- An **expr** followed by a newline (token **NEWLINE**)

- The sequence **ID** (an identifier), '=', **expr**, **NEWLINE**

- A **NEWLINE** token

Now we have to define what an expression, rule **expr**, looks like. It turns out that there is a grammar design pattern for arithmetic expressions (see Section 11.5, *Arithmetic Expression Grammars*, on page 266). The pattern prescribes a series of rules, one for each operator precedence level and one for the lowest level describing expression atoms such as integers. Start with an overall rule called **expr** that represents a complete expression. Rule **expr** will match operators with the weakest precedence, plus and minus, and will refer to a rule that matches subexpressions for operators with the next highest precedence. In this case, that next operator is multiply. We can call the rule **multExpr**. Rules **expr**, **multExpr**, and **atom** look like this:

tour/basic/Expr.g

```
expr:    multExpr (('+'|'-') multExpr)*
    ;

multExpr
    :    atom ('*' atom)*
    ;

atom:    INT
    |    ID
    |    '(' expr ')'
    ;
```

Turning to the lexical level, let's define the vocabulary symbols (tokens): identifiers, integers, and the newline character. Any other whitespace is ignored. Lexical rules all begin with an uppercase letter in ANTLR and typically refer to character and string literals, not tokens, as parser rules do. Here are all the lexical rules we'll need:

tour/basic/Expr.g

```
ID   :    ('a'..'z'|'A'..'Z')+ ;
INT  :    '0'..'9'+ ;
NEWLINE:'\r'? '\n' ;
WS   :    (' '|'\t'|'\n'|'\r')+ {skip();} ;
```

Rule **WS** (whitespace) is the only one with an action (skip();) that tells ANTLR to throw out what it just matched and look for another token.

The easiest way to work with ANTLR grammars is to use ANTLRWorks,[1] which provides a sophisticated development environment (see also Section 1.5, *ANTLRWorks Grammar Development Environment*, on page 12). Figure 3.1, on the facing page, shows what grammar **Expr** looks like inside ANTLRWorks. Notice that the syntax diagram view of a rule makes it easy to understand exactly what the rule matches.

At this point, we have no Java code to execute. All we have is an ANTLR grammar. To convert the ANTLR grammar to Java, invoke ANTLR from

---

1. See http://www.antlr.org/works.

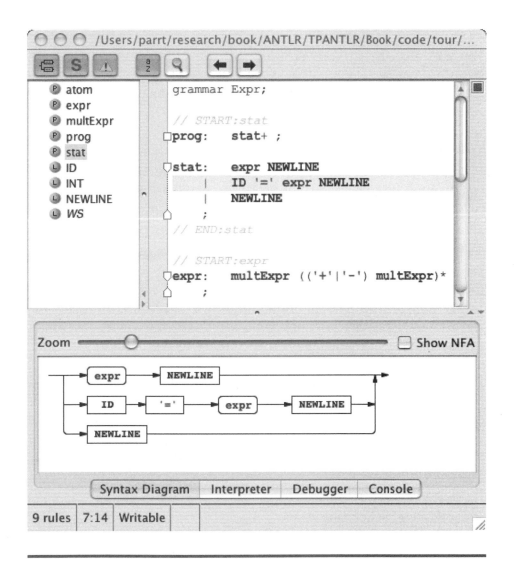

Figure 3.1: ANTLRWORKS GUI GRAMMAR DEVELOPMENT TOOL SHOWING EXPR.G AND SYNTAX DIAGRAM FOR RULE STAT

the command line (make sure antlr-3.0.jar, antlr-2.7.7, and stringtemplate-3.0.jar are in your CLASSPATH):

```
$ java org.antlr.Tool Expr.g
ANTLR Parser Generator   Version 3.0   1989-2007
$
```

You can also use ANTLRWorks to generate code using the Generate menu's Generate Code option, which will generate code in the same directory as your grammar file. In the next section, we will see what ANTLR generates from the grammar.

What Does ANTLR Generate?

From a combined grammar, ANTLR generates a parser and lexer (written in Java, in this case) that you can compile. Better yet, the code ANTLR generates is human-readable. I strongly suggest you look at the generated code because it will really help demystify ANTLR. ANTLR will generate the following files:

ANTLR generates recognizers that mimic the recursive-descent parsers that you would build by hand; most other parser generators, on the other hand, generate tables full of integers because they simulate state machines.

Generated File	Description
ExprParser.java	The recursive-descent parser generated from the grammar. From grammar **Expr**, ANTLR generates ExprParser and ExprLexer.
Expr.tokens	The list of token-name, token-type assignments such as INT=6.
Expr__.g	The automatically generated **lexer** grammar that ANTLR derived from the combined grammar. The generated file begins with a header: lexer grammar Expr;.
ExprLexer.java	The recursive-descent lexer generated from Expr__.g.

If you look inside ExprParser.java, for example, you will see a method for every rule defined in the grammar. The code for rule **multExpr** looks like the following pseudocode:

```
void multExpr() {
    try {
        atom();
        while ( «next input symbol is *» ) {
            match('*');
            atom();
        }
    }
    catch (RecognitionException re) {
        reportError(re);  // automatic error reporting and recovery
        recover(input,re);
    }
}
```

The pseudocode for rule **atom** looks like this:

```
void atom() {
    try {
        // predict which alternative will succeed
        // by looking at next (lookahead) symbol: input.LA(1)
        int alt=3;
        switch ( «next input symbol» ) {
            case INT: alt=1; break;
            case ID:  alt=2; break;
            case '(': alt=3; break;
            default: «throw NoViableAltException»
        }
        // now we know which alt will succeed, jump to it
        switch (alt) {
            case 1 : match(INT); break;
            case 2 : match(ID); break;
            case 3 :
                match('(');
                expr(); // invoke rule expr
                match(')');
                break;
        }
    }

    catch (RecognitionException re) {
        reportError(re); // automatic error reporting and recovery
        recover(input,re);
    }
}
```

Notice that rule references are translated to method calls, and token references are translated to match(TOKEN) calls.

All the FOLLOW_multExpr_in_expr160 variable and pushFollow() method references are part of the error recovery strategy, which always wants to know what tokens could come next. In case of a missing or extra token, the recognizer will resynchronize by skipping tokens until it sees a token in the proper "following" set. See Chapter 10, *Error Reporting and Recovery*, on page 231 for more information.

*The generated code here is general and more complicated than necessary for this simple parser. A future version of ANTLR will optimize these common situations down to simpler code. For example, clearly, the two **switch** statements could be collapsed into a single one.*

ANTLR generates a file containing the token types just in case another grammar wants to use the same token type definitions, as you will do in Section 3.3, *Evaluating Expressions Encoded in ASTs*, on page 63 when building a tree parser.

Token types are integers that represent the "kind" of token, just like ASCII values represent characters:

tour/basic/Expr.tokens

```
INT=6
WS=7
NEWLINE=4
ID=5
'('=12
')'=13
'*'=11
'='=8
'-'=10
'+'=9
```

Testing the Recognizer

Running ANTLR on the grammar just generates the lexer and parser, ExprParser and ExprLexer. To actually try the grammar on some input, we need a test rig with a main() method such as this one:

tour/basic/Test.java

```java
import org.antlr.runtime.*;

public class Test {
    public static void main(String[] args) throws Exception {
        // Create an input character stream from standard in
        ANTLRInputStream input = new ANTLRInputStream(System.in);
        // Create an ExprLexer that feeds from that stream
        ExprLexer lexer = new ExprLexer(input);
        // Create a stream of tokens fed by the lexer
        CommonTokenStream tokens = new CommonTokenStream(lexer);
        // Create a parser that feeds off the token stream
        ExprParser parser = new ExprParser(tokens);
        // Begin parsing at rule prog
        parser.prog();
    }
}
```

Classes ANTLRInputStream and CommonTokenStream are standard ANTLR classes in the org.antlr.runtime package. ANTLR generated all the other classes instantiated in the test rig.

Once you have compiled the generated code and the test rig, Test.java, run Test, and type a simple expression followed by newline and then the end-of-file character appropriate for your platform:[2]

---

2. The end-of-file character is Ctrl+D on Unix and Ctrl+Z on Windows.

```
⇐  $ javac Test.java ExprLexer.java ExprParser.java
⇐  $ java Test
⇐  (3+4)*5
⇐  EOF
⇒  $
```

ANTLR doesn't emit any output because there are no actions and grammar. If, however, you type an invalid expression—one that does not follow the grammar—the ANTLR-generated parser will emit an error. The parser will also try to recover and continue matching expressions. The same is true of the generated lexer. For example, upon seeing invalid character @, the lexer reports the following:

```
⇐  $ java Test
⇐  3+@
⇐  EOF
⇒  line 1:2 no viable alternative at character '@'
   line 1:3 no viable alternative at input '\n'
   $
```

The recognizer found two errors in this case. The first error is a lexical error: an invalid character, @. The second error is a parser error: a missing **atom** (the parser saw 3+\n, not a valid atom such as an integer). A lexer or parser emits the phrase "no viable alternative" when it can't figure out what to do when confronted with a list of alternatives. This means that the next input symbols don't seem to fit any of the alternatives.

For mismatched tokens, recognizers indicate the incorrect token found on the input stream and the expected token:

```
⇐  $ java Test
⇐  (3
⇐  EOF
⇒  line 1:2 mismatched input '\n' expecting ')'
   $
```

The error message is saying that the newline token was unexpected and that the parser expected) instead. The 1:2 error prefix indicates that the error occurred on line 1 and in character position 2 within that line. Because the character position starts from 0, position 2 means the third character.

At this point we have a program that will accept valid input or complain if we give it invalid input. In the next section, you will learn how to add actions to the grammar so you can actually evaluate the expressions.

3.2 Using Syntax to Drive Action Execution

You've made significant progress at this point because you've got a parser and lexer, all without writing any Java code! As you can see, writing a grammar is much easier than writing your own parsing code. You can think of ANTLR's notation as a domain-specific language specifically designed to make recognizers and translators easy to build.

To move from a recognizer to a translator or interpreter, we need to add actions to the grammar, but which actions and where? For our purposes here, we'll need to perform the following actions:

1. Define a hashtable called memory to store a variable-to-value map.
2. Upon expression, print the result of evaluating it.
3. Upon assignment, evaluate the right-side expression, and map the variable on the left side to the result. Store the results in memory.
4. Upon **INT**, return its integer value as a result.
5. Upon **ID**, return the value stored in memory for the variable. If the variable has not been defined, emit an error message.
6. Upon parenthesized expression, return the result of the nested expression as a result.
7. Upon multiplication of two atoms, return the multiplication of the two atoms' results.
8. Upon addition of two multiplicative subexpressions, return the addition of the two subexpressions' results.
9. Upon subtraction of two multiplicative subexpressions, return the subtraction of the two subexpressions' results.

We now just have to implement these actions in Java and place them in the grammar according to the location implied by the "Upon. . . " phrase. Begin by defining the memory used to map variables to their values (action 1):

```
tour/eval/Expr.g
```

```
@header {
import java.util.HashMap;
}

@members {
/** Map variable name to Integer object holding value */
HashMap memory = new HashMap();
}
```

We don't need an action for rule **prog** because it just tells the parser to look for one or more **stat** constructs. Actions 2 and 3 from the previous itemized list need to go in **stat** to print and store expression results:

tour/eval/Expr.g

```
prog:   stat+ ;

stat:   // evaluate expr and emit result
        // $expr.value is return attribute 'value' from expr call
        expr NEWLINE {System.out.println($expr.value);}

        // match assignment and stored value
        // $ID.text is text property of token matched for ID reference
    |   ID '=' expr NEWLINE
        {memory.put($ID.text, new Integer($expr.value));}

        // do nothing: empty statement
    |   NEWLINE
    ;
```

For the rules involved in evaluating expressions, it's really convenient to have them return the value of the subexpression they match. So, each rule will match and evaluate a piece of the expression, returning the result as a method return value. Look at **atom**, the simplest subexpression first:

tour/eval/Expr.g

```
atom returns [int value]
    :   // value of an INT is the int computed from char sequence
        INT {$value = Integer.parseInt($INT.text);}

    |   ID // variable reference
        {
        // look up value of variable
        Integer v = (Integer)memory.get($ID.text);
        // if found, set return value else error
        if ( v!=null ) $value = v.intValue();
        else System.err.println("undefined variable "+$ID.text);
        }

        // value of parenthesized expression is just the expr value
    |   '(' expr ')' {$value = $expr.value;}
    ;
```

Per the fourth action from the itemized list earlier, the result of an **INT atom** is just the integer value of the **INT** token's text. An **INT** token with text 91 results in the value 91. Action 5 tells us to look up the **ID** token's text in the memory map to see whether it has a value.

If so, just return the integer value stored in the map, or else print an error. Rule **atom**'s third alternative recursively invokes rule **expr**. There is nothing to compute, so the result of this **atom** evaluation is just the result of calling expr(); this satisfies action 6. As you can see, $value is the result variable as defined in the **returns** clause; $expr.value is the result computed by a call to **expr**. Moving on to multiplicative subexpressions, here is rule **multExpr**:

tour/eval/Expr.g

```
/** return the value of an atom or, if '*' present, return
 *  multiplication of results from both atom references.
 *  $value is the return value of this method, $e.value
 *  is the return value of the rule labeled with e.
 */
multExpr returns [int value]
    :   e=atom {$value = $e.value;} ('*' e=atom {$value *= $e.value;})*
    ;
```

Rule **multExpr** matches an **atom** optionally followed by a sequence of * operators and **atom** operands. If there is no * operator following the first atom, then the result of **multExpr** is just the **atom**'s result. For any multiplications that follow the first atom, all we have to do is keep updating the **multExpr** result, $value, per action 7. Every time we see a * and an **atom**, we multiply the **multExpr** result by the **atom** result.

The actions in rule **expr**, the outermost expression rule, mirror the actions in **multExpr** except that we are adding and subtracting instead of multiplying:

tour/eval/Expr.g

```
/** return value of multExpr or, if '+'|'-' present, return
 *  multiplication of results from both multExpr references.
 */
expr returns [int value]
    :   e=multExpr {$value = $e.value;}
        (   '+' e=multExpr {$value += $e.value;}
        |   '-' e=multExpr {$value -= $e.value;}
        )*
    ;
```

These actions satisfy the last actions, 8 and 9, from the itemized list earlier in this section. One of the big lessons to learn here is that syntax drives the evaluation of actions in the parser. The structure of an input sequence indicates what kind of thing it is. Therefore, to execute actions only for a particular construct, all we have to do is place actions in the grammar alternative that matches that construct.

What does ANTLR do with grammar actions? ANTLR simply inserts actions right after it generates code for the preceding element—parsers must execute embedded actions after matching the preceding grammar element. ANTLR spits them out verbatim except for the special attribute and template reference translations (see Section 6.6, *References to Attributes within Actions*, on page 146 and Section 9.9, *References to Template Expressions within Actions*, on page 227).

ANTLR's handling of actions is straightforward. For example, ANTLR translates rule return specifications such as this:

```
multExpr returns [int value]
  : ...
  ;
```

to the following Java code:

```
public int multExpr() throws RecognitionException {
    int value = 0; // rule return value, $value
    ...
    return value;
}
```

ANTLR translates labels on rule references, such as e=multExpr, to method call assignments, such as e=multExpr(). References to rule return values, such as $e.value, become e when there is only one return value and e.value when there are multiple return values.

Take a look at the pseudocode for rule **expr**. The highlighted lines in the output derive from embedded actions:

```
public int expr() {
►   int value = 0; // our return value, automatically initialized
    int e = 0;
    try {
        e=multExpr();
►       value = e; // if no + or -, set value to result of multExpr
        // Expr.g:27:9: ( '+' e= multExpr | '-' e= multExpr )*
loop3:
        while ( true ) {
            int alt=3;
            if ( «next input symbol is +» ) { alt=1; }
            else if ( «next input symbol is -» ) { alt=2; }
            switch ( alt ) {
            case 1 :
                match('+');
                e=multExpr();
►               value += e; // add in result of multExpr
                break;
```

```
            case 2 :
                match('-');
                e=multExpr();
                value -= e; // subtract out result of multExpr
                break;
            default :
                break loop3;
            }
        }
    }
    catch (RecognitionException re) {
        reportError(re);
        recover(input,re);
    }
    return value;
}
```

OK, we're ready to test the grammar. We have added actions only to the grammar, so the main() program in Test can stay the same. It still just invokes the **prog** start rule. Note that if we change the grammar, we have to recompile the generated files, such as ExprParser.java and ExprLexer.java. Running expressions into the program now returns the expected computations:

```
⇐   $ java Test
⇐   3+4*5
⇐   EOF
⇒   23
⇐   $ java Test
⇐   (3+4)*5
⇐   EOF
⇒   35
    $
```

Variable assignments will store expression results, and then we can pull the results back later by referencing the variable, as shown in the following input file:

tour/eval/input

```
a=3
b=4
2+a*b
```

Running those expressions into the test rig with IO redirection gives the proper result:

```
$ java Test < input
14
$
```

Upon invalid input, ANTLR reports an error and attempts to recover. Recovering from an error means resynchronizing the parser and pretending that nothing happened. This means the parser should still execute actions after recovering from an error. For example, if you type 3++4, the parser fails at the second + because it can't match it against **atom**:

```
⇐   $ java Test
⇐   3++4
⇐   EOF
⇒   line 1:2 no viable alternative at input '+'
    7
    $
```

The parser recovers by throwing out tokens until it sees a valid **atom**, which is 4 in this case. It can also recover from missing symbols by pretending to insert them. For example, if you leave off a right parenthesis, the parser reports an error but then continues as if you had typed the):

```
⇐   $ java Test
⇐   (3
⇐   EOF
⇒   line 1:2 mismatched input '\n' expecting ')'
    3
    $
```

This concludes your first complete ANTLR example. The program uses a grammar to match expressions and uses embedded actions to evaluate expressions. Now let's look at a more sophisticated solution to the same problem. The solution is more complicated but worth the trouble because it demonstrates how to build a tree data structure and walk it with another grammar. This multipass strategy is useful for complicated translations because they are much easier to handle if you break them down into multiple, simple pieces.

3.3 Evaluating Expressions Using an AST Intermediate Form

Now that you've seen how to build a grammar and add actions to implement a translation, this section will guide you through building the same functionality but using an extra step involving trees. We'll use that same parser grammar to build an intermediate data structure, replacing the embedded actions with tree construction rules. Once we have that tree, we'll use a tree parser to walk the tree and execute embedded actions.

ANTLR will generate a tree parser from a tree grammar automatically for us. The parser grammar converts a token stream into a tree that the tree grammar parses and evaluates.

Although the previous section's approach was more straightforward, it does not scale well to a full programming language. Adding constructs such as function calls or **while** loops to the language means that the interpreter must execute the same bits of code multiple times. Every time the input program invoked a method, the interpreter would have to reparse that method. That approach works but is not as flexible as building an intermediate representation such as an abstract syntax tree (AST) and then walking that data structure to interpret the expressions and assignments. Repeatedly walking an intermediate-form tree is much faster than reparsing an input program. See Section 1.1, *The Big Picture*, on page 4 for more about ASTs.

An intermediate representation is usually a tree of some flavor and records not only the input symbols but also the relationship between those symbols as dictated by the grammatical structure. For example, the following AST represents expression 3+4:

In many cases, you'll see trees represented in text form. For example, the text representation of 3+4 is (+ 3 4). The first symbol after the (is the root and the subsequent symbols are its children. The AST for expression 3+4*5 has the text form (+ 3 (* 4 5)) and looks like this:

As you can see, the structure of the tree implicitly encodes the precedence of the operators. Here, the multiplication must be done first because the addition operation needs the multiplication result as its right operand.

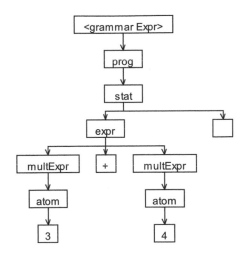

Figure 3.2: PARSE TREE FOR 3+4

An AST is to be distinguished from a *parse tree*, which represents the sequence of rule invocations used to match an input stream. Figure 3.2 shows the parse tree for 3+4 (created by ANTLRWorks).

The leaves of a parse tree are input symbols, and the nonleaves are rule names (the very top node, <grammarExpr>, is something ANTLRWorks adds to show you what grammar the parse tree comes from). The top rule node, **prog**, indicates that 3+4 is a **prog** overall. More specifically, it is a **stat**, which in turn is an **expr** followed by a newline, and so on. So the parse tree records how the recognizer navigates the rules of the grammar to match the input. Compare this to the much smaller and simpler AST for 3+4 where all nodes in the AST are input symbol nodes. The structure of the tree encodes the meaning that '+' is an operator with two children. This is much easier to see without all of the "noise" introduced by the grammar rule nodes.

In practice, it is also useful to decouple the grammar from the trees that it yields; hence, ASTs are superior to parse trees. A tweak in a grammar usually alters the structure of a parse tree while leaving an AST unaffected, which can make a big difference to the code that walks your trees.

Once you have the tree, you can walk it in multiple ways in order to evaluate the tree that the expression represents. In general, I recommend using a grammar to describe the tree structure just as you use a parser grammar to describe a one-dimensional input language. From the tree grammar, ANTLR can generate a tree walker using the same top-down recursive-descent parsing strategy used for lexers and parsers.

In the following sections, you'll learn how to build ASTs, how to walk them with a tree grammar, and how to embed actions within a tree grammar to emit a translation. At the end, you'll have a translator that is functionally equivalent to the previous one.

Building ASTs with a Grammar

Building ASTs with ANTLR is straightforward. Just add AST construction rules to the parser grammar that indicate what tree shape you want to build. This declarative approach is much smaller and faster to read and write than the informal alternative of using arbitrary embedded actions. When you use the output=AST option, each of the grammar rules will implicitly return a node or subtree. The tree you get from invoking the starting rule is the complete AST.

Let's take the raw parser grammar without actions from Section 3.1, *Recognizing Language Syntax*, on page 44 and augment it to build a suitable AST. As you we along, we'll discuss the appropriate AST structure. We begin by telling ANTLR to build a tree node for every token matched on the input stream:

```
grammar Expr;
options {
    output=AST;
    // ANTLR can handle literally any tree node type.
    // For convenience, specify the Java type
    ASTLabelType=CommonTree; // type of $stat.tree ref etc...
}
...
```

For each token the recognizer matches, it will create a single AST node. Given no instructions to the contrary, the generated recognizer will build a flat tree (a linked list) of those nodes. To specify a tree structure, simply indicate which tokens should be considered operators (subtree roots) and which tokens should be excluded from the tree. Use the ^ and ! token reference suffixes, respectively.

Starting with the raw parser grammar without actions, modify the expression rules as follows:

`tour/trees/Expr.g`

```
expr:   multExpr (('+'^|'-'^) multExpr)*
    ;

multExpr
    :   atom ('*'^ atom)*
    ;

atom:   INT
    |   ID
    |   '('! expr ')'!
    ;
```

We only need to add AST operators to tokens +, -, *, (, and). The ! operator suffix on the parentheses tells ANTLR to avoid building nodes for those tokens. Parentheses alter the normal operator precedence by changing the order of rule method calls. The structure of the generated tree, therefore, encodes the arithmetic operator precedence, so we don't need parentheses in the tree.

For the **prog** and **stat** rule, let's use tree rewrite syntax (see Section 4.3, *Rewrite Rules*, on page 88) because it is clearer. For each alternative, add a -> AST construction rule as follows:

`tour/trees/Expr.g`

```
/** Match a series of stat rules and, for each one, print out
 *  the tree stat returns, $stat.tree.  toStringTree() prints
 *  the tree out in form: (root child1 ... childN)
 *  ANTLR's default tree construction mechanism will build a list
 *  (flat tree) of the stat result trees.  This tree will be the input
 *  to the tree parser.
 */
prog:   ( stat {System.out.println($stat.tree.toStringTree());} )+ ;

stat:   expr NEWLINE        -> expr
    |   ID '=' expr NEWLINE -> ^('=' ID expr)
    |   NEWLINE             ->
    ;
```

The grammar elements to the right of the -> operator are tree grammar fragments that indicate the structure of the tree you want to build. The first element within a ^(...) tree specification is the root of the tree. The remaining elements are children of that root. You can think of the rewrite rules as grammar-to-grammar transformations. We'll see in a moment that those exact tree construction rules become alternatives in the tree grammar. The **prog** rule just prints the trees and, further, does not need any explicit tree construction. The default tree construction behavior for **prog** builds what you want: a list of statement trees to parse with the tree grammar.

The rewrite rule for the first alternative says that **stat**'s return value is the tree returned from calling **expr**. The second alternative's rewrite says to build a tree with '=' at the root and **ID** as the first child. The tree returned from calling **expr** is the second child. The empty rewrite for the third alternative simply means don't create a tree.

The lexical rules and the main program in Test do not need any changes. Let's see what the translator does with the previous file, input:

`tour/trees/input`

```
a=3
b=4
2+a*b
```

First ask ANTLR to translate Expr.g to Java code and compile as you did for the previous solution:

```
$ java org.antlr.Tool Expr.g
ANTLR Parser Generator  Version 3.0  1989-2007
$ javac Test.java ExprParser.java ExprLexer.java
$
```

Now, redirect file input into the test rig, and you will see three trees printed, one for each input assignment or expression. The test rig prints the tree returned from start rule **prog** in text form:

```
$ java Test < input
(= a 3)
(= b 4)
(+ 2 (* a b))
$
```

The complete AST built by the parser (and returned from **prog**) looks like the following in memory:

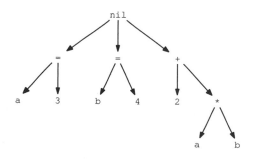

The nil node represents a list of subtrees. The children of the nil node track the elements in a list.

Now we have a parser that builds appropriate ASTs, and we need a way to walk those trees to evaluate the expressions they represent. The next section shows you how to build a tree grammar that describes the AST structure and how to embed actions, like you did in Section 3.2, *Using Syntax to Drive Action Execution*, on page 52.

Evaluating Expressions Encoded in ASTs

In this section, we'll write a tree grammar to describe the structure of the ASTs we built using a parser grammar in the previous section. Then, we'll add actions to compute subexpression results. Like the previous solution, each expression rule will return these partial results. From this augmented grammar, ANTLR will build a tree parser that executes your embedded actions.

Parsing a tree is a matter of walking it and verifying that it has not only the proper nodes but also the proper two-dimensional structure. Since it is harder to build parsers that directly recognize tree structures, ANTLR uses a one-dimensional stream of tree nodes computed by iterating over the nodes in a tree via a depth-first walk. ANTLR inserts special imaginary **UP** and **DOWN** nodes to indicate when the original tree dropped down to a child list or finished walking a child list. In this manner, ANTLR reduces tree parsing to conventional one-dimensional token stream parsing. For example, the following table summarizes how ANTLR serializes two sample input trees.

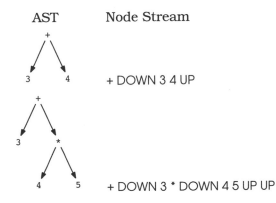

AST   Node Stream

+ DOWN 3 4 UP

+ DOWN 3 * DOWN 4 5 UP UP

The ANTLR notation for a tree grammar is identical to the notation for a regular grammar except for the introduction of a two-dimensional tree construct. The beauty of this is that we can make a tree grammar by cutting and pasting from the parser grammar. We just have to remove recognition grammar elements to the left of the -> operator, leaving the AST rewrite fragments. These fragments build ASTs in the parser grammar and recognize that structure in the tree grammar.

Let's build your first tree grammar in a separate file, which we'll call Eval.g. Tree grammars begin very much like parser grammars with a grammar header and some options:

```
tree grammar Eval; // yields Eval.java

options {
    tokenVocab=Expr; // read token types from Expr.tokens file
    ASTLabelType=CommonTree; // what is Java type of nodes?
}
...
```

The **tokenVocab** option indicates that the tree grammar should preload the token names and associated token types defined in Expr.tokens. (ANTLR generates that file after processing Expr.g.) When we say **ID** in the tree grammar, we want the resulting recognizer to use the same token type that the parser used. **ID** in the tree parser must match the same token type it did in the parser.

Before writing the rules, define a memory hashtable to store variable values, like we did for the parser grammar solution:

tour/trees/Eval.g

```
@header {
import java.util.HashMap;
}

@members {
/** Map variable name to Integer object holding value */
HashMap memory = new HashMap();
}
```

As you'll learn in Section 7.1, *Proper AST Structure*, on page 150, ASTs should be simplified and normalized versions of the token stream that implicitly encode grammatical structure. Consequently, tree grammars are usually much simpler than the associated parser grammars that build their trees. In fact, in this case, all the expression rules from the parser grammar collapse to a single **expr** rule in the tree grammar (see Section 8.3, *Building a Tree Grammar for the C- Language*, on page 187 for more about the expression grammar design pattern). This parser grammar normalizes expression trees to have an operator at the root and its two operands as children. We need an **expr** rule that reflects this structure:

`tour/trees/Eval.g`

```
expr returns [int value]
    :   ^('+' a=expr b=expr) {$value = a+b;}
    |   ^('-' a=expr b=expr) {$value = a-b;}
    |   ^('*' a=expr b=expr) {$value = a*b;}
    |   ID
        {
        Integer v = (Integer)memory.get($ID.text);
        if ( v!=null ) $value = v.intValue();
        else System.err.println("undefined variable "+$ID.text);
        }
    |   INT                 {$value = Integer.parseInt($INT.text);}
    ;
```

Rule **expr** indicates that an expression tree is either a simple node created from an **ID** or an **INT** token or that an expression tree is an operator subtree. With the simplification of the grammar comes a simplification of the associated actions. The **expr** rule normalizes all computations to be of the form "result = a <operator> b." The actions for **ID** and **INT** nodes are identical to the actions we used in the parser grammar's **atom** rule.

The actions for rules **prog** and **stat** are identical to the previous solution. Rule **prog** doesn't have an action—it just matches a sequence of expression or assignment trees. Rule **stat** does one of two things:

1. It matches an expression and prints the result.

2. It matches an assignment and maps the result to the indicated variable.

Here is how to say that in ANTLR notation:

`tour/trees/Eval.g`

```
prog:   stat+ ;

stat:   expr
        {System.out.println($expr.value);}
    |   ^('=' ID expr)
        {memory.put($ID.text, new Integer($expr.value));}
    ;
```

Rule **stat** does not have a third alternative to match the **NEWLINE** (empty) expression like the previous solution. The parser strips out empty expressions by not building trees for them.

What about lexical rules? It turns out you don't need any because tree grammars feed off a stream of tree nodes, not tokens.

At this point, we have a parser grammar that builds an AST and a tree grammar that recognizes the tree structure, executing actions to evaluate expressions. Before we can test the grammars, we have to ask ANTLR to translate the Eval.g grammar to Java code. Execute the following command line:

```
$ java org.antlr.Tool Eval.g
ANTLR Parser Generator  Version 3.0  1989-2007
$
```

This results in the following two files:

Generated File	Description
Eval.java	The recursive-descent tree parser generated from the grammar.
Eval.tokens	The list of token-name, token-type assignments such as INT=6. Nobody will be using this file in this case, but ANTLR always generates a token vocabulary file.

We now need to modify the test rig so that it walks the tree built by the parser. At this point, all it does is launch the parser, so we must add code to extract the result tree from the parser, create a tree walker of type Eval, and start walking the tree with rule **prog**. Here is the complete test rig that does everything we need:

`tour/trees/Test.java`

```java
import org.antlr.runtime.*;
import org.antlr.runtime.tree.*;

public class Test {
    public static void main(String[] args) throws Exception {
        // Create an input character stream from standard in
        ANTLRInputStream input = new ANTLRInputStream(System.in);
        // Create an ExprLexer that feeds from that stream
        ExprLexer lexer = new ExprLexer(input);
        // Create a stream of tokens fed by the lexer
        CommonTokenStream tokens = new CommonTokenStream(lexer);
        // Create a parser that feeds off the token stream
        ExprParser parser = new ExprParser(tokens);
        // Begin parsing at rule prog, get return value structure
        ExprParser.prog_return r = parser.prog();

        // WALK RESULTING TREE
        CommonTree t = (CommonTree)r.getTree(); // get tree from parser
        // Create a tree node stream from resulting tree
        CommonTreeNodeStream nodes = new CommonTreeNodeStream(t);
        Eval walker = new Eval(nodes); // create a tree parser
        walker.prog();                 // launch at start rule prog
    }
}
```

The test rig extracts the AST from the parser by getting it from the return value object **prog** returns. This object is of type prog_return, which ANTLR generates within ExprParser:

```
// from the parser that builds AST for the tree grammar
public static class prog_return extends ParserRuleReturnScope {
    CommonTree tree;
    public Object getTree() { return tree; }
};
```

In this case, rule **prog** does not have a user-defined return value, so the constructed tree is the sole return value.

We have a complete expression evaluator now, so we can try it. Enter some expressions via standard input:

```
⇐  $ java Test
⇐  3+4
⇐  EOF
⇒  (+ 3 4)
   7
⇐  $ java Test
⇐  3*(4+5)*10
⇐  EOF
⇒  (* (* 3 (+ 4 5)) 10)
   270
   $
```

You can also redirect file input into the test rig:

```
$ java Test < input
(= a 3)
(= b 4)
(+ 2 (* a b))
14
$
```

The output of the test rig first shows the tree structure (in serialized form) for each input statement. Serialized form (= a 3) represents the tree built for a=3. The tree has = at the root and two children: a and 3. The rig then emits the expression value computed by the tree parser.

In this chapter, we built two equivalent expression evaluators. The first implementation evaluated expressions directly in a parser grammar, which works great for simpler translations and is the fastest way to build a translator. The second implementation separated parsing and evaluation into two phases. The first phase parsed as before but built ASTs instead of evaluating expressions immediately. The second phase walked the resulting trees to do the evaluation. You will need this second approach when building complicated translators that are easier to understand when broken into subproblems.

In fact, some language tasks, such as programming language interpreters, need to repeatedly walk the input by their very nature. Building a simple and concise intermediate form is much faster than repeatedly parsing the token stream.

At this point, you have an overall sense of how to work with ANTLR and how to write simple grammars to recognize and translate input sentences. But, you have a lot more to learn, as you will see in the next few chapters. In particular, the first two chapters of Part II are important because they explain more about ANTLR grammars, embedded actions, and attributes. If you'd like to jump deeper into ANTLR before reading more of this reference guide, please see the tree-based interpreter tutorial on the wiki, which extends this expression evaluator to support function definitions and function calls.[3]

---

3. See http://www.antlr.org/wiki/display/ANTLR3/Simple+tree-based+interpeter.

Part II

ANTLR Reference

Chapter 4

ANTLR Grammars

ANTLR's highest-level construct is a grammar, which is essentially a list of rules describing the structure of a particular language. From this list of rules, ANTLR generates a recursive-descent parser that recognizes sentences in that language (recursive-descent parsers are the kind of parsers you write by hand). The language might be a programming language or simply a data format, but ANTLR does not intuitively know anything about the language described by the grammar. ANTLR is merely building a recognizer that can answer this question: is an input sequence a valid sentence according to the grammar? In other words, does the input follow the rules of the language described by the grammar? You must embed code within the grammar to extract information, perform a translation, or interpret the incoming symbols in some other way according to the intended application.

This chapter defines the syntax of ANTLR grammars and begins with an introduction to the specification of languages with formal grammars. This chapter covers the following:

- Overall ANTLR file structure
- Grammar lexical elements such as comments, rule names, token names, and so on
- Individual rule syntax including parameters and return values
- Rule elements, actions, alternatives, and EBNF subrules
- Rewrite rule syntax
- Lexical and tree matching rules
- Dynamically scoped attribute syntax
- Grammar-level actions

You'll need to learn the information in this chapter well because building grammar rules and embedding actions will be your core activities. Readers familiar with v2 can scan through looking for margin notes. These notes identify new, improved, and modified features for v3. The wiki also has a good migration page.[1] If you're unfamiliar with ANTLR altogether, you should do an initial quick scan of this chapter and the next to familiarize yourself with the general pieces. Then try modifying a few existing v3 grammar examples.[2]

4.1 Describing Languages with Formal Grammars

Before diving into the actual syntax of ANTLR, let's discuss the general idea of describing languages with grammars and define some common terms. We'll start by explicitly stating the behavior of a translator.

A translator is a program that reads some input and emits some output. By *input*, we mean a sequence of *vocabulary symbols*, not random characters. The vocabulary symbols are analogous to the words in the English language. An input sequence is formally called a *sentence*. Technically, each sentence represents a complete input sequence implicitly followed by the end-of-file symbol. For example, a complete Java class definition file is a sentence, as is a data file full of comma-separated values. A *language* then is simply a well-defined set of sentences. A *translator* is a program that maps each input sentence, s, in its input language to a specific output sentence, t.[3]

Translating complete sentences such as Java class definitions in a single step is generally impractical. Translators decompose sentences into multiple subsequences, or *phrases*, that are easier to translate. A phrase, x, exists somewhere in sentence s, s="...x..." (at the outermost level, s="x"). Translators further decompose phrases into subphrases, subsubphrases, and so on. For example, the statements in a Java method are phrases of the method, which is itself a phrase of the overall class definition sentence. Breaking sentences down into phrases and subphrases is analogous to breaking large methods into smaller, more manageable methods.

---

1. See http://www.antlr.org/wiki/display/ANTLR3/Migrating+from+ANTLR+2+to+ANTLR+3.
2. See http://www.antlr.org.
3. This translator definition covers compilers, interpreters, and in some sense almost any program that generates output.

To map each phrase x to some output phrase y, a translator computes y as a function of x. The mapping function can be anything from a simple lookup to an involved computation. A lookup might map input symbol x="int" to y="integer" and a computation might map x="i+1-1" to y="i". In order to execute the correct mapping function, the translator needs to identify x. Identifying x within a sentence means *recognizing* it or distinguishing it from the other phrases within a linear sequence of symbols.

To recognize phrase x, a translator needs to know what x looks like. The best way to tell a computer what phrases and sentences look like is to use a formal, text-based description called a *grammar*. Grammars conform to a DSL that was specifically designed for describing other languages. Such a DSL is called a *metalanguage*. English is just too loose to describe other languages, and besides, computers can't yet grok English prose.

A grammar describes the syntax of a language. We say that a grammar "generates a language" because we use grammars to describe what languages look like. In practice, however, the goal of formally describing a language is to obtain a program that recognizes sentences in the language. ANTLR converts grammars to such recognizers.

A grammar is a set of rules where each rule describes some phrase (subsentence) of the language. The rule where parsing begins is called the *start rule* (in ANTLR grammars, any and all rules can be the starting rule). Each rule consists of one or more *alternatives*.

For example, a rule called **variableDef** might have two alternatives, one for a simple definition and another for a definition with an initialization expression. Often the rules in a grammar correspond to abstract language phrases such as **statement** and **expression**. There will also be a number of finer-grained helper rules, such as **multiplicativeExpression** and **declarator**. Rules reference other rules as well as tokens to match the phrase and subphrase structure of the various sentences.

The most common grammar notation is called *Backus-Naur Form* (BNF). ANTLR uses a grammar dialect derived from YACC [Joh79] where rules begin with a lowercase letter and token types begin with an uppercase letter.

Here is a sample rule with two alternatives:

```
/** Match either a simple declaration followed by ';' or match
 *  a declaration followed by an initialization expression.
 *  Rules: variableDef, declaration, expr.
 *  Tokens: SEMICOLON, EQUALS
 */
variableDef
    :   declaration SEMICOLON
    |   declaration EQUALS expr SEMICOLON
    ;
```

BNF notation is cumbersome for specifying things like repeated elements because you must use recursion. ANTLR supports *Extended BNF* (EBNF) notation that allows optional and repeated elements. EBNF also supports parenthesized groups of grammar elements called *subrules*. See Section 4.3, *Extended BNF Subrules*, on page 83 and, in particular, Figure 4.3, on page 84.

EBNF grammars are called *context-free grammars* (CFGs). They are called context-free because we can't restrict rules to certain contexts. For example, we can't constrain an expression rule to situations where the recognizer has matched or will match another rule. Such a grammar is called *context-sensitive grammar*, but no one uses them in practice because there is no efficient context-sensitive recognition algorithm. Instead, we'll use semantic and syntactic predicates to achieve the same effect (see Chapter 13, *Semantic Predicates*, on page 309 and Chapter 14, *Syntactic Predicates*, on page 323).

The remainder of this chapter describes ANTLR's EBNF grammar syntax using the concepts and terminology defined in this section.

4.2 Overall ANTLR Grammar File Structure

ANTLR generates recognizers that apply grammatical structure to a stream of input symbols, which can be characters, tokens, or tree nodes. ANTLR presents you with a single, consistent syntax for lexing, parsing, and tree parsing. In fact, ANTLR generates the same kind of recognizer for all three. Contrast this with having to use different syntax for lexer and parser as you do with tools lex [Les75] and YACC [Joh79].

This section describes ANTLR's consistent grammar syntax for the four kinds of ANTLR grammars (*grammarType*): **lexer**, **parser**, **tree**, and combined lexer and parser (no modifier). All grammars have the same basic structure:

```
/** This is a document comment */
grammarType grammar name;
«optionsSpec»
«tokensSpec»
«attributeScopes»
«actions»

/** doc comment */
rule1 : ... | ... | ... ;
rule2 : ... | ... | ... ;
...
```

The order of the grammar sections must be as shown, with the rules appearing after all the other sections.

From a grammar T, ANTLR generates a recognizer with a name indicating its role. Using the Java language target, ANTLR generates TLexer.java, TParser.java, and T.java for **lexer**, **parser**, and **tree** grammars, respectively. For combined grammars, ANTLR generates both TLexer.java and TParser.java as well as an intermediate temporary file, T__.g, containing the lexer specification extracted from the combined grammar. ANTLR always generates a vocabulary file in addition, called T.tokens, that other grammars use to keep their token types in sync with T.

A target is one of the languages in which ANTLR knows how to generate code.

The following simple (combined) grammar illustrates some of the basic features of ANTLR grammars:

grammars/simple/T.g

```
grammar T;
options {
    language=Java;
}
@members {
String s;
}
r : ID '#' {s = $ID.text; System.out.println("found "+s);} ;
ID: 'a'..'z'+ ;
WS: (' '|'\n'|'\r')+ {skip();} ; // ignore whitespace
```

Grammar T matches an identifier followed by a pound symbol. The action sets an instance variable and prints the text matched for the identifier. There is another action, this one in the lexer. {skip();} tells the lexer to skip the whitespace token and look for another.

To have ANTLR translate grammar T to Java code (or any other target according to the grammar's **language** option in T.g), use the following command line:

```
$ java org.antlr.Tool T.g
ANTLR Parser Generator  Version 3.0  1989-2007
$
```

The following main program illustrates how to have grammar T parse data from the standard input stream.

grammars/simple/Test.java

```
import org.antlr.runtime.*;

public class Test {
    public static void main(String[] args) throws Exception {
        ANTLRInputStream input = new ANTLRInputStream(System.in);
        TLexer lexer = new TLexer(input);
        CommonTokenStream tokens = new CommonTokenStream(lexer);
        TParser parser = new TParser(tokens);
        parser.r();
    }
}
```

Support classes ANTLRInputStream and CommonTokenStream provide streams of characters and tokens to the lexer and parser. Parsers begin parsing when control programs, such as Test, invoke one of the methods generated from grammar rules. The first rule invoked is usually called the *start symbol*. By convention, the first rule is usually the start symbol, though you can invoke any rule first. Here, parser.r() invokes rule r as the start symbol.

To test some input against grammar T, launch Java class Test in the usual way, and then type an identifier followed by space and then # and then a newline. To close standard input, do not forget to type the end-of-file character appropriate for your operating system, such as Ctrl+D on Unix. Here is a sample session:

```
⇐   $ java Test
⇐   abc #
⇐   EOF
⇒   found abc
    $
```

Grammar Lexicon

The lexicon of ANTLR is familiar to most programmers because it follows the syntax of C and its derivatives with some extensions for grammatical descriptions.

Comments

There are single-line, multiline, and Javadoc-style comments:

```
/** This grammar is an example illustrating the three kinds
 *  of comments.
 */
grammar T;

/* a multi-line
   comment
 */

/** This rule matches a declarator for my language */
decl : ID ; // match a variable name
```

Identifiers

Token names always start with a capital letter and so do lexer rules. Nonlexer rule names always start with a lowercase letter. The initial character can be followed by uppercase and lowercase letters, digits, and underscores. Only ASCII characters are allowed in ANTLR names. Here are some sample names:

```
ID, LPAREN, RIGHT_CURLY // token names/rules
expr, simpleDeclarator, d2, header_file // rule names
```

Literals

ANTLR does not distinguish between character and string literals as most languages do. All literal strings one or more characters in length are enclosed in single quotes such as ';', 'if', '>=', and '\'' (refers to the one-character string containing the single quote character). Literals never contain regular expressions.

This changed in v3. In v2, char literals used single quotes, and string literals used double quotes.

Literals can contain Unicode escape sequences of the form \uXXXX, where XXXX is the hexadecimal Unicode character value. For example, '\u00E8' is the French letter *e* with a grave accent: 'è'. ANTLR also understands the usual special escape sequences: '\n' (newline), '\r' (carriage return), '\b' (backspace), and '\f' (form feed). ANTLR itself does not currently allow non-ASCII input characters. If you need non-ASCII characters within a literal, you must use the Unicode escape sequences at the moment.

The recognizers that ANTLR generates, however, assume a character vocabulary containing all Unicode characters.

Actions

Actions are code blocks written in the target language. You can use actions in a number of places within a grammar, but the syntax is always the same: arbitrary text surrounded by curly braces. To get the close curly character, escape it with a backslash: {System.out.println("\}");}. The action text should conform to the target language as specified with the **language** option.

The only interpretation ANTLR does inside actions relates to symbols for grammar attribute and output template references. See Chapter 6, *Attributes and Actions*, on page 117.

Templates

To emit structured text, such as source code, from a translator, use StringTemplate templates (see Chapter 9, *Generating Structured Text with Templates and Grammars*, on page 195). Set the **output** option to **template**. Each parser or tree parser rule then implicitly returns a template, which you can set with template rewrites. These rewrite templates are most often references to template names defined in a StringTemplate group elsewhere, but you can also specify in-line template literals. Template literals are either single-line strings in double quotes, "...", or multiline strings in double angle brackets, <<...>>, as shown in the highlighted section in the following grammar:

New in v3.

```
/** Insert implied "this." on front of method call */
methodCall
    :   ID '(' ')' -> template(m={$ID.text}) "this.<m>();"
    ;
methodBody
    :   '{' ACTION '}'
        -> template(body={$ACTION.text})
►           <<
►           {
►               <body>
►           }
►           >>
    ;
```

We'll explore the full syntax for template construction rules that follow the -> operator in Chapter 9, *Generating Structured Text with Templates and Grammars*, on page 195. For now, just be aware that templates are enclosed in either double quotes or double angle brackets.

The next section describes how to define rules within a grammar.

4.3 Rules

The rules of a grammar collectively define the set of valid sentences in a language. An individual rule, then, describes a partial sentence (sometimes called a *phrase* or *substructure*). Each rule has one or more alternatives. The alternatives can, in turn, reference other rules just as one function can call another function in a programming language. If a rule directly or indirectly invokes itself, the rule is considered recursive. The syntax for rules in lexers, parsers, and tree parsers is the same except that tree grammar rules may use tree structure elements, as we'll see below.

Because of ANTLR's unified recognition strategy, lexer grammar rules can also use recursion. Recursive rules in the lexer are useful for matching things such as nested comments. Contrast this with most lexer generators such as lex that are limited to nonrecursive regular expressions rather than full grammars.

Besides specifying syntactic phrase structure, ANTLR rules have a number of components for specifying options, attributes, exception handling, tree construction, and template construction. The general structure of a rule looks like the following:

```
/** comment */
access-modifier rule-name[«arguments»] returns [«return-values»]
    «throws-spec»
    «options-spec»
    «rule-attribute-scopes»
    «rule-actions»
    :   «alternative-1» -> «rewrite-rule-1»
    |   «alternative-2» -> «rewrite-rule-2»
    ...
    |   «alternative-n» -> «rewrite-rule-n»
    ;
    «exceptions-spec»
```

The simplest rules specify pure syntactic structure:

```
/** A decl is a type followed by ID followed by 0 or more
 *  ',' ID sequences.
 */
decl:   type ID (',' ID)* ;  // E.g., "int a", "int a,b"
type:   'int'   // match either an int or float keyword
    |   'float'
    ;
ID  :   'a'..'z'+ ;
```

As an optimization, ANTLR collapses rules and subrules, whose alternatives are single token references without actions, into token sets, as demonstrated in the following rule:

```
type:   'int' | 'float' | 'void' ;
```

ANTLR generates a bit set test or token type range check instead of a **switch** statement.

Elements within Alternatives

The elements within an alternative specify what to do at any moment just like statements in a programming language. Elements either match a construct on the input stream or execute an action. These actions perform a translation or aid in the recognition process, such as updating or testing a symbol table. You can suffix elements with operators that alter the recognition of that element or specify what kind of abstract syntax tree to create (see Chapter 7, *Tree Construction*, on page 149). Figure 4.1, on the facing page, summarizes the core elements and their variations.

Element Sets

Token and character elements can be combined into sets using subrule notation, a range operator, or the "not" operator, as summarized in the following table.

Syntax	Description
$'x'..'y'$	*Lexer*. Match any single character between range x and y, inclusively.
$(A \mid B \mid \ldots \mid C)$	*Parser or tree parser*. Match any token from the list of tokens within the subrule. These subrules are collapsed to a set only when there are no actions and each alternative is exactly one token reference.
$('x'..'y' \mid 'a' \mid \ldots \mid 'b')$	*Lexer*. Match any single character from the list of characters and ranges within the subrule.
$\sim x$	*Any grammar*. Match any single character or token *not* in x where x can be a single element, a range, or a subrule set.

Element Labels

Actions that need to refer to rule, token, or character references within a grammar can do so by referencing labels attached to those elements. To label an element, assign the element to a label name: $x=T$. For example, the following rule defines labels on a string literal, a token reference, and a rule reference:

```
classDef
    :   c='class' name=ID '{' m=members '}'
    ;
```

Actions can reference these labels via $c, $name, and $m, where the first two labels have type Token and the last label has type members_return.

Syntax	Description
T	*Parser or tree parser*. Match token T at the current input position. Tokens always begin with a capital letter.
T	*Lexer*. Invoke lexer rule T.
T[«args»]	*Lexer*. Invoke **fragment** lexer rule T, passing in a list of arguments. It does not work for non-**fragment** rules.
'literal'	*Any grammar*. Match the string literal at the current input position. A string literal is simply a token with a fixed string.
r	*Parser or tree parser*. Match rule **r** at current input position, which amounts to invoking the rule just like a function call.
r[«args»]	*Parser or tree parser*. Match rule **r** at current input position, passing in a list of arguments just like a function call. The arguments inside the square brackets are in the syntax of the target language and are usually a comma-separated list of expressions.
.	*Any grammar*. The wildcard. Match a single token in a parser. Match any single character in a lexer. In a tree parser, match an entire subtree. For example, the following rule matches a function without parsing the body: func : ^(FUNC ID args .) ;. The wildcard skips the entire last child (the body subtree).
{«action»}	*Any grammar*. Execute an action immediately after the preceding alternative element and immediately before the following alternative element. The action conforms to the syntax of the target language. ANTLR ignores what is inside the action except for attribute and template references such as $x.y. Actions are not executed if the parser is backtracking; instead, the parser rewinds the input after backtracking and reparses in order to execute the actions once it knows which alternatives will match.
{«p»}?	*Any grammar*. Evaluate semantic predicate «p». Throw FailedPredicateException if «p» evaluates to false at parse time. Expression «p» conforms to the target language syntax. ANTLR might also hoist semantic predicates into parsing decisions to guide the parse. These predicates are invaluable when symbol table information is needed to disambiguate syntactically ambiguous alternatives. Cf. Chapter 13, *Semantic Predicates*, on page 309 for more information.

Figure 4.1: ANTLR RULE ELEMENTS

ANTLR generates members_return while generating code for rule **members**. See Chapter 6, *Attributes and Actions*, on page 117 for more information about the predefined properties of token and rule labels.

When an action must refer to a collection of tokens matched by an alternative, ANTLR provides a convenient labeling mechanism that automatically adds elements to a list in the order they are matched, for example, $x+=T$.[4] In the following example, all **ID** tokens are added to a single list called ids.

New in v3.

```
decl:   type ids+=ID (',' ids+=ID)* ';'
    ;
```

In an action, the type of ids is List and will contain all Token objects associated with **ID** tokens matched at the time of reference. ANTLR generates the following code for rule **decl** where the highlighted sections result from the ids label:

```
public void decl() throws RecognitionException {
▶       Token ids=null;
▶       List list_ids=null;
        try {
            // match type
            type();
            // match ids+=ID
▶           ids=(Token)input.LT(1);
            match(input,ID,FOLLOW_ID_in_decl13);
▶           if (list_ids==null) list_ids=new ArrayList();
▶           list_ids.add(ids);
            ...
        }
        catch (RecognitionException re) {
            «error-handling»
        }
}
```

You can also collect rule AST or template return values using the += operator:

```
options {output=AST;} // or output=template
// collect ASTs from expr into a list called $e
elist:  e+=expr (',' e+=expr)* ;
```

ANTLR will emit an error if you use a += label without the **output** option. In an action, the type of e will be List and will contain either tree nodes (for example, CommonTree) or StringTemplate instances.

---

4. This was suggested by John D. Mitchell, a longtime supporter of ANTLR and research collaborator.

Syntax	Description
$T!$	*Parser.* Match token T, but do not include a tree node for it in the tree created for this rule.
$r!$	*Parser.* Invoke rule r, but do not include its subtree in the tree created for the enclosing rule.
$T^\wedge$	*Parser.* Match token T and create an AST node using the parser's tree adapter. Make the node the root of the enclosing rule's tree regardless of whether T is in a subrule or at the outermost level.
$r^\wedge$	*Parser.* Invoke rule r, and make its return AST node the root of the enclosing rule's tree regardless of whether r is in a subrule or at the outermost level. Rule r should must a single node, not a subtree.

Figure 4.2: TREE CONSTRUCTION OPERATORS FOR RULE ELEMENTS

Tree Operators

If you are building trees, you can suffix token and rule reference elements in parsers with AST construction operators. These operators indicate the kind of node to create in the tree and its position relative to other nodes. These operators are extremely convenient in some kinds of rules such as expression specifications. But, in general, the rewrite rules provide a more readable tree construction specification. Figure 4.2 summarizes the tree operators and rewrite rules.

See Chapter 7, *Tree Construction*, on page 149 for more information about tree construction using these operators.

Extended BNF Subrules

ANTLR supports EBNF grammars: BNF grammars augmented with repetition and optional operators as well as parenthesized subrules to support terse grammatical descriptions. All parenthesized blocks of grammar elements are considered subrules. Because single elements suffixed with an EBNF operator have implied parentheses around them, they too are subrules. Subrules are like anonymous embedded rules and support an **options** section. The ANTLR EBNF syntax is summarized in Figure 4.3, on the next page.

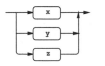

$(\text{«}x\text{»}|\text{«}y\text{»}|\text{«}z\text{»})$
Match any alternative within the subrule exactly once.

$x?$
Element x is optional.

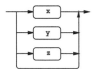

$(\text{«}x\text{»}|\text{«}y\text{»}|\text{«}z\text{»})?$
Match nothing or any alternative within subrule.

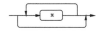

$x*$
Match element x zero or more times.

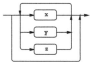

$(\text{«}x\text{»}|\text{«}y\text{»}|\text{«}z\text{»})*$
Match an alternative within subrule zero or more times.

$x+$
Match element x one or more times.

$(\text{«}x\text{»}|\text{«}y\text{»}|\text{«}z\text{»})+$
Match an alternative within subrule one or more times.

Figure 4.3: EBNF GRAMMAR SUBRULES WHERE «...» REPRESENTS A GRAMMAR FRAGMENT

Here is an example that matches an optional **else** clause for an **if** statement:

```
stat:   'if' '(' expr ')' ( 'else' stat )? // optional else clause
    |   ...
    ;
```

In the lexer, you will commonly use subrules to match repeated character groups. For example, here are two common rules for identifiers and integers:

```
/** Match identifiers that must start with '_' or a letter. The first
 *  characters are followed by zero or more letters, digits, or '_'.
 */
ID : ('a'..'z'|'A'..'Z'|'_') ('a'..'z'|'A'..'Z'|'_'|'0'..'9')* ;
INT: '0'..'9'+ ;
```

Subrules allow all the rule-level options listed in Figure 4.4, on page 98, and use this syntax:

```
( options {«option-assignments»} : «subrule-alternatives» )
```

The only addition is the handy **greedy** option. This option alters how ANTLR resolves nondeterminisms between subrule alternatives and the subrule exit branch. A *nondeterminism* is a situation in which the recognizer cannot decide which path to take because an input symbol predicts taking multiple paths (see Section 11.5, *Ambiguities and Nondeterminisms*, on page 264). Greedy decisions match as much input as possible in the current subrule even if the element following the subrule can match that same input. A nongreedy decision instead chooses to exit the subrule as soon as it sees input consistent with what follows the subrule. This option is useful only when ANTLR detects a nondeterminism; otherwise, ANTLR knows there is only one viable path. The default is to be greedy in all recognizer types.

You'll use nongreedy subrules in rules that can match any character until it sees some character sequence. For example, the following is a rule that matches multiline comments. The subrule matches any character until it finds the final '*/':

```
ML_COMMENT
    :   '/*' ( options {greedy=false;} : . )* '*/'
    ;
```

Because the subrule can also match '*/', ANTLR considers the subrule nondeterministic. By telling ANTLR to be nongreedy, the subrule matches characters until it sees the end of the comment.

What you really want to type, though, and what you will see in other systems, is the terse notation: '.*' and '.+'. Unfortunately, following the usual convention that all subrules are greedy makes this notation useless. Such greedy subrules would match all characters until the end of file. Instead, ANTLR considers them idioms for "Match any symbol until you see what lies beyond the subrule." ANTLR automatically makes these two subrules nongreedy. So, you can use '.*' instead of manually specifying the option.

Actions Embedded within Rules

To execute an action before anything else in the rule and to define local variables, use an **init** action. Similarly, to execute something after any alternative has been executed and right before the rule returns, use an **after** action. For example, here is a rule that initializes a return value to zero before matching an alternative. It then prints the return value after matching one of the alternatives:

*New in v3. The **after** action is new, and the **init** action was simply a code block in v2.*

```
r returns [int n]
@init {
    $n=0; // init return value
}
@after {
    System.out.println("returning value n="+$n);
}
    :    ... {$n=23;}
    |    ... {$n=9;}
    |    ... {$n=1;}
    |    // use initialized value of n
    ;
```

One of the most common uses for the **init** action is to initialize return values. See Chapter 6, *Attributes and Actions*, on page 117 for more information.

Rule Arguments and Return Values

Just like function calls, ANTLR parser and tree parser rules can have arguments and return values. ANTLR lexer rules cannot have return values, and only **fragment** lexer rules (see Section 4.3, *Lexical Rules*, on page 92) can have parameters. Those rules that can define return values can return multiple values, whereas functions in most languages can return only a single value. For example, consider the following rule with two arguments and two return values:

New in v3. In v2, you could have only one return value.

```
r[int a, String b] returns [int c, String d]
    : ... {$c=$a; $d=$b;}
    ;
```

To set the return value, use the relevant attribute on the left side of an assignment such as $c=...;$. See Chapter 6, *Attributes and Actions*, on page 117 for more information about the use of attributes.

For rule r, ANTLR generates the following code where the highlighted executable lines derive from rule r's parameters and return values:

```
public static class r_return extends ParserRuleReturnScope {
►    public int c;
►    public String d;
};
public r_return r(int a, String b) throws RecognitionException {
►    r_return retval = new r_return();
►    retval.start = input.LT(1);
     try {
         ...
►        retval.c=a; retval.d=b;
     }
     catch (RecognitionException re) {
         reportError(re);
         recover(input,re);
     }
     finally {
►        retval.stop = input.LT(-1);
     }
     return retval;
}
```

Rule references use syntax similar to function calls. The only difference is that, instead of parentheses, you use square brackets to pass rule parameters. For example, the following rule invokes rule r with two parameters and then, in an action, accesses the second return value, $v.d:

```
s   :   ... v=r[3,"test"] {System.out.println($v.d);}
    ;
```

Dynamic Rule Attribute Scopes

Besides the predefined rule attributes, rules can define scopes of attributes that are visible to all rules invoked by a rule. Here's a simple example that makes attribute name available to any rule invoked directly or indirectly by **method**:

New in v3.

```
method
@scope {
    String name;
}
    :   'void' ID {$method::name = $ID.text;} '(' args ')' body
    ;
```

Down in a deeply nested expression rule, for example, you can directly access the method's name without having to pass the method name all the way down to that rule from **method**:

```
atom:   ID {System.out.println("ref "+$ID.text+" in "+$method::name);}
    ;
```

If for some reason you wanted your language to allow nested method definitions, each method definition would automatically get its own name variable. Upon entry to **method**, the recognizer pushes the old name value onto a stack and makes space for a new name. Upon exit, **method** pops off the current name value. See Section 6.5, *Dynamic Attribute Scopes for Interrule Communication*, on page 135 for more information.

Rewrite Rules

ANTLR parsers can generate ASTs or StringTemplate templates by specifying an **output** option (**AST** and **template**, respectively). In either case, all rules have an implied return value that is set manually in an action or, more commonly, in a *rewrite rule* (*rewrite alternative* would be more accurate, but *rewrite rule* sounds better). Every alternative, whether it is in a subrule or the outermost rule level, can have a rewrite rule. Regardless of location, the rewrite rule always sets the return object for the entire rule. Symbol -> begins each rewrite rule. For example, the following rule matches the unary minus operator followed by an identifier. The rewrite rule makes a tree with the operator at the root and the identifier as the first and only child.

New in v3.

```
unaryID : '-' ID -> ^('-' ID) ;
```

As a more complicated example, consider the following rule that specifies how to match a class definition. It also provides a rewrite rule that describes the shape of the desired AST with 'class' at the root and the other elements as children.

```
classDefinition
    :   'class' ID ('extends' sup=typename)?
        ('implements' i+=typename (',' i+=typename)*)?
        '{'
        (   variableDefinition
        |   methodDefinition
        |   ctorDefinition
        )*
        '}'
        -> ^('class' ID ^('extends' $sup)? ^('implements' $i+)?
            variableDefinition* ctorDefinition* methodDefinition*
            )
    ;
```

Rewrite rules for AST construction are parser-grammar-to-tree-grammar mappings. When generating templates, on the other hand, rewrite rules specify the template to create and a set of argument assignments that set the attributes of the template. The following expression rule from a tree grammar illustrates how to create template instances:

```
expr:   ^(CALL c=expr args=exprList) -> call(m={$c.st},args={$args.st})
    |   ^(INDEX a=expr i=expr) -> index(list={$a.st},e={$i.st})
    |   primary -> {$primary.st} // return ST computed in primary
    ;
```

The rewrite rule in the first alternative of rule **expr** instantiates the template called call and sets that template's two attributes: m and args. The argument list represents the interface between ANTLR and StringTemplate. The assignments reference arbitrary actions in order to set the attribute values. In this case, m is set to the template returned from invoking rule **expr**. args is set to the template returned from invoking **exprList**. The third alternative's rewrite rule does not reference a template by name. Instead, the specified action evaluates to a StringTemplate instance. In this case, it evaluates to the template returned from invoking **primary**.

The template definitions for call and index are defined elsewhere in a StringTemplate group, but you can specify in-line templates if necessary. Here are some sample templates in StringTemplate group format:

```
call(m,args) ::=   "<m>(<args>)"
index(list,e) ::=  "<list>[e]"
```

See Chapter 7, *Tree Construction*, on page 149 and Chapter 9, *Generating Structured Text with Templates and Grammars*, on page 195 for details about using rewrite rules.

Rule Exception Handling

When an error occurs within a rule, ANTLR catches the exception, reports the error, attempts to recover (possibly by consuming more tokens), and then returns from the rule. In other words, every rule is wrapped in a **try/catch** block:

```
void rule() throws RecognitionException {
    try {
        «rule-body»
    }
    catch (RecognitionException re) {
        reportError(re);
        recover(input,re);
    }
}
```

To replace that **catch** clause, specify an exception after the rule definition:

```
r   :   ...
    ;
    catch[RecognitionException e] { throw e; }
```

This example shows how to avoid reporting an error and avoid recovering. This rule rethrows the exception, which is useful when it makes more sense for a higher-level rule to report the error.

You can specify other exceptions as well:

```
r   :   ...
    ;
    catch[FailedPredicateException fpe] { ... }
    catch[RecognitionException e] { ...; }
```

When you need to execute an action even if an exception occurs (and even when the parser is backtracking), put it into the **finally** clause:

```
r   :   ...
    ;
    // catch blocks go first
    finally { System.out.println("exit rule r"); }
```

The **finally** clause is the last part a rule executes before returning. The clause executes after any dynamic scopes close and after memoization occurs; see Section 6.5, *Dynamic Attribute Scopes for Interrule Communication*, on page 135 and Section 14.5, *Memoization*, on page 335. If you want to execute an action after the rule finishes matching the alternatives but before it does its cleanup work, use an **after** action (Section 6.2, *Embedding Actions within Rules*, on page 124).

ANTLR also knows how to do single-token insertion and deletion in order to recover in the middle of an alternative without having to exit the surrounding rule. This all happens automatically.

See Chapter 10, *Error Reporting and Recovery*, on page 231 for a complete list of exceptions and for more general information about their reporting and recovery.

Syntactic Predicates

A syntactic predicate indicates the syntactic context that must be satisfied if an alternative is to match. It amounts to specifying the lookahead language for an alternative (see Section 2.7, *Categorizing Recognizers*, on page 34 for more information about lookahead). In general, a parser will need to backtrack over the elements within a syntactic predicate to properly test the predicate against the input stream. Alternatives predicated with syntactic predicates are attempted in the order specified. The first alternative that matches wins. The syntax of a syntactic predicate looks like an ordinary subrule, but with a suffix operator of =>. Syntactic predicates must be on the extreme left edge of an alternative. For example, consider rule **stat** whose two alternatives are ambiguous:

```
stat:   (decl)=>decl ';'
    |   expr ';'
    ;
```

The syntactic predicate on the first alternative tells ANTLR that a successful match of **decl** predicts that alternative. The parser attempts rule **decl**. If it matches, the parser rewinds the input and begins parsing the first alternative. If the predicate fails, the parser assumes that the second alternative matches.

This example illustrates the resolution of the C++ ambiguity that statements such as T(i); can be either declarations or expressions syntactically. To resolve the issue, the language reference says to choose declaration over expression if both are valid. Because ANTLR chooses the first alternative whose predicate matches, the decl ';' alternative matches input T(i);.

The last alternative in a series of predicated alternatives does not need a predicate because it is assumed to be the default if nothing else before it matches. Alternatives that are not mutually ambiguous, even in the same block alternatives, do not need syntactic predicates. For example, adding a few more alternatives to rule **stat** does not confuse ANTLR:

```
stat:   (decl)=>decl ';'
    |   expr ';'
    |   'return' expr ';'
    |   'break' ';'
    ;
```

Even when the second ambiguous alternative is last, ANTLR still knows to choose it if the first alternative fails:

```
stat:   (decl)=>decl ';'
    |   'return' expr ';'
    |   'break' ';'
    |   expr ';'
    ;
```

As a convenience and to promote clean-looking grammars, ANTLR provides the **backtrack** option. This option tells ANTLR to automatically insert syntactic predicates where necessary to disambiguate decisions that are not *LL(*)* (cf. Section 2.7, *Categorizing Recognizers*, on page 34). Here is an alternative, functionally equivalent version of rule **stat**:

```
stat
options {
    backtrack=true;
}
    :   decl ';'
    |   'return' expr ';'
    |   'break' ';'
    |   expr ';'
    ;
```

See Chapter 14, *Syntactic Predicates*, on page 323 for more information about how syntactic predicates guide the parse.

Lexical Rules

Lexer rules differ from parser and tree parser rules in a number of important ways, though their syntax is almost identical. Most obviously, lexer rules are always token names and must begin with a capital letter. For example, the following rule matches ASCII identifiers:

```
ID  :   ('a'..'z'|'A'..'Z'|'_') ('a'..'z'|'A'..'Z'|'_'|'0'..'9')* ;
```

To distinguish methods generated from rules in the lexer from the token type definitions, ANTLR prefixes methods with m. Rule **ID**'s method is mID(), for example.

Unlike a parser grammar, there is no start symbol in a lexer grammar. The grammar is simply a list of token definitions that the lexer can match at any moment on the input stream. ANTLR generates a method called nextToken() (that satisfies the TokenSource interface). nextToken() amounts to a big **switch** statement that routes the lexer to one of the lexer rules depending on which token is approaching.

Just as with parser grammars, it is useful to break up large rules into smaller rules. This makes rules more readable and also reusable by other rules. The next section describes how to factor rules into helper rules.

Fragment Lexer Rules

Because ANTLR assumes that all lexer rules are valid tokens, you must prefix factored "helper rules" with the **fragment** keyword. This keyword tells ANTLR that you intend for this rule to be called only by other rules and that it should not yield a token to the parser. The following rule specifies the syntax of a Unicode character and uses a **fragment** rule to match the actual hex digits:

Changed in v3. v2 called these helper rules protected, a truly horrible name.

```
UNICODE_CHAR
    :   '\\' 'u' HEX_DIGIT HEX_DIGIT HEX_DIGIT HEX_DIGIT
    ;
fragment
HEX_DIGIT
    :   '0'..'9'|'a'..'f'|'A'..'F'
    ;
```

If **UNICODE_CHAR** were to be used only by another rule, such as **STRING**, then it too would be a **fragment** rule.

It makes no sense to allow parameters and return values on token definition rules because, in general, no one is invoking those rules explicitly. Method nextToken() is implicitly invoking those rules, and it would not know what parameters to pass and could not use the return value. **fragment** rules, on the other hand, are never implicitly invoked—other lexer rules must explicitly invoke them. Consequently, **fragment** rules can define parameters, though they can't define return values because lexer rules always return Token objects. For example, here is a rule that matches (possibly nested) code blocks in curly braces and takes a parameter dictating whether it should strip the curlies:

```
fragment
CODE[boolean stripCurlies]
    :   '{' ( CODE[stripCurlies] | ~('{'|'}') )* '}'
        {
        if ( stripCurlies ) {
            setText(getText().substring(1, getText().length()));
        }
        }
    ;
```

Another rule would invoke **CODE** via CODE[false] or CODE[true].

Also note that lexer rule **CODE** is recursive because it invokes itself. This is the only way to properly match nested code blocks. You could add embedded actions to count the number of open and close braces, but that is inelegant. ANTLR generates recursive-descent recognizers for lexers just as it does for parsers and tree parsers. Consequently, ANTLR supports recursive lexer rules, unlike other tools such as lex.

Lexer rules can call other lexer rules, but that doesn't change the token type of the invoking rule. When lexer rule T calls another lexer rule or fragment rule, the return type for T is still T, not the token type of the other lexer rule.

Ignoring Whitespace and Comments

One of the most difficult lexing issues to deal with is the paradox that the parser must ignore whitespace and comments but at the same time provide access to those tokens for use during translation. To solve this problem, ANTLR allows each token object to exist on different *channels*, sort of like different radio frequencies. The parser can "tune" to any single channel; hence, it ignores any off-channel tokens. Objects implementing the TokenStream interface, such as CommonTokenStream, provide access to these off-channel tokens for use by actions. The following token definition matches whitespace and specifies with an action that the token should go on to the standard hidden channel (see class Token for the definitions of DEFAULT_CHANNEL and HIDDEN_CHANNEL):

Improved in v3.

```
WS   :   (' '|'\t'|'\r'|'\n')+ {$channel=HIDDEN;} ;
```

Character streams in the ANTLR runtime library automatically track newlines so that you do not have to manually increment a line counter. Further, the current character position within the current line is always available via getCharPositionInLine() in Lexer. Character positions are indexed from 0. Note that tab characters are not taken into consideration—the character index tracks tabs as one character.

Improved in v3.

For efficiency reasons, lexer rules can also indicate that the token should be matched but no actual Token object should be created. Method skip() in an embedded lexer rule action forces the lexer to throw out the token and look for another. Most language applications can ignore whitespace and comments, allowing you to take advantage of this efficiency. Here is an example whitespace rule:

```
WS   :   (' '|'\t'|'\r'|'\n')+ {skip();} ;
```

Rather than throwing out tokens, sometimes you'd like to emit more than a single token per lexer invocation.

Emitting More Than One Token per Lexer Rule

Lexer rules can force the lexer to emit more token per rule invocation by manually invoking method emit(). This feature solves some fairly difficult problems such as inserting *imaginary tokens* (tokens for which there is no input counterpart). The best example is lexing Python. Because Python uses indentation to indicate code blocks, there are no explicit begin and end tokens to group statements within a block. For example, in the following Python code, the if statement and the method call to g() are at the same outer level. The print statement and method call to f() are the same inner, nested level.

```
if foo:
    print "foo is true"
    f()
g()
```

Without begin and end tokens, parsing this input presents a problem for the parser when it tries to group statements. The lexer needs to emit imaginary **INDENT** and **DEDENT** tokens to indicate the begin and end of code blocks. The token sequence must be as follows:

```
IF ID : NL INDENT PRINT STRINGLITERAL NL ID ( ) NL DEDENT ID ( ) NL
```

The parser rule for matching code blocks would look like this:

```
block : INDENT statement+ DEDENT ;
```

The lexer can emit the **INDENT** token when it sees whitespace that is more deeply indented than the previous statement's whitespace; however, there is no input character to trigger the **DEDENT** token. In fact, the lexer must emit a **DEDENT** token when it sees less indentation than the previous statement. The lexer might even have to emit multiple **DEDENT** tokens depending on how far out the indentation has moved from the previous statement. The **INDENT** rule in the lexer might look something like this:

New in v3. In v2, your lexer could emit only one token at a time.

```
INDENT
    :   // turn on rule only if at left edge
        {getCharPositionInLine()==0}?=>
        (' '|'\t')+ // match whitespace
        {
        if ( «indentation-bigger-than-before» ) {
            // can only indent one level at a time
            emit(«INDENT-token»);
            «track increased indentation»
        }
        else if ( «indentation-smaller-than-before» ) {
            int d = «current-depth» - «previous-depth»;
            // back out of d code blocks
            for (int i=1; i<=d; i++) {
                emit(«DEDENT-token»);
            }
            «reduce indentation»
        }
        }
    ;
```

After matching a lexer rule, if you have not emitted a token manually in an action, nextToken() will emit a token for you. The token is based upon the text and token type for the rule. Note that, for efficiency reasons, the CommonTokenStream class does not support multiple token emissions for the same invocation of nextToken(). Read the following from class Lexer when you try to implement multiple token emission:

```
/** The goal of all lexer rules/methods is to create a token object.
 *  This is an instance variable as multiple rules may collaborate to
 *  create a single token.  nextToken will return this object after
 *  matching lexer rule(s).  If you subclass to allow multiple token
 *  emissions, then set this to the last token to be matched or
 *  something nonnull so that the auto token emit mechanism will not
 *  emit another token.
 */
protected Token token;

/** Currently does not support multiple emits per nextToken invocation
 *  for efficiency reasons.  Subclass and override this method and
 *  nextToken (to push tokens into a list and pull from that list rather
 *  than a single variable as this implementation does).
 */
public void emit(Token token) {
    this.token = token;
}
```

Tree Matching Rules

For translation problems that require multiple passes over the input stream, you should create parsers that build ASTs. ASTs not only are a terse representation of the input stream but also encode the grammatical structure applied to that input string. Rather than building a tree walker by hand or using a simple visitor pattern that has no contextual information, use a tree grammar that specifies the two-dimensional structure of the tree created by the parser. Again, ANTLR uses essentially the same syntax with the addition of a new construct that specifies the two-dimensional structure of a subtree: a root and one or more children. The syntax uses parentheses with a caret symbol on the front to distinguish it from an EBNF subrule:

Changed in v3. Using $^\wedge$ makes much more sense than the # symbol v2 used.

```
^( root child1 child2 ... childn )
```

For example, rule **expr**:

```
expr:   ^('+' expr expr)
    |   ^('*' expr expr)
    |   INT
    ;
```

matches ASTs consisting of expression subtrees with '+' and '*' operators as interior nodes (subtree roots) and **INT** nodes as leaves. Here is the tree for 3+4*5:

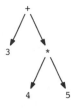

Trees have self-similar structures in that a small subtree and a big subtree are identical in structure. In this case, they both have operators at the root and two children as operands, which can also be subtrees. That self-similar structure is reflected in the recursive nature of the **expr** rule.

As a larger example, consider the following rules taken from a Java-like language grammar:

```
expression
    :   ^(unary_op expression)
    |   ^(CALL expression expressionList)
    |   ^(INDEX expression expression)
    |   primary
    ;

unary_op
    :   UNARY_MINUS|UNARY_PLUS|UNARY_NOT|UNARY_BNOT
    ;

primary
    :   ID
    |   INT
    |   FLOAT
    |   'null'
    ;
```

As you can see, tree grammars look like parser grammars with the addition of a few tree expressions. If the input to a tree grammar were a flat tree (a linked list), then the tree grammar would not have any tree constructs and would look identical to a parser grammar. In that sense, a tree grammar reduces to a parser grammar when the input looks like a one-dimensional token stream.

Tree grammar rules can have parameters and return values just like parser grammar rules, and actions can contain attribute references. The difference is that references to T for some token T yield pointers to the tree node matched for that reference. Further, ANTLR v3 does not allow tree grammars to create new trees. A future version will allow this in order to support tree transformations.

Option	Description
backtrack	When **true**, indicate that ANTLR should backtrack when static $LL(*)$ grammar analysis fails to yield a deterministic decision for this rule or subrules within the rule. This is usually used in conjunction with the **memoize** option. The default is to use the grammar's **backtrack** option. See Section 5.3, *backtrack Option*, on page 107.
memoize	Record partial parsing results to guarantee that, while backtracking, the parser never parses a rule more than once for a given input position. The default is to use the grammar's **memoize** option. See Section 5.4, *memoize Option*, on page 108.
k	Limit the decision generated for this rule, and any contained subrules, to use a maximum, fixed-lookahead depth of k. This turns off $LL(*)$ analysis in favor of classical $LL(k)$. If the overall grammar has fixed lookahead, a rule can override this by setting k=*. The default is to use the grammar's **k** option. See Section 5.11, *k Option*, on page 115.

Figure 4.4: SUMMARY OF ANTLR RULE-LEVEL OPTIONS

See Section 5.5, *tokenVocab Option*, on page 108 for a sample test program that invokes a tree parser.

Rule Options

Sometimes rules need options such as turning on memoization. The syntax mirrors the options specification for grammars:

```
decl
options {
    memoize=true;
}
    :   type ID (',' ID)*
    ;
```

The set of options available to rules are summarized in Figure 4.4.

The following sections return to the outer grammar level to discuss **tokens** and **scope** specifications.

4.4 Tokens Specification

Use the grammar **tokens** specification to introduce new tokens or to give better names to token literals (see Section 2.6, *Vocabulary Symbols Are Structured Too*, on page 27 for more about tokens). The **tokens** specification has the following form:

```
tokens {
    token-name1;
    token-name2 = 'string-literal';
    ...
}
```

It allows you to introduce *imaginary tokens*, which are token names that are not associated with any particular input character(s). Imaginary tokens usually become subtree root nodes that act as operators for a series of operands (children). For example, **VARDEF** is a convenient root node for the declaration int i;. It would have the type (int) and variable name (i) as children. Using ANTLR's tree grammar notation, the tree looks like this:

```
^(VARDEF int i)
```

and could be built with a parser grammar such as this:

```
grammar T;
tokens {
    VARDEF;
}
var : type ID ';' -> ^(VARDEF type ID) ;
```

The **tokens** specification also allows you to provide an alias for a string literal, which is useful when the alias is more descriptive than the literal. For example, token name **MOD** is more descriptive than the literal '%':

```
grammar T;
tokens {
    MOD='%'; // alias MOD to '%'
}
expr : INT (MOD INT)* ;
```

4.5 Global Dynamic Attribute Scopes

Usually the only way to pass information from one rule to another is via parameters and return values. Unfortunately, this can be particularly inconvenient when rules are far away in the call chain. One of the best examples is determining whether an identifier is defined in the current scope. A rule deeply nested in the expression call chain such as **atom** needs to access the current scope. The scope is probably updated in multiple rules such as **block, classDefinition**, and **methodDefinition**. There could be twenty rule invocations between **classDefinition** and **atom**. Passing the current scope down through all the twenty rules is a hassle and makes the grammar harder to read.

In a manner similar to an instance variable, ANTLR allows you to define global attribute scopes. These scopes are visible to actions in all rules. The specification uses the following syntax:

New in v3.

```
scope name {
    type1 attribute-name1;
    type2 attribute-name2;
    ...
}
```

So, for example, you might define a global scope to handle lists of symbols:

```
scope SymbolScope {
    List symbols;
}
```

Multiple rules would access that scope:

```
classDefinition
scope SymbolScope;
    : ...
    ;

methodDefinition
scope SymbolScope;
    : ...
    ;

block
scope SymbolScope;
    : ...
    ;
```

The key difference between the symbols list in SymbolScope and an instance variable is that the recognizer pushes a new list onto a stack of scopes upon entry to each method that declares scope SymbolScope;. See Chapter 6, *Attributes and Actions*, on page 117 for information about the usage and purpose of global dynamic scopes.

4.6 Grammar Actions

ANTLR generates a method for each rule in a grammar. The methods are wrapped in a class definition for object-oriented target languages. ANTLR provides named actions so you can insert fields and instance methods into the generated class definition (or global variables in the case of languages such as C). The syntax is as follows:

Improved in v3. The new name and scope based scheme is much clearer and more flexible than the global action mechanism in v2.

```
@action-name { ... }
@action-scope-name::action-name { ... }
```

The following example defines a field and method for the Java target using the **members** action:

```
grammar T;
options {language=Java;}
@members {
    int n;
    public void foo() {...}
}
a : ID {n=34; foo();} ;
```

To place the generated code in a particular Java package, use action **header**:

```
grammar T;
options {language=Java;}
@header {
package org.antlr.test;
}
```

When building a combined grammar, containing lexer and parser, you need a way to set the **members** or **header** for both. To do this, prefix the action with the action scope, which is one of the following: **lexer**, **parser**, or **treeparser**. For example, @header {...} is shorthand for @parser::header {...} if it is in a parser or combined parser. Here is how to add members to the lexer from a combined grammar and also set the package for both:

```
grammar T;
@header {import org.antlr.test;} // not auto-copied to lexer
@lexer::header{import org.antlr.test;}
@lexer::members{int aLexerField;}
```

See Section 6.2, *Grammar Actions*, on page 121 for more details. This chapter described the general structure of an ANTLR grammar as well as the details of the various grammar-level specifications. It also provided details on the structure of a rule, the rule elements, and the rule operators. The next chapter describes the grammar-level options that alter the way ANTLR generates code.

Chapter 5

ANTLR Grammar-Level Options

In the **options** section of an ANTLR grammar, you can specify a series of key/value assignments that alter the way ANTLR generates code. These options globally affect all the elements contained within the grammar, unless you override them in a rule. This chapter describes all the available options.

The options section must come after the **grammar** header and must have the following form:

```
options {
name1 = value1;
name2 = value2;
...
}
```

Option names are always identifiers, but values can be identifiers, single-quoted string literals, integers, and the special literal star, * (currently usable only with option k). Values are all literals and, consequently, can't refer to option names. For single-word string literals such as 'Java', you can use the shorthand Java, as shown here:

```
options {
  language=Java;
}
```

The list following this paragraph summarizes ANTLR grammar-level options. The subsections that follow describe them all in more detail; they're ordered from most commonly used to least commonly used.

language

Specify the target language in which ANTLR should generate recognizers. ANTLR uses the **CLASSPATH** to find directory org/antlr/codegen/templates/Java, in this case, used to generate Java. The default is Java. See Section 5.1, *language Option*, on page 105.

output

Generate output templates, **template**, or trees, **AST**. This is available only for combined, **parser**, and **tree** grammars. Tree grammars cannot currently output trees, only templates. The default is to generate nothing. See Section 5.2, *output Option*, on page 106.

backtrack

When **true**, indicates that ANTLR should backtrack when static *LL(*)* grammar analysis fails to yield a deterministic decision. This is usually used in conjunction with the **memoize** option. The default is **false**. See Section 5.3, *backtrack Option*, on page 107.

memoize

Record partial parsing results to guarantee that while backtracking the parser never parses the same input with the same rule more than once. This guarantees linear parsing speed at the cost of nonlinear memory. The default is **false**. See Section 5.4, *memoize Option*, on page 108.

tokenVocab

Specify where ANTLR should get a set of predefined tokens and token types. This is needed to have one grammar use the token types of another. Typically a **tree** grammar will use the token types of the **parser** grammar that creates its trees. The default is to not import any token vocabulary. See Section 5.5, *tokenVocab Option*, on page 108.

rewrite

When the output of your translator looks very much like the input, the easiest solution involves modifying the input buffer in-place. Re-creating the entire input with actions just to change a small piece is too much work. **rewrite** works in conjunction with output=template. Template construction actions usually just set the return template for the surrounding rule (see Section 9.4, *The ANTLR StringTemplate Interface*, on page 203). When you use rewrite=true, the recognizer also replaces the input matched by the rule with the template. See Section 5.6, *rewrite Option*, on page 110. The default is **false**.

superClass

Specify the superclass of the generated recognizer. This is not the supergrammar—it affects only code generation. The default is Lexer, Parser, or TreeParser depending on the grammar type. See Section 5.7, *superClass Option*, on page 111.

filter

Lexer only. All lexer rules are tried in order specified, looking for a match. Upon finding a matching rule, nextToken() returns that rule's Token object. If no rule matches, the lexer consumes a single character and again looks for a matching rule. The default is not to filter, **false**. See Section 5.8, *filter Option*, on page 112.

ASTLabelType

Set the target language type for all tree labels and tree-valued expressions. The default is Object. See Section 5.9, *ASTLabelType Option*, on page 113.

TokenLabelType

Set the target language type for all token labels and token-valued expressions. The default is interface Token. Cf. Section 5.10, *Token-LabelType Option*, on page 114.

k

Limit the recognizer generated from this grammar to use a maximum, fixed-lookahead depth of k. This turns off $LL(*)$ analysis in favor of classical $LL(k)$. The default is * to engage $LL(*)$. See Section 5.11, *k Option*, on page 115.

5.1 language Option

The **language** option specifies the target language in which you want ANTLR to generate code. By default, **language** is Java. You must write your embedded grammar actions in the language you specify with the **language** option. For example:

```
grammar T;
options {language=Java;}
a : ... {«action-in-Java-language»} ... ;
```

Because of ANTLR's unique StringTemplate-based code generator, new targets are relatively easy to build; hence, you can choose from numerous languages such as Java, C, C++, C#, Objective-C, Python, and Ruby.[1]

The **language** option value informs ANTLR that it should look for all code generation templates in a directory with the same name such as org/antlr/codegen/templates/Java or org/antlr/codegen/templates/C.

---

1. See http://www.antlr.org/wiki/display/ANTLR3/Code+Generation+Targets for the latest information about ANTLR language targets.

Inside this directory, you will find a set of StringTemplate group files that tell ANTLR how to generate code for that language. For example, file Java.stg contains all the templates needed to generate recognizers in Java. To make a variation on an existing target, copy the directory to a new directory, and tweak the template files within. If you move files to directory TerenceJava, then say language=TerenceJava in your grammar to use the altered templates. All target directories must have a prefix of org/antlr/codegen/templates and be visible via the CLASSPATH environment variable.

5.2 output Option

The **output** option controls the kind of data structure that your recognizer will generate. Currently the only possibilities are to build abstract syntax trees, **AST**, and StringTemplate templates, **template**. When this option is used, every rule yields an AST or template.

Using output=AST allows you to use tree construction operators and rewrite rules described in Chapter 7, *Tree Construction*, on page 149. For example, the following simple grammar builds a tree with an imaginary root node, **DECL**, and a child node created from input token **ID**:

```
grammar T;

options {
        output=AST;
}

decl : ID -> ^(DECL ID) ;
ID : 'a'..'z'+ ;
```

Rules without defined return values generally have **void** return types unless the output option is used. For example, here is a piece of the generated code for this grammar:

```
public static class decl_return extends ParserRuleReturnScope {
    Object tree;
    public Object getTree() { return tree; }
};
public decl_return decl() throws RecognitionException {...}
```

When using output=template, rule definitions yield templates instead of trees:

```
public static class decl_return extends ParserRuleReturnScope {
    public StringTemplate st;
    /** To avoid unnecessary dependence on StringTemplate library,
     *  superclass uses Object not StringTemplate as return type.
     */
    public Object getTemplate() { return st; }
};
public decl_return decl() throws RecognitionException {...}
```

For more about generating templates, see Chapter 9, *Generating Structured Text with Templates and Grammars*, on page 195.

This option is available only for combined, **parser**, or **tree** grammars.

5.3 backtrack Option

The **backtrack** option informs ANTLR that, should *LL(*)* analysis fail, it should try the alternatives within the decision in the order specified at parse time, choosing the first alternative that matches. Once the parser chooses an alternative, it rewinds the input and matches the alternative a second time, this time "with feeling" to execute any actions within that alternative. Actions are not executed during the "guessing" phase of backtracking because there is no general way to undo arbitrary actions written in the target language.   *New in v3.*

No nondeterminism warnings are reported by ANTLR during grammar analysis time because, by definition, there is no uncertainty in backtracking mode—ANTLR simply chooses the first alternative that matches at parse time. You can look upon this option as a rapid prototyping feature because ANTLR accepts just about any grammar you give it. Later you can optimize your grammar so that it more closely conforms to the needs of *LL(*)*.

The nice aspect of using backtrack=true is that the generated recognizer will backtrack only in decisions that are not *LL(*)*. Even within decisions that are not completely *LL(*)*, a recognizer will backtrack only on those input sequences that render the decision non-*LL(*)*. ANTLR implements this option by implicitly adding a syntactic predicate to the front of every alternative that does not have a user-specified predicate there already (see Chapter 14, *Syntactic Predicates*, on page 323 for more information). The grammar analysis converts syntactic predicates to semantic predicates.

The analysis uses semantic predicates only when syntax alone is insufficient to distinguish between alternatives. Therefore, the generated code uses backtracking (syntactic predicates) only when *LL(*)* fails.

You should use backtracking sparingly because it can turn the usual linear parsing complexity into an exponential algorithm. It can mean the difference between having a parser that terminates in your lifetime and one that does not. To use the strength of backtracking but with the speed of a linear parser at the cost of some memory utilization, use the **memoize** option discussed in the next section.

5.4 memoize Option

Backtracking is expensive because of repeated rule evaluations for the same input position. By recording the result of such evaluations, the recognizer can avoid recomputing them in the future. This recording process is a form of dynamic programming called *memoization* (see Section 14.5, *Memoization*, on page 335). When the **memoize** option is **true**, ANTLR generates code at the beginning of each parsing method to check for prior attempts:

New in v3.

```
if ( backtracking>0 && alreadyParsedRule(input, rule-number) ) {return;}
```

and inserts code at the end of the rule's method to memoize whether this rule completed successfully for the current input position:

```
if ( backtracking>0 ) {
    memoize(input, rule-number, rule-starting-input-position);
}
```

Using the **memoize** option at the grammar level turns on memoization for each rule in the grammar. This results in considerable parsing overhead to store partial results even when backtracking never invokes the same rule at the same input position. It is often more efficient to turn on the **memoize** option at the rule level rather than globally at the grammar level. Options specified at the rule level override the same options given at the grammar level. See Chapter 14, *Syntactic Predicates*, on page 323 for more information.

5.5 tokenVocab Option

For large language projects, the parser typically creates an intermediate representation such as an abstract syntax tree (AST). This AST is walked one or more times to perform analysis and ultimately generate code. I highly recommend you use a tree grammar to walk ASTs over a simple depth-first tree walk or visitor pattern (see Section 4.3, *Tree Matching Rules*, on page 96). Because a tree grammar must live in a different file than the parser that feeds it ASTs, there must be a way to synchronize the token types. Referring to **ID** in the tree grammar must have the same meaning as it does in the parser and lexer.

A grammar can import the vocabulary of another grammar using the **tokenVocab** option. The value associated with this option is the name of another grammar, not the name of a file. Consider the following simple grammar:

grammars/vocab/P.g

```
grammar P;
options {
    output=AST;
}
expr:   INT ('+'^ INT)* ;
INT :   '0'..'9'+;
WS  :   ' ' | '\r' | '\n' ;
```

From grammar **P**, ANTLR generates the recognizer files and a .tokens file that contains a list of token name and token type pairs for all tokens and string literals used in grammar **P**. There are two tokens in this case:

grammars/vocab/P.tokens

```
INT=4
WS=5
'+'=6
```

To walk the trees generated by **P**, a tree grammar must import the token vocabulary using tokenVocab=P, as shown in the following simple tree grammar:

grammars/vocab/Dump.g

```
tree grammar Dump;
options {
    tokenVocab=P;
    ASTLabelType=CommonTree;
}
expr:   ^( '+' expr {System.out.print('+');} expr )
    |   INT {System.out.print($INT.text);}
    ;
```

ANTLR looks for .tokens files in the library directory specified by the -lib command-line option to ANTLR, which defaults to the current directory.

For example, to generate code for the tree grammar, use the following (with or without the -lib option):

```
java org.antlr.Tool -lib . Dump.g
```

For completeness, here is a test program that prints the tree generated by the parser and then invokes the tree parser to dump the expression back out to text:

grammars/vocab/Test.java

```
// Create an input character stream from standard input
ANTLRInputStream input = new ANTLRInputStream(System.in);
PLexer lexer = new PLexer(input);       // create lexer
// Create a buffer of tokens between the lexer and parser
CommonTokenStream tokens = new CommonTokenStream(lexer);
PParser parser = new PParser(tokens); // create parser
PParser.expr_return r = null;
r = parser.expr(); // parse rule expr and get return structure
CommonTree t = (CommonTree)r.getTree();// extract AST
System.out.println(t.toStringTree());  // print out
// Create a stream of nodes from a tree
CommonTreeNodeStream nodes = new CommonTreeNodeStream(t);
Dump dumper = new Dump(nodes);          // create tree parser
dumper.expr();                          // parse expr
System.out.println();
```

Here is a sample session:

```
⇐    $ java Test
⇐    3+4+5
⇐    EOF
⇒    (+ (+ 3 4) 5)
     3+4+5
     $
```

5.6 rewrite Option

For many translations, the output looks very different from the input. The translator generates and then buffers up bits of translated input that it subsequently organizes into larger and larger chunks. This leads to the final chunk representing the complete output. In other cases, however, the output looks very much like the input. The easiest approach is to have the translator just tweak the input. For example, you might want to instrument source code for debugging, as shown in Section 9.7, *Rewriting the Token Buffer In-Place*, on page 217. What you want to do is rewrite a few pieces of the input buffer during translation and then print the modified buffer.

To get this functionality, set option **rewrite** to true. Recognizers in this mode automatically copy the input to the output except where you specify translations using template rewrite rules. This option works only with output=template and in parsers or tree parsers. The following grammar (minus the lexical rules) translates int tokens to Integer, leaving the rest of the input alone:

grammars/rewrite/T.g

```
grammar T;
options {output=template; rewrite=true;}

decl:   type ID ';' ;                    // no translation here

type:   'int' -> template() "Integer" // translate int to Integer
    |   ID                            // leave this alone
    ;
```

Input int i; becomes Integer i;, but String i; stays the same. Without using rewrite mode, rule **decl** returns nothing because rules return nothing by default. Rewrite mode, on the other hand, is altering the token buffer—the main program can print the altered buffer. Here is the core of a test rig:

grammars/rewrite/Test.java

```
ANTLRInputStream input = new ANTLRInputStream(System.in);
TLexer lexer = new TLexer(input);
// use TokenRewriteStream not CommonTokenStream!!
TokenRewriteStream tokens = new TokenRewriteStream(lexer);
TParser parser = new TParser(tokens);
parser.decl();
System.out.print(tokens.toString()); // emit rewritten source
```

Note that this mode works only with TokenRewriteStream, not CommonTokenStream.

5.7 superClass Option

Sometimes it is useful to have your recognizers derive from a class other than the standard ANTLR runtime superclasses. You might, for example, define a class that overrides some of the standard methods to alter the behavior of your recognizers.

The **superClass** option specifies the class name that ANTLR should use as the superclass of the generated recognizer. The superclass is usually Lexer, Parser, or TreeParser but is DebugParser or DebugTreeParser if you use the -debug command-line option. Whatever superclass you use instead must derive from the appropriate class mentioned here in order for the recognizer to compile and work properly. Here is a sample partial grammar that defines a superclass:

```
grammar T;
options {
    superClass=MyBaseParser;
}
```

ANTLR generates TParser as follows:

```
public class TParser extends MyBaseParser {...}
```

Naturally this option makes sense only for targets that are object-oriented programming languages. Note that the superclass is not a supergrammar—it is any Java class name.

5.8 filter Option

In general, programmers use ANTLR to specify the entire grammatical structure of an input file they want to process, but this is often overkill. Even for complicated files, sometimes it is possible to extract a few items of interest without having to describe the entire grammatical structure (as long as these items are lexically easy to identify). Some people call this *fuzzy parsing* because the recognizer does not match the exact structure of the input according to the full language syntax—the recognizer matches only those constructs of interest.[2]

The idea is to provide a series of lexical rules as with a normal grammar but have the lexer ignore any text that does not match one of the rules. You can look at **filter=true** mode as a normal lexer that has an implicit rule to catch and discard characters that do not match one of the other rules. nextToken() keeps scanning until it finds a matching lexical rule at which point it returns a Token object. If more than one rule matches the input starting from the current input position, the lexer resolves the issue by accepting the rule specified first in the grammar file; in other words, specify rules in the order of priority.

The krugle.com code search engine uses ANTLR v3's filter option to extract variable, method, and class definitions from, for example, Java and Python code spidered from the Internet.

---

2. See http://www.antlr.org/download/examples-v3.tar.gz for a full fuzzy Java parser that extracts class, method, and variable definitions as well as method call sites.

The following **lexer** grammar illustrates how to extract Java method calls:

```
lexer grammar FuzzyJava;
options {filter=true;}

CALL
    :    name=QID WS? '('
         {System.out.println("found call "+$name.text);}
    ;

SL_COMMENT
    :    '//' .* '\n'
    ;

WS  :    (' '|'\t'|'\r'|'\n')+
    ;

fragment
QID :    ID ('.' ID)*
    ;

fragment
ID  :    ('a'..'z'|'A'..'Z'|'_') ('a'..'z'|'A'..'Z'|'_'|'0'..'9')*
    ;
```

The **SL_COMMENT** rule is necessary because the program should not track method calls within comments. The multiline comments and strings would also be checked to do this for real.

Lexical rules can use skip() to force nextToken() to throw out the current token and look for another. The lexer returns the first nonskipped token to the parser.

Lexical **filter** mode is generally not used with a parser because the lexer yields an incomplete stream of tokens.

5.9 ASTLabelType Option

ANTLR makes no assumption about the actual type of tree nodes built during tree AST construction—by default, all node variables pointers are of type Object. ANTLR relies on the TreeAdaptor interface to know how to create nodes and hook them together to form trees (the CommonTreeAdaptor is a predefined implementation). Although this makes ANTLR very flexible, it can make embedded grammar actions inconvenient because of constant typecasting.

For example, in the following grammar, the type of expression $ID.tree is Object by default:

```
grammar T;
options {output=AST;}

/** we are creating CommonTree nodes, but ANTLR can't be sure;
 *  it assumes Object.
 */
e : ID {CommonTree t = (CommonTree)$ID.tree;} ;
ID: 'a'..'z'+ ;
```

The generated code for matching the **ID** token and building the AST will look something like this:

```
ID1=(Token)input.LT(1);
match(input,ID,FOLLOW_ID_in_e17);
ID1_tree = (Object)adaptor.create(ID1);
```

where ID1_tree is defined as follows:

```
Object ID1_tree=null;
```

The embedded action is translated to this:

```
CommonTree t = (CommonTree)ID1_tree;
```

To avoid having to use typecasts everywhere in your grammar actions, specify the type of your tree nodes via the **ASTLabelType** option. For example, if you are building CommonTree nodes with the CommonTreeAdaptor class, use option ASTLabelType=CommonTree. ANTLR will define variables such as ID1_tree to be of type CommonTree. And then actions can refer to tree nodes with the proper type:

```
e : ID {CommonTree t = $ID.tree;} ;
```

5.10 TokenLabelType Option

By default, ANTLR generates lexers that create CommonToken objects. If you have overridden Lexer method emit() to create special tokens, then you will want to avoid lots of typecasts in your embedded actions by using the **TokenLabelType** option. Here is a simple example:

```
grammar T;
options {TokenLabelType=MyToken;}

e : ID {$ID.methodFromMyToken();} ;
ID: 'a'..'z'+ ;
```

In this case, $ID will evaluate to type MyToken.

5.11 k Option

Use the **k** option to limit ANTLR's grammar analysis to classical *LL(k)* parsing. This option is mostly useful for optimizing the speed of your parser by limiting the amount of lookahead available to the parser. In general, however, using this option will force alterations in the grammar to avoid nondeterminism warnings, which can lead to unnatural grammars.

The argument to the **k** option is either a star or an integer representing the desired fixed-lookahead depth. By default, ANTLR assumes this:

```
grammar T;
options {
    k=*;
}
...
```

This chapter described the various grammar-level options that alter how ANTLR perceives input grammars and how it generates code. The next chapter looks at grammar actions and where ANTLR inserts them in the generated code. Further, it describes how actions can access information about the rule elements matched on the input stream.

Chapter 6

Attributes and Actions

In the previous two chapters, we examined the general structure of ANTLR grammar files and how to properly build rules, but a grammar by itself is not particularly useful. The resulting recognizer can answer only yes or no as to whether an input sentence conforms to the language specified by the grammar. To build something useful such as an interpreter or translator, you must augment grammars with actions. Grammar actions perform computations on the input symbols or emit new output symbols.

This chapter describes the syntax of actions, the significance of their locations, and the manner in which they can access data elements derived from the recognition process. In addition, this chapter defines dynamic scopes that allow distant rules to read and write mutually accessible variables. Dynamic scopes allow rules to communicate without having to define and pass parameters through intermediate rules. In particular, this chapter answers all the following common questions:

- "How can we insert actions among the rule elements to perform a translation or build an interpreter?"

- "How can we access information about the input symbols matched by various rule elements?"

- "How can rules pass data back and forth?"

- "What information about rule references and token references does ANTLR automatically create for us?"

6.1 Introducing Actions, Attributes, and Scopes

You must execute some code to do anything beyond recognizing the syntax of a language. You must, therefore, embed code directly in your grammar as *actions*. Actions usually directly operate on the input symbols, but they can also trigger method calls to appropriate external code.

Actions are blocks of text written in the target language and enclosed in curly braces. The recognizer triggers them according to their locations within the grammar. For example, the following rule emits found a decl after the parser has seen a valid declaration:

```
decl: type ID ';' {System.out.println("found a decl");} ;
type: 'int' | 'float' ;
```

The action performs a translation, but it's an uninteresting translation because every declaration results in the same output. To perform a useful translation, actions must refer to the input symbols. Token and rule references both have predefined attributes associated with them that are useful during translation. For example, you can access the text matched for rule elements:

```
decl: type ID ';'
    {System.out.println("var "+$ID.text+":"+$type.text+";");}
  ;
type: 'int' | 'float' ;
```

where text is a predefined attribute. $ID is a Token object, and $type is a data aggregate that contains all the predefined properties for that particular reference to rule **type**. Given input int x;, the translator emits var x:int;.

When references to rule elements are unique, actions can use $*elementName* to access the associated attributes. When there is more than one reference to a rule element, $*elementName* is ambiguous, and you must label the elements to resolve the ambiguity. For example, to allow user-defined types in the language described by rule **decl**, you could add another rule that matches two identifiers in a row. To access both ID tokens, you must label them and then refer to their labels in the action:

```
decl: type ID ';'
    {System.out.println("var "+$ID.text+":"+$type.text+";");}
  | t=ID id=ID ';'
    {System.out.println("var "+$id.text+":"+$t.text+";");}
  ;
```

When a rule matches elements repeatedly, translators commonly need to build a list of these elements. As a convenience, ANTLR provides the += label operator that automatically adds all associated elements to an *New in v3.* ArrayList, whereas the = label operator always refers to the last element matched. The following variation of rule **decl** captures all identifiers into a list called ids for use by actions:

```
decl: type ids+=ID (',' ids+=ID)* ';' ; // ids is list of ID tokens
```

Beyond these predefined attributes, you can also define your own rule attributes that behave like and are implemented as rule parameters and return values (or inherited and synthesized attributes, as academics refer to them). In the following example, rule **declarator** defines a parameter attribute called typeText that is available to actions as $typeText (see Section 4.3, *Rule Arguments and Return Values*, on page 86 for more about rule parameter and return value definition syntax):

```
decl: type declarator[$type.text] ';' ;
declarator[String typeText]
    : '*' ID {System.out.println("var "+$ID.text+":^"+$typeText+";");}
    | ID     {System.out.println("var "+$ID.text+":"+$typeText+";");}
    ;
```

Rule references use square brackets instead of parentheses to pass parameters. The text inside the square brackets is a comma-separated expression list written in the target language. ANTLR does no interpretation of the action except for the usual attribute reference translation such as $type.text.

Actions can access rule return values just like predefined attributes:

```
field
    : d=decl ';' {System.out.println("type "+$d.type+", vars="+$d.vars);}
    ;
decl returns [String type, List vars]
    : t=type ids+=ID (',' ids+=ID)* {$type = $t.text; $vars = $ids;}
    ;
```

Given input int a, b;, the translator emits type int, vars=[a, b] (the square brackets come from Java's standard List toString()).

All the attributes described thus far are visible only in the rule that defines them or as a return value. In many situations, however, you'll want to access tokens matched previously by other rules. For example, consider a **statement** rule that needs to access the name of the immediately enclosing method.

One solution involves defining an instance variable that is set by the **method** rule and accessed by the **statement** rule:

```
@members {
    String methodName;
}
method: type ID {methodName=$ID.text;} body
    ;
body:   '{' statement+ '}' ;
statement
    :   decl {...methodName...} ';' // ref value set in method
    |   ...
    ;
```

In this way, you can avoid having to define and pass parameters all the way down to rule **statement**. Because this sort of thing is so common, ANTLR formalizes such communication by allowing you to define rule attributes that any rule invoked can access (this notion is technically called *dynamic scoping*). Here is the functionally equivalent version of the earlier grammar using a dynamic rule scope:

```
method
scope {
    String name;
}
    :   type ID {$method::name=$ID.text;} body
    ;
body:   '{' statement+ '}' ;
statement
    :   decl {...$method::name...} ';' // ref value set in method
    |   ...
    ;
```

Note that the $method:: syntax clearly distinguishes a dynamically scoped attribute from a normal rule attribute.

A rule scope acts exactly like a list of local variables that just happens to be visible to rules further down in the call chain. As such, recursive indications of rule **method** each get their own copy of name, which distinguishes it from the first, simpler implementation that used just an instance variable. This feature turns out to be extremely useful because distant rules can communicate without having to define and pass arguments through the intermediate rules; see Section 6.5, *Dynamic Attribute Scopes for Interrule Communication*, on page 135.

The following sections describe all the concepts introduced here in more detail.

6.2 Grammar Actions

Actions are snippets of code that you write in the target language and embed in your grammar. ANTLR then inserts them into the generated recognizer according to their positions relative to the surrounding grammar elements. ANTLR inserts the actions verbatim except for some special expressions prefixed with $ or %.

Actions specified outside rules generally define global or class member program elements such as variables and methods. Most translators need at least a few helper methods and instance variables. Actions embedded within rules define executable statements, and the recognizer executes them as it recognizes input symbols.

Consider the following simple grammar that illustrates most of the locations within a grammar where you can put actions:

```
parser grammar T;

@header {
package p;
}

@members {
int i;
public TParser(TokenStream input, int foo) {
    this(input);
    i = foo;
}
}

a[int x] returns [int y]
@init {int z=0;}
@after {System.out.println("after matching rule; before finally");}
    :   {«action1»} A {«action2»}
    ;
    catch[RecognitionException re] {
        System.err.println("error");
    }
    finally { «do-this-no-matter-what» }
```

ANTLR generates TParser.java from grammar T; the code on the next page shows the surrounding infrastructure for class TParser where the highlighted lines indicate the actions copied from grammar T into the generated recognizer.

attributes/actions/TParser.java

```
▶ package p;

  import org.antlr.runtime.*;
  import java.util.Stack;
  import java.util.List;
  import java.util.ArrayList;

  public class TParser extends Parser {
      public static final String[] tokenNames = new String[] {
          "<invalid>", "<EOR>", "<DOWN>", "<UP>", "A"
      };
      public static final int A=4;
      public static final int EOF=-1;
          public TParser(TokenStream input) {
              super(input);
          }
      public String[] getTokenNames() { return tokenNames; }
      public String getGrammarFileName() { return "T.g"; }

▶     int i;
▶     public TParser(TokenStream input, int foo) {
▶         this(input);
▶         i = foo;
▶     }
```

For rule a, ANTLR generates the following method a() definition:

attributes/actions/TParser.java

```
      // T.g:15:1: a[int x] returns [int y] : A ;
      public int a(int x) throws RecognitionException {
          int y = 0; // auto-initialized by ANTLR
▶         int z=0;
          try {
              // T.g:18:4: A
▶             action1
              match(input,A,FOLLOW_A_in_a40);
▶             action2
▶             System.out.println("exiting");
          }
          catch (RecognitionException re) {
▶             System.err.println("error");
          }
          finally {
▶             do-this-no-matter-what
          }
          return y;
      }
```

Action placement is fairly straightforward if you view grammars as programs in a very high-level domain-specific language. Actions outside rules become member declarations, and actions with rules are executable statements inserted into the generated rule methods. The next two subsections describe actions and the significance of their locations in more detail.

Using Named Global Actions

ANTLR gives names to all the locations in the generated code that you can fill with user-defined code. The following list summarizes the action names and their purposes:

Improved in v3. Actions are named to indicate where in the output file ANTLR inserts the action.

header

Specify code that should appear before the class definition (this is usually where package definitions and imports go).

members

Specify instance variables and methods.

rulecatch

Replace default **catch** clauses generated for syntax errors with this action. Cf. Chapter 10, *Error Reporting and Recovery*, on page 231.

synpredgate

Replace the expression that gates actions on and off during syntactic predicate evaluation. This indicates when it is OK to execute embedded user actions. By default, embedded actions are executed by the recognizer only when the backtracking depth is 0:

```
if ( backtracking==0 ) { «embedded-user-action» }
```

To change the condition, set the **synpredgate** action:

```
@synpredgate { «ok-to-execute-action-expression» }
```

This replaces the backtracking==0 default expression.

In combined grammars, **header** and **members** actions refer to the parser component only, not the implicitly generated lexer. If you need to override this default, you can prefix these actions with an action scope name. The action scope is one of **lexer**, **parser**, or **treeparser**. It specifies to which recognizer you would like to associate the action. For example, @header is shorthand for @parser::header in a combined grammar. Use @lexer::header to specify packages and other header code needed by the lexer.

The various action names might differ depending on the ANTLR target language, but they all support at least the previously mentioned action names. Also note that some targets might not support the **treeparser** action scope.

Embedding Actions within Rules

Actions are treated like any other rule elements and, as such, can appear just about anywhere among the alternatives of a rule. Actions are executed immediately after the preceding rule element and immediately before the following rule element. For example, in the following rule, an action is executed after each reference to token **ID**:

```
@members {
Map symbols = new HashMap();
}
decl: type a=ID {symbols.put($a,$type.text);}
      (',' b=ID {symbols.put($b,$type.text);} )* ';'
    ;
```

The goal of this code is to map Token objects to the text name of their type, implementing a primitive symbol table. The first action, symbols.put($a,$type.text), is executed only once and immediately after the recognition of the first **ID** token. The second action,symbols. put($b,$type.text), is executed once for every iteration of the loop generated for the EBNF (...)* zero-or-more subrule. Every time through the loop $b points to the most recently matched identifier. Given input float a, b, c;, rule **decl** yields a hashtable where all three Token objects associated with a,b, and c point at the string float.

Because Java allows you to define variables in-line as opposed to the start of a code block, you can define variables inside any action. The variables are visible to the immediately surrounding alternative, but not other alternatives and not surrounding alternatives if the action is within a subrule. Targets such as the C target, however, are limited to defining variables with **init** actions.

Beyond the actions executed among the rule elements, some special actions execute just before the rule starts, just after the rule finishes, and upon syntax error within the rule.

The following example shows the utility of the **init** and **after** actions:

```
@members {
boolean inMethod = false;
}

methodDefinition returns [int numStats]
@init {
inMethod = true;
}
@after {
inMethod = false;
}
    :   ...
    ;
```

Any rule invoked from the **methodDefinition** rule can use the boolean instance variable inMethod to test its context (that is, whether the rule is being matched within the context of a method). This is a good way to distinguish between local variables and fields of a class definition, for example.

ANTLR inserts **init** actions after all definitions and initialization generated for the rule and right before the code generated for the rule body. ANTLR inserts **after** actions after all the rule cleanup code that sets return values and so on. The **after** action can, for example, access the tree computed by the rule. ANTLR inserts **after** actions before the code that cleans up the dynamic scopes used by the rule; see Section 6.5, *Rule Scopes*, on page 137 for an example that illustrates the **after** action's position relative to dynamic scope cleanup code. Subrules can't define **init** or **after** actions.

For completeness, note that rules can also specify actions as part of the exception handlers, but please see Chapter 10, *Error Reporting and Recovery*, on page 231 for more information.

6.3 Token Attributes

All tokens matched by parser and lexer rules have a collection of predefined, read-only attributes. The attributes include useful token properties such as the token type and text matched for a token. Actions can access these attributes via $*label.attribute* where *label* labels a token reference. As shorthand, actions can use $*T.attribute* where *T*

Improved in v3. Token references now have a rich set of predefined attributes.

is a unique token reference visible to the action. The following example illustrates token attribute expression syntax:

```
r   :   INT {int x = $INT.line;}
        ( ID {if ($INT.line == $ID.line) ...;} )?
        a=FLOAT b=FLOAT {if ($a.line == $b.line) ...;}
    ;
```

The action within the (...)? subrule can see the **INT** token matched before it in the outer level.

Because there are two references to the **FLOAT** token, a reference to $FLOAT in an action is not unique; you must use labels to specify which token reference you are interested in.

Token references within different alternatives are unique because only one of them can be matched for any invocation of the rule. For example, in the following rule, actions in both alternatives can reference $ID directly without using a label:

```
r   :   ... ID {System.out.println($ID.text);}
    |   ... ID {System.out.println($ID.text);}
    ;
```

To access the tokens matched for literals, you must use a label:

```
stat:   r='return' expr ';' {System.out.println("line="+$r.line);} ;
```

Most of the time you access the attributes of the token, but sometimes it is useful to access the Token object itself because it aggregates all the attributes. Further, you can use it to test whether an optional subrule matched a token:

```
stat: 'if' expr 'then' stat (el='else' stat)?
      {if ( $el!=null ) System.out.println("found an else");}
    | ...
    ;
```

Figure 6.1, on the next page, summarizes the attributes available for tokens; this includes lexer rule references in a lexer.

For lexer rules, note that labels on elements are sometimes characters, not tokens. Therefore, you can't reference token attributes on all labels. For example, the following rule defines three labels, of which $a and $c are character labels and evaluate to type int, not Token. If the literal is more than a single character like 'hi', then the label is a token reference, not a character reference:

```
lexer grammar T;
R : a='c' b='hi' c=. {$a, $b.text, $c} ;
```

Attribute	Type	Description
text	String	The text matched for the token; translates to a call to getText().
type	int	The token type (nonzero positive integer) of the token such as INT; translates to a call to getType().
line	int	The line number on which the token occurs, counting from 1; translates to a call to getLine().
pos	int	The character position within the line at which the token's first character occurs counting from zero; translates to a call to getCharPositionInLine().
index	int	The overall index of this token in the token stream, counting from zero; translates to a call to getTokenIndex().
channel	int	The token's channel number. The parser tunes to only one channel, effectively ignoring off-channel tokens. The default channel is 0 (Token.DEFAULT_CHANNEL), and the default hidden channel is Token.HIDDEN_CHANNEL.
tree	Object	When building trees, this attribute points to the tree node created for the token; translates to a local variable reference that points to the node, and therefore, this attribute does not live inside the Token object itself.

Figure 6.1: PREDEFINED TOKEN AND LEXER RULE ATTRIBUTES

ANTLR generates the following code for the body of the method:

```
// a='c'
int a = input.LA(1);
match('c');
// b='hi'
int bStart = getCharIndex();
match("hi");
Token b = new CommonToken(input, Token.INVALID_TOKEN_TYPE,
    Token.DEFAULT_CHANNEL, bStart, getCharIndex()-1);
// c=.
int c = input.LA(1);
matchAny();
// {$a, $b.text, $c}
a, b.getText(), c
```

6.4 Rule Attributes

When a recognizer matches a rule, it gathers a few useful attributes such as the text matched for the entire rule (**text**), the first symbol matched for the rule (**start**), and the last symbol matched by the rule (**stop**). The recognizer automatically sets the attributes for you. With a few exceptions, you cannot write to these attributes. You can, however, define more attributes in the form of rule parameters and return values. Actions within the rule use them to pass data between rules. User-defined attributes behave exactly like method parameters and return values except that rules can have multiple return values. The following subsections describe the predefined attributes and how to create rule parameters and return values.

Improved in v3. Rules now have a richer set of predefined attributes, and the general attribute mechanism is more consistent in v3.

Predefined Rule Attributes

For translation applications, actions often need to know about the complete input text matched by a rule. When generating trees or templates, actions also need to get the subtree or subtemplate created by a rule invocation. ANTLR predefines a number of read-only attributes associated with rule references that are available to actions. As you might expect, actions can access rule attributes only for references that precede the action. The syntax is $r.attribute$ for rule name r or a label assigned to a rule reference. For example, $expr.text returns the complete text matched by a preceding invocation of rule **expr**.

The predefined attributes of the currently executing rule are also available via shorthand: $attribute$ or $enclosingRuleName.attribute$. Consider the following rule that illustrates where you can put actions:

```
r
@init {
Token myFirstToken = $start; // do me first
}
@after {
Token myLastToken = $r.stop; // do me after rule matches
}
    :   ID {String s = $r.text;} INT {String t = $text;}
    ;
```

In the generated code, you will see that these attribute references translate to field accesses of the retval aggregate. For example, the **init** action is translated as follows:

```
Token myFirstToken = ((Token)retval.start);
```

The recognizer automatically computes the predefined attributes, and your actions should not attempt to modify them. One exception is that your **after** action can set attributes **tree** and **st** when generating ASTs (see Chapter 7, *Tree Construction*, on page 149) or templates (see Chapter 9, *Generating Structured Text with Templates and Grammars*, on page 195). Setting them in any other action has no effect because they are set by the rule's bookkeeping code right before the **after** action.

Figure 6.2, on the following page, describes the predefined attributes that are available to actions.

Predefined Lexer Rule Attributes

Lexer rules always have an implicit return value of type Token that is sent back to the parser. However, lexer rules that refer to other lexer rules can access those portions of the overall token matched by the other rules and returned as implicit tokens. The following rule illustrates a composite lexer rule that reuses another token definition:

```
PREPROC_CMD
    :    '#' ID {System.out.println("cmd="+$ID.text);}
    ;
ID :    ('a'..'z'|'A'..'Z')+
    ;
```

ANTLR translates rule **PREPROC_CMD**'s production to the following code that creates a temporary token for use by the embedded action (note that $ID.text is automatically translated to ID1.getText()):

```
match('#');
int ID1Start = getCharIndex();
mID();
Token ID1 = new CommonToken(
    input, ID, Token.DEFAULT_CHANNEL, ID1Start, getCharIndex()-1);
System.out.println("cmd="+ID1.getText());
```

The attributes of a lexer rule reference are the same as a token reference in a parser grammar (see Section 6.3, *Token Attributes*, on page 125). The only exception is that **index** is undefined. The lexer does not know where in the token stream the token will eventually appear. Figure 6.3, on page 131 summarizes the attributes available to attribute expressions referring to the surrounding rule.

Attribute	Type	Description
text	String	The text matched from the start of the rule up until the point of the $text expression evaluation. Note that this includes the text for all tokens including those on hidden channels, which is what you want because usually that has all the whitespace and comments. When referring to the current rule, this attribute is available in any action including any exception actions.
start	Token	The first token to be potentially matched by the rule that is on the main token channel; in other words, this attribute is never a hidden token. For rules that end up matching no tokens, this attribute points at the first token that could have been matched by this rule. When referring to the current rule, this attribute is available to any action within the rule.
stop	Token	The last nonhidden channel token to be matched by the rule. When referring to the current rule, this attribute is available only to the **after** action.
tree	Object	The AST computed for this rule, normally the result of a -> rewrite rule. When referring to the current rule, this attribute is available only to the **after** action.
st	StringTemplate	The template computed for this rule, usually the result of a -> rewrite rule. When referring to the current rule, this attribute is available only to the **after** action.

Figure 6.2: PREDEFINED PARSER RULE ATTRIBUTES

Attribute	Type	Description
text	String	The text matched thus far from the start of the token at the outermost rule nesting level; translated to getText().
type	int	The token type of the surrounding rule, even if this rule does not emit a token (because it is invoked from another rule).
line	int	The line number, counting from 1, of this rule's first character.
pos	int	The character position in the line, counting from 0, of this rule's first character.
channel	int	The default channel number, 0, unless you set it in an action in this rule.

Figure 6.3: LEXER RULE ATTRIBUTES AVAILABLE TO EXPRESSIONS

Predefined Tree Grammar Rule Attributes

Tree grammar rules have the same attributes as parser grammar rules except that the input symbols are tree nodes instead of tokens and **stop** is not defined. So, for example, $ID refers to the tree node matched for token **ID** rather than a Token object. Figure 6.4, on the next page, summarizes the predefined attributes for tree grammar rules.

Rule Parameters

Besides the predefined attributes, rules can define user-defined attributes in the form of parameters whose values are set by invoking rules. For example, the following rule has a single parameter that the embedded action uses to generate output:

```
declarator[String typeName]
    :   ID {System.out.println($ID.text+" has type "+$typeName);}
    ;
```

Rule parameters often contain information about the rule's context. The rule can use that information to guide the parse.

Attribute	Type	Description
text	String	The text derived from the first node matched by this rule. Each tree node knows the range of input tokens from which it was created. Parsers automatically set this range to the first and last token matched by the rule that created the tree (see Section 7.3, *Default AST Construction*, on page 157). This attribute includes the text for all tokens including those on hidden channels, which is what you want because usually that has all the whitespace and comments. When referring to the current rule, this attribute is available in any action including exception actions. Note that **text** is not well defined for rules like this: `slist : stat+ ;` because **stat** is not a single node or rooted with a single node. $slist.text gets only the first **stat** tree.
start	Object	The first tree node to be potentially matched by the rule. For rules that end up matching no nodes, this attribute points at the first node that could have been matched by this rule. When referring to the current rule, this attribute is available to any action within the rule.
st	StringTemplate	The template computed for this rule, usually the result of a -> rewrite rule. When referring to the current rule, this attribute is available only to the **after** action.

Figure 6.4: PREDEFINED ATTRIBUTES FOR TREE GRAMMAR RULES

To illustrate this, consider the following rule with parameter needBody that indicates whether a body is expected after the method header:

```
methodDefinition[boolean needBody]
    :    modifiers typename ID '(' formalArgs ')'
         ( {$needBody}?=>  body
         | {!$needBody}?=> ';' // abstract method
         )
    ;
```

where {$needBody}?=> is a gated semantic predicate that turns on the associated alternative according to the value of parameter needBody.

ANTLR generates the following method structure for rule **methodDefinition**:

```
public void methodDefinition(boolean needBody)
    throws RecognitionException {
    ...
}
```

These parameter attributes are visible to the entire rule including exception, **init**, and **after** actions.

In lexers, only **fragment** rules can have parameters because they are the only rules you can explicitly invoke in the lexer. Non-**fragment** rules are implicitly invoked from the automatically generated **nextToken** rule.

Use square brackets to surround parameter lists. For example, here is a rule that invokes **methodDefinition**:

```
classDefinition
    :    methodDefinition[true]
    |    fieldDefinition
    ;
```

Although it is probably not very good form, you are able to set parameter values in actions. Naturally, actions can't access the parameters of rule references; here, $methodDefinition.needBody makes no sense.

Rule Return Values

Rules can define user-defined attributes in the form of rule return values. Actions access these return values via rule label properties.

For example, the following grammar defines rule **field** that invokes rule

Improved in v3. You can now return multiple return values from a rule.

decl and accesses its return values:

```
field
    :   d=decl {System.out.println("type "+$d.type+", vars="+$d.vars);}
    ;
/** Compute and return a list of variables and their type. */
decl returns [String type, List vars]
    :   t=type ids+=ID (',' ids+=ID)* ';'
        {$type = $t.text; $vars = $ids;}
    ;
```

ANTLR generates the following (slightly cleaned up) code for rule **field**:

```
public void field() throws RecognitionException {
    decl_return d = null;
    try {
        d=decl();
        System.out.println("type "+d.type+", vars="+d.vars);
    }
    catch (RecognitionException re) {
        reportError(re);
        recover(input,re);
    }
}
```

and generates a return value structure to represent the multiple return values of rule **decl**:

```
public static class decl_return extends RuleReturnScope {
    public String type;
    public List vars;
};
```

Rule **decl** then creates a new instance of this aggregate to hold the return values temporarily:

```
public decl_return decl() throws RecognitionException {
►       // create return value data aggregate
►       decl_return retval = new decl_return();
►       retval.start = input.LT(1);
        try {
            ...
            // set $stop to previous token (last symbol matched by rule)
►           retval.stop = input.LT(-1);
►           retval.type = input.toString(t.start,t.stop); // $type = $t.text
►           retval.vars = list_ids; // $vars = $ids
        }
        catch (RecognitionException re) {
            reportError(re);
            recover(input,re);
        }
        return retval;
}
```

The highlighted lines are generated directly or indirectly from the embedded action and use of the += label operator.

In the future, expect ANTLR to optimize the object creation away if only one return value is used or set.

Actions within **decl** that access return values translate to field references of this data aggregate; they can read and write these values. Invoking rules can't set return values. Here, executing $d.type="int"; from within rule **field** makes no sense.

6.5 Dynamic Attribute Scopes for Interrule Communication

Rule attributes have very limited visibility—rule **r** can pass information (via parameters) only to rule **s** if **r** directly invokes **s**. Similarly, **s** can pass information back to only that rule that directly invokes **s** (via return values). This is analogous to the normal programming language functionality whereby methods communicate directly through parameters and return values. For example, the following reference to local variable x from a deeply nested method call is illegal in Java:

New in v3.

```
void f() {
    int x = 0;
    g();
}
void g() {
    h();
}
void h() {
    int y = x; // INVALID reference to f's local variable x
}
```

Variable x is available only within the scope of f(), which is the text lexically delimited by curly brackets. For this reason, Java is said to use *lexical scoping*. Lexical scoping is the norm for most programming languages.[1] Languages that allow methods further down in the call chain to access local variables defined earlier are said to use *dynamic scoping*. The term *dynamic* refers to the fact that a compiler cannot statically determine the set of visible variables. This is because the set of variables visible to a method changes depending on who calls that method. For general programming languages, I am opposed to dynamic scoping, as are most people, because it is often difficult to decide which variable you are actually accessing. Languages such as Lisp and Perl have been criticized for dynamic scoping.

New in v3.

---

1. See http://en.wikipedia.org/wiki/Scope_(programming)#Static_scoping.

In a general-purpose language like Java, to allow h() to access x, either you have to pass x all the way down as a parameter, which is very inconvenient, or you can define an instance variable that f() and h() can both access:

```
int x;
void f() {
    x = 0; // same as this.x = 0
    g();
}
void g() {
    h();
}
void h() {
    int y = x; // no problem, x is this.x
}
```

It turns out that, in the grammar realm, distant rules often need to communicate with each other, mostly to provide context information to rules matched below in the rule invocation chain (that is, below in the parse tree). For example, an expression might want to know whether an identifier was previously defined. An expression might want to know whether it is an assignment right-side or a loop conditional. For the first problem, a symbol table instance variable works nicely, but for the latter problem, it is bad "information hiding" programming practice to define a bunch of instance variables visible to all rules just to provide context to a specific few. Further, the definition of the context variable is often far from the rule that sets its value.

Recognizing the importance of context in language translation problems, ANTLR gives you both locality of definition and wide visibility through dynamic scoping.[2] ANTLR allows you to define rule attributes that look like local variables but that are visible to any rule invoked from that rule no matter how deeply nested. The following grammar is functionally equivalent to the earlier Java code:

New in v3.

```
f
scope {int x;}
    : {$f::x = 0;} g
    ;
g : h ;
h : {int y = $f::x;} ;
```

Here, $f::x accesses the dynamically scoped attribute x defined in rule f.

---

2. See http://en.wikipedia.org/wiki/Scope_(programming)#Dynamic_scoping.

In contrast to unrestricted dynamic scoping, all references to dynamically scoped attributes must include the scope containing the definition. This syntax neatly sidesteps the primary concern that it is difficult to decide which dynamically scoped variable is being accessed. The $f:: prefix on dynamically scoped references also highlights that it is a nonlocal reference.

Rule Scopes

To define a dynamic scope of attributes in a rule, specify a list of variable definitions without initialization values inside a **scope** action:

```
r
scope {
    «attribute1»;
    «attribute2»;
    ...
    «attributeN»;
}
    : ...
    ;
```

To illustrate the use of dynamic scopes, consider the real problem of defining variables and ensuring that variables in expressions are defined. The following grammar defines the symbols attribute where it belongs in the **block** rule but adds variable names to it in rule **decl**. Rule **stat** then consults the list to see whether variables have been defined.

attributes/rulescope/T.g

```
grammar T;

prog:   block
    ;

block
scope {
    /** List of symbols defined within this block */
    List symbols;
}
@init {
    // initialize symbol list
    $block::symbols = new ArrayList();
}
    :   '{' decl* stat+ '}'
        // print out all symbols found in block
        // $block::symbols evaluates to a List as defined in scope
        {System.out.println("symbols="+$block::symbols);}
    ;
```

```
/** Match a declaration and add identifier name to list of symbols */
decl:   'int' ID {$block::symbols.add($ID.text);} ';'
    ;

/** Match an assignment then test list of symbols to verify
 *  that it contains the variable on the left side of the assignment.
 *  Method contains() is List.contains() because $block::symbols
 *  is a List.
 */
stat:   ID '=' INT ';'
        {
        if ( !$block::symbols.contains($ID.text) ) {
            System.err.println("undefined variable: "+$ID.text);
        }
        }
    ;
ID  :   'a'..'z'+ ;
INT :   '0'..'9'+ ;
WS  :   (' '|'\n'|'\r')+ {$channel = HIDDEN;} ;
```

Here's the given input:

```
{
  int i;
  int j;
  i = 0;
}
```

The translator emits the following:

```
symbols=[i, j]
```

Given this input:

```
attributes/rulescope-recursive/input2
```
```
{
  int i;
  int j;
  i = 0;
  x = 4;
}
```

the translator gives an error message about the undefined variable reference:

```
undefined variable: x
symbols=[i, j]
```

In this example, defining symbols as an instance variable would also work, but it is not the same solution as using a dynamically scoped variable. Dynamically scoped variables act more like a local variable.

There is a copy of symbols for each invocation of rule **block**, whereas there is only one copy of an instance variable per grammar. This might not be a problem in general, but having only a single copy of symbols would not work if **block** were invoked recursively. For nested blocks, you want each block to have its own list of variable definitions so that you can reuse the same variable name in an inner block. For example, the following nested code block redefines i in the inner scope. This new definition must hide the definition in the outer scope.

attributes/rulescope-recursive/input

```
{
  int i;
  int j;
  i = 0;
  {
    int i;
    int x;
    x = 5;
  }
  x = 3;
}
```

The following modified grammar supports nested code blocks by allowing rule **stat** to recursively invoke **block**. The invocation of **block** automatically creates an entirely new copy of the symbols attribute. The invocation still pushes symbols on the same stack, though, so that it maintains a single stack of all scopes.

attributes/rulescope-recursive/T.g

```
grammar T;

@members {
/** Track the nesting level for better messages */
int level=0;
}

prog:   block
    ;
block
scope {
    List symbols;
}
@init {
    $block::symbols = new ArrayList();
    level++;
}
```

```
@after {
    System.out.println("symbols level "+level+" = "+$block::symbols);
    level--;
}
    :   '{' decl* stat+ '}'
    ;
decl:   'int' ID {$block::symbols.add($ID.text);} ';'
    ;
stat:   ID '=' INT ';'
        {
        if ( !$block::symbols.contains($ID.text) ) {
            System.err.println("undefined variable level "+level+
                                ": "+$ID.text);
        }
        }
    |   block
    ;
ID  :   'a'..'z'+ ;
INT :   '0'..'9'+ ;
WS  :   (' '|'\n'|'\r')+ {$channel = HIDDEN;} ;
```

Instance variable level tracks the recursion level of rule **block** so that
the print action can identify the level in which the symbols are defined.
The print action is also now in an **after** action for symmetry with the **init**
action. For the earlier input, the translator emits the following:

```
symbols level 2 = [i, x]
undefined variable level 1: x
symbols level 1 = [i, j]
```

Note that the undefined variable message is still there because the list
of symbols for the inner block disappears just like a local variable after
the invocation of that recursive invocation of rule **block**.

This example is a nice illustration of dynamically scoped variables, but
for completeness, the check for undefined variables should really look
at all scopes on the stack rather than just the current scope. For example, a reference to j within the nested code block yields an undefined
variable error. The action needs to walk backward up the stack of symbols attributes until it finds a scope containing variable reference. If the
search reaches the bottom of the stack, then the variable is undefined
in any scope.

To access elements other than the top of the dynamically scoped attribute stack, use syntax $x[i]::y where x is the scope name, y is the
attribute name, and i is the absolute index into the stack with 0 being
the bottom of the stack. Expression $x.size()-1 is the index of the top of
the stack. The following method, defined in the **members** action, com-

putes whether a variable is defined in the current scope or any earlier scope:

```
boolean isDefined(String id) {
    for (int s=level-1; s>=0; s--) {
        if ( $block[s]::symbols.contains(id) ) {
            System.out.println(id+" found in nesting level "+(s+1));
            return true;
        }
    }
    return false;
}
```

Then rule **stat** should reference the method to properly identify undefined variables:

```
stat:   ID '=' INT ';'
        {
        if ( !isDefined($ID.text) ) {
            System.err.println("undefined variable level "+level+
                                ": "+$ID.text);
        }
        }
    |   block
    ;
```

Given the following input:

attributes/rulescope-resolve/input

```
{
  int i;
  int j;
  {
    int i;
    int x;
    x = 5;
    i = 9;
    j = 4;
  }
  x = 3;
}
```

the program emits this:

```
x found in nesting level 2
i found in nesting level 2
j found in nesting level 1
symbols level 2 = [i, x]
undefined variable level 1: x
symbols level 1 = [i, j]
```

The next section describes how to handle the case where multiple rules need to share dynamically scoped attributes.

Global Scopes

There is a separate attribute stack for each rule that defines a dynamic scope. In the previous section, only rule **block** defined a scope; therefore, there was only one stack of scopes. Each invocation of **block** pushed a new symbols list onto the stack. The isDefined() method walked up the single stack trying to resolve variable references. This simple technique works because there is only one kind of variable definition scope in the language described by the grammar: code blocks enclosed in curly braces.

Consider the scoping rules of the C programming language. Ignoring **struct** definitions and parameters for simplicity, there are a global scope, function scopes, and nested code blocks. The following extension to the previous grammar matches a language with the flavor of C:

```
prog:   decl* func*
    ;
func:   'void' ID '(' ')' '{' decl* stat+ '}'
    ;
...
```

This deceptively simple grammar matches input such as the following:

attributes/globalscope/input

```
int i;
void f()
{
  int i;
  {
    int i;
    i = 2;
  }
  i = 1;
}
void g() {
  i = 0;
}
```

Variable i is defined in three different nested scopes: at the global level, in function f(), and in a nested code block. When trying to resolve references to i, you need to look in the closest enclosing scope and then in outer scopes. For example, the reference to i in i=1; should be resolved in f()'s scope rather than the preceding nested code block. The reference to i in g() should resolve to the global definition.

Your first attempt at using dynamic scopes to solve this problem might involve defining a dynamic scope in each rule that matches declarations:

```
prog
scope {
    List symbols;
}
    :    decl* func*
    ;
func
scope {
    List symbols;
}
    :    'void' ID '(' ')' '{' decl* stat+ '}'
    ;
block
scope {
    List symbols;
}
    :    '{' decl* stat+ '}'
    ;
...
```

The problem with this solution is that there are three different stacks, one for each C language scope. To properly resolve variable references, however, you must maintain a single stack of variable scopes (as is clear by examining method isDefined()).

ANTLR provides a mechanism for multiple rules to share the same dynamic scope stack. Simply define a named scope outside any rule. In this case, define CScope with two attributes:

*In the future, expect ANTLR to allow initialization code within **scope** definitions such as constructors.*

attributes/globalscope/T.g

```
// rules prog, func, and block share the same global scope
// and, therefore, push their scopes onto the same stack
// of scopes as you would expect for C (a code block's
// scope hides the function scope, which in turn, hides
// the global scope).
scope CScope {
    String name;
    List symbols;
}
```

where attribute name records the name of the scope such as "global" or the associated function name.

Method isDefined() can then print a more specific name rather than just the level number:

attributes/globalscope/T.g

```
@members {
/** Is id defined in a CScope?  Walk from top of stack
 *  downwards looking for a symbols list containing id.
 */
boolean isDefined(String id) {
    for (int s=$CScope.size()-1; s>=0; s--) {
        if ( $CScope[s]::symbols.contains(id) ) {
            System.out.println(id+" found in "+$CScope[s]::name);
            return true;
        }
    }
    return false;
}
}
```

Instead of manually tracking the scope level, you can use $CScope.size()-1 as isDefined() does.

The rules that define variables within a C scope (**prog**, **func**, and **block**) must indicate that they want to share this scope by specifying scope CScope;. The following rules properly use a global dynamic scope to share a single stack of attributes:

attributes/globalscope/T.g

```
prog
scope CScope;
@init {
    // initialize a scope for overall C program
    $CScope::symbols = new ArrayList();
    $CScope::name = "global";
}
@after {
    // dump global symbols after matching entire program
    System.out.println("global symbols = "+$CScope::symbols);
}
    :   decl* func*
    ;

func
scope CScope;
@init {
    // initialize a scope for this function
    $CScope::symbols = new ArrayList();
}
```

```
@after {
    // dump variables defined within the function itself
    System.out.println("function "+$CScope::name+" symbols = "+
                       $CScope::symbols);
}
    :   'void' ID {$CScope::name=$ID.text;} '(' ')' '{' decl* stat+ '}'
    ;

block
scope CScope;
@init {
    // initialize a scope for this code block
    $CScope::symbols = new ArrayList();
    $CScope::name = "level "+$CScope.size();
}
@after {
    // dump variables defined within this code block
    System.out.println("code block level "+$CScope.size()+" = "+
                       $CScope::symbols);
}
    :   '{' decl* stat+ '}'
    ;
```

These rules push a new attribute scope onto the stack (identified by $CScope) upon invocation and pop the scope off upon returning. For example, here is the code generated for the global scope, the stack of scopes, and the **prog** rule:

```
/** Put all elements within a scope into a class */
protected static class CScope_scope {
    String name;
    List symbols;
}
/** The stack of scopes; each element is of type CScope_scope */
protected Stack CScope_stack = new Stack();

/** Code generated for rule prog */
public void prog() throws RecognitionException {
    CScope_stack.push(new CScope_scope());
►   ((CScope_scope)CScope_stack.peek()).symbols = new ArrayList();
►   ((CScope_scope)CScope_stack.peek()).name = "global";
    try {
        ...
        // from @after action
        System.out.println("global symbols = "+
            ((CScope_scope)CScope_stack.peek()).symbols);
        CScope_stack.pop();
    }
}
```

where the highlighted code is the **init** action from rule **prog. init** actions are executed after the new scope becomes available, and **after** actions are executed right before the scope disappears.

The global dynamic scope mechanism works well for many simple symbol table implementation such as this, but in general, a more sophisticated symbol table is required for real applications (for example, symbol table scopes generally must persist beyond parser completion).[3]

The following, final section summarizes all the special symbols related to attributes and scopes that you can reference within actions.

6.6 References to Attributes within Actions

ANTLR ignores everything inside user-defined actions except for expressions beginning with $ and %. The list that follows summarizes the special symbols and expressions that ANTLR recognizes and translates to code in the target language. % references are template expressions and are described in Section 9.9, *References to Template Expressions within Actions*, on page 227.

$*tokenRef*
> An expression of type Token that points at the Token object matched by the indicated grammar token reference, which is identified either by a token label or a reference to a token name mentioned in the rule. This is useful to test whether a token was matched in an optional subrule also. Example: ID {$ID} (ELSE stat)? {if ($ELSE!=null) ...}

$*tokenRef.attr*
> Refers to the predefined token attribute *attr* of the referenced token, identified either by a token label or by a reference to a token name mentioned in the rule. See Figure 6.1, on page 127 for the list of valid attributes. Example: id=ID {$id.text} INT {$INT.line}

$*listLabel*
> An expression that evaluates to type List and is a list of all elements collected thus far by the *listLabel*. A list label is identified by labels using the += operator; this is valid only within a parser or tree grammar. Example: ids+=ID (',' ids+=ID)* {$ids}

---

3. See http://www.cs.usfca.edu/~parrt/course/652/lectures/symtab.html for more information about symbol tables.

$ruleRef

Isolated $rulename is not allowed in a parser or tree grammar unless the rule has a dynamic scope and there is no reference to rulename in the enclosing alternative, which would be ambiguous. The expression is of type Stack. Example (checks how deeply nested rule **block** is): $block.size()

$ruleRef.attr

Refers to the predefined or user-defined attribute of the referenced rule, which is identified either by a rule label or by a reference to a rule mentioned in the rule. See Figure 6.2, on page 130 for the list of available rule attributes. Example: e=expr {$e.value, $expr.tree}

$lexerRuleRef

Within a lexer, this is an expression of type Token that contains all the predefined properties of the token except the token stream index matched by invoking the lexer rule. The lexer rule reference can be either a rule label or a reference to a lexer rule mentioned within the rule. As with token references, you can refer to predefined attributes of the returns token. Example: (DIGIT {$DIGIT, $DIGIT.text})+

$attr

attr is a return value, parameter, or predefined rule property of the enclosing rule. Example: r[int x] returns [Token t]: {$t=$start; $x} ;

$enclosingRule.attr

The fully qualified name of a return value, parameter, or predefined property. Example: r[int x] returns [Token t]: {$r.t=$r.start; $r.x;} ;

$globalScopeName

An isolated global dynamic scope reference. This is useful when code needs to walk the stack of scopes or check its size. Example: $symbols.size()

$x::y

Refer to the y attribute within the dynamic scope identified by x, which can either be a rule scope or be a global scope. In all cases, the scope prefix is required when referencing a dynamic attribute. Example: $CScope::symbols

$x[-1]::y

Attribute y (just under top of stack) of the previous x scope. Example: $block[-1]::symbols

$x[-i]::y$

Attribute y of a previous scope of x. The previous scope is i down from the top of stack. The minus sign must be present; that is, i cannot simply be negative. You must use the minus sign! Example: $block[-level]::symbols

$x[i]::y$

Attribute y of a the scope of x up from the bottom of the stack. In other words, i is an absolute index in the range 0..size-1. Example: $block[2]::symbols

$x[0]::y$

Attribute y of a bottommost scope of x. Example: $block[0]::symbols

In general, most attributes are writable, but attributes of token and rule references are read-only. Further, predefined rule attributes other than **tree** and **st** are read-only. The following example illustrates the writable and readable attributes:

```
r   :   s[42]
        {$s.x}             // INVALID: cannot access parameter
        {$s.y=3;}          // INVALID: cannot set return value
        {$r.text="ick";}   // INVALID: cannot set predefined attribute
        ID
        {$ID.text="ick";} // INVALID: cannot set predefined attribute
    ;
s[int x] returns [int y, int z]
@init {$y=0; $z=0;}
    :   {$y = $x*2;} {Token t = $start;} {$tree = ...;}
        {$start = ...;}    // INVALID: cannot set predefined attribute
    ;
```

This chapter described embedded actions and attributes in detail. Together with Chapter 4, *ANTLR Grammars*, on page 71, you've now learned all the basic building blocks for constructing grammars. Most language applications need more infrastructure from ANTLR, however, than simple actions. Complicated translators typically involve multiple passes over the input. A parser grammar builds an intermediate-form tree, and then one or more tree grammars walk that tree. In a final stage, a tree grammar emits output via template construction rules. In the next three chapters, we'll examine how to construct a tree, how to walk a tree via tree grammars, and how to emit output via templates.

Chapter 7

Tree Construction

Complex problems are much easier to solve when you break them down into several, smaller problems. This is particularly true when building language translators. Translators usually have logically separate phases that execute one after the other like the stages in a processor's pipeline. It is just too difficult to translate one programming language to another in one step, for example. Each phase computes some information, fills a data structure, or emits output.

In fact, many language problems cannot even be solved with a single pass. Resolving references to programming language variables defined further ahead is the most obvious example. A translator must walk the input program once to get variable definitions and a second time to resolve references to those variables. Rather than repeatedly rescanning the characters and reparsing the token stream, it is much more efficient to construct and walk a condensed version of the input. This condensed version is called an *intermediate form* and is usually some kind of tree data structure. The tree not only records the input symbols, but it also records the structure used to match them.

Encoding structure in the intermediate-form tree makes walking it much easier and faster than scanning a linear list of symbols as a parser does. Figuring out that 3+4 is an expression from token stream INT + INT is much harder for a computer than looking at a tree node that explicitly says "Hi, I'm an addition expression with two operands." The most convenient way to encode input structure is with a special tree called an *abstract syntax tree* (AST). ASTs contain only those nodes associated with input symbols and are, therefore, not parse trees.

Parse trees also record input structure, but they have nodes for all rule references used to recognize the input. Parse trees are much bigger and highly sensitive to changes to the parser grammar.

Translators pass an AST between phases, and consequently, all of the phases following the AST-building parser are tree walkers. These phases can alter or simply extract information from the AST. For example, the first tree-walking phase might update a symbol table to record variable and method definitions. The next phase might alter the AST so that nodes created from variable and method references point to their symbol table entries. The final phase typically emits output using all the information collected during previous phases.

This chapter describes how to structure ASTs and then defines the tree node types ANTLR can deal with. Once you are familiar with those details, you need to learn how to use AST operators, AST rewrite rules, and actions within your parser grammar to build trees. In the next chapter, we'll build tree-walking translator phases using tree grammars.

7.1 Proper AST Structure

Before learning to build ASTs, let's consider what ASTs should look like for various input structures. Keep in mind the following primary goals as you read this section and when you design ASTs in general. ASTs should do the following:

- Record the meaningful input tokens (and only the meaningful tokens)

- Encode, in the two-dimensional structure of the tree, the grammatical structure used by the parser to match the associated tokens but not the superfluous rule names themselves

- Be easy for the computer to recognize and navigate

These goals give general guidance but do not directly dictate tree structure. For that, think about how computers deal with programs most naturally: as simple instruction streams. The next two sections describe how to break high-level programming language constructs into subtrees with simple instructions as root nodes.

Encoding Arithmetic Expressions

Although humans prefer to think of arithmetic expressions using notation such as 3+4*5, computers prefer to think about the canonical operations needed to compute the result. The following pseudomachine instruction sequence multiplies 4 and 5 (storing the result in register r1) and then adds 3 to r1 (storing the result in register r2):

```
mul 4, 5, r1
add 3, r1, r2
```

Compilers do not generate such machine instructions directly from the input symbols—that would be way too complex to implement in one step. Compilers and other translators break down such difficult translations into multiple steps. The first step is to create a tree intermediate representation that is somewhere between source code and machine code in precision. Trees are much more convenient to examine and manipulate than low-level machine code. Here is what the typical AST looks like for 3+4*5:

Think of that machine instruction sequence as a "dismembered" tree with r1 as a symbolic reference to another subtree.

The structure of this tree dictates the order of operations because you cannot compute the addition without knowing both operands. The right operand is itself a multiply operation, and therefore, you must compute the multiply first.

Working backward from the machine instructions toward the AST, substitute the multiply instruction for r1 in the add (second) operation, and replace the instruction names with the operators:

```
+ 3, (* 4, 5), r2
```

If you consider the operators to be subtree roots, you get the following AST using ANTLR tree notation (the tree itself represents r2, so the r2 reference on the end is unnecessary):

```
^('+' 3 ^('*' 4 5))
```

This notation is merely a text representation of the previous AST image and has the following form:

```
^(root child1 child2 ... childN)
```

Most people have no problem agreeing that this AST is an acceptable way to represent the expression in memory, but what about more abstract concepts such as variable definitions like int i;?

Encoding Abstract Instructions

To deal with language constructs that are more abstract than expressions, we need to invent some high-level pseudomachine instructions that represent the operation implied by the source language construct. Each subtree should be like an imperative command in English with a verb and object such as "define an integer variable i." Always think of subtrees as operations with operands that tell the computer precisely what to do, just like we saw with the expression AST above. The following AST is one possible representation of the variable definition:

The VARDEF root node is an *imaginary node*, a node containing a token type for which there is no corresponding input symbol. int i; is implicitly a definition operation by its grammatical structure rather than explicitly because of an input symbol such as plus or multiply. For language constructs more abstract than expressions and statements, expect to invent pseudo-operations and the associated imaginary nodes.

Source code is meant for human consumption; hence, a single source-level construct often represents multiple lower-level operations. Consider a variation on the variable definition syntax that allows you to define multiple variables without having to repeat the type: int i,j;. You must unravel this into two operations when building an AST where the AST does not include the comma and semicolon.

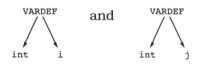

The punctuation characters are not included because they only exist to make the syntax clear to the parser (that is, to make a programmer's intentions clear). Once the parser has identified the structure, though, the punctuation symbols are superfluous and should not be included in the tree.

The VARDEF subtrees are in keeping with the third goal, that of creating trees that are easy to process. "Easy to process" usually means the node has an obvious operation and structure. To illustrate this, consider that Fortran syntax, a(i), is identical for both array indexes and function calls. Because the syntax alone does not dictate the operation, you will typically define semantic predicates in your parser grammar that query the symbol table to distinguish between the two based upon the type of the identifier (array or function name). The identifier type dictates the operation. Once you have discovered this information, do not throw it away. Use it to create different AST operation nodes. For example, the following AST does not satisfy the third goal because the operation is not obvious—the operation is still ambiguous.

```
    '('
    / \
   a   i
```

The '(' token also just does not make much sense as an operator. Instead, build an AST that makes the operation clear such as an array index:

```
  INDEX
   / \
  a   i
```

or a function call:

```
  CALL
   / \
  a   i
```

Besides nodes created from tokens and imaginary root nodes, you will also create lists of nodes and subtrees. Usually there is some obvious root node to which you should add the list elements as children. For example, the earlier variable definitions might be children of a class definition root node that also groups together method definitions:

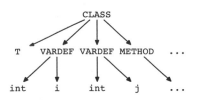

Using ANTLR's tree description language, that tree is written like this:

```
^( CLASS ID ^(VARDEF int i) ^(VARDEF int j) ^(METHOD ...) ... )
```

During construction, you will often have a rule that creates a list of subtrees. Until a valid root node can take on the list elements as children, you must use a special "nil operation" root node (trees must always have a single root node). Consider the variable definition subtrees created by, say, rule **definitions**. This rule would simulate a list using a tree with a nil root:

```
^( nil ^(VARDEF int i) ^(VARDEF int j) )
```

There is another situation in which you will want to create an imaginary node: to represent optional but missing subtrees. In general, you should not put something into the AST unless there is a corresponding input construct, but sometimes you must add extra nodes in order to remove ambiguity; remember, one of your goals is to make the subtrees easy to recognize during subsequent phases. Consider the **for** loop in Java, which has the following basic form:

```
forStat
    : 'for' '(' declaration? ';' expression? ';' expression? ')'
      slist
    ;
```

Because every element is optional, you might be tempted to leave missing expressions out of the AST. Unfortunately, this makes the AST ambiguous. If the tree has only one expression child, which is it? The conditional or the update expression? Instead, you need to leave a marker representing a missing expression (or variable definition). For the input for (int i=0; ; i++) {...}, create a tree that looks like the following where an imaginary node, EXPR, represents the missing conditional expression:

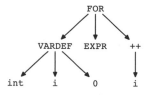

Similarly, if the initializer were missing from the variable definition, you could include an EXPR node on the end in its place. In this case, however, the optional initializer expression is last, and simply leaving it off would not be a problem.

You might also consider adding an EXPR node on top of all expressions because it might be a good place to squirrel away computation results or other information about the expression after it.

In summary, your goal is to identify and break apart the input constructs into simple operations and encode them in the AST. Your AST will contain nodes created from tokens, nodes with imaginary token types, subtrees with a root and children, and lists of these. Subtree roots represent operations, real or abstract, and subtree children represent operands. Do not include syntactic sugar tokens, such as semicolons, from the source language in the AST.

Now that you know something about what AST structures look like, let's examine the contents and types of the nodes themselves and how they are assembled into trees.

7.2 Implementing Abstract Syntax Trees

ANTLR assumes nothing about the actual Java type and implementation of your AST nodes and tree structure but requires that you specify or implement a TreeAdaptor. The adaptor plays the role of both factory and tree navigator. ANTLR-generated parsers can build trees, and tree parsers can walk them through the use of a single adapter object. Because ANTLR assumes tree nodes are of type Object, you could even make your Token objects double as AST nodes, thus avoiding a second allocation for the tree nodes associated with tokens.

Improved in v3. ANTLR v2 used cumbersome child-sibling trees for memory efficiency reasons, but v3 uses a simpler "list of children" approach.

ANTLR allows you to define your own tree nodes but provides a default tree node implementation, CommonTree, that is useful in most situations. Each node has a list of children and a payload consisting of the token from which the node was created.

For imaginary nodes, the parser creates a CommonToken object using the imaginary token type and uses that as the payload. CommonTree Adaptor creates CommonTree objects, which satisfy interface Tree. Tree has, among a few other things, the ability to add and get children:

```
/** Get ith child indexed from 0..getChildCount()-1 */
Tree getChild(int i);

/** How many children does this node have? */
int getChildCount();
```

```
/** Add t as a child to this node.  If t is null, do nothing.  If t
 *  is nil, add all children of t to this node's children.
 */
void addChild(Tree t);

/** Indicates the node is a nil node but may still have children,
 *  meaning the tree is a flat list.
 */
boolean isNil();
```

The generic Tree functionality of CommonTree that has nothing to do with payload is contained in BaseTree, a Tree implementation with no user data. CommonTreeAdaptor works with any tree node that implements Tree. BaseTree is useful if you want the core tree functionality but with a payload other than the Token.

An example makes the use of a tree adapter clearer. The following simple program creates a list of identifiers via create() and prints it via toStringTree(). The root node of a list is a "nil" node, which the adapter creates using nil().

trees/XYZList.java

```
import org.antlr.runtime.tree.*;

public class XYZList {
    public static void main(String[] args) {
        int ID = 1; // define a fictional token type
        // create a tree adapter to use for tree construction
        TreeAdaptor adaptor = new CommonTreeAdaptor();
        // a list has no root, creating a nil node
        CommonTree list = (CommonTree)adaptor.nil();
        // create a Token with type ID, text "x" then use as payload
        // in AST node; this variation on create does both.
        list.addChild((CommonTree)adaptor.create(ID,"x"));
        list.addChild((CommonTree)adaptor.create(ID,"y"));
        list.addChild((CommonTree)adaptor.create(ID,"z"));
        // recursively print the tree using ANTLR notation
        // ^(nil x y z) is shown as just x y z
        System.out.println(list.toStringTree());
    }
}
```

The unrestricted tree node data type comes at the cost of using the adapter to create and connect nodes, which is not the simplest means of building trees. Since you annotate grammars to build trees instead of manually coding the tree construction, this is not a burden.

When executed, the program emits the following:

```
$ java XYZList
x y z
$
```

If you'd like to use your own tree node type because you want to add some fields to each node, define your node as a subclass of CommonTree:

`trees/MyNode.java`

```java
import org.antlr.runtime.tree.*;
import org.antlr.runtime.Token;

public class MyNode extends CommonTree {
    /** If this is an ID node, symbol points at the corresponding
     *  symbol table entry.
     */
    public Symbol symbol;

    public MyNode(Token t) {
        super(t);
    }
}
```

Then, subclass CommonTreeAdaptor, and override create() so that it builds your special nodes:

```java
/** Custom adaptor to create MyNode nodes */
class MyNodeAdaptor extends CommonTreeAdaptor {
    public Object create(Token payload) {
        return new MyNode(payload);
    }
}
```

Finally, you must inform ANTLR that it should use your custom adapter:

```java
MyParser parser = new MParser(tokens,symtab); // create parser
MyNodeAdaptor adaptor = new MyNodeAdaptor();  // create adaptor
parser.setTreeAdaptor(adaptor);               // use my adaptor
parser.startRule();                           // launch!
```

If you'd like to build radically different trees or use an existing, say, XML DOM tree, then you will have to build a custom TreeAdaptor so ANTLR knows how to create and navigate those trees.

7.3 Default AST Construction

By default, ANTLR does not create ASTs, so you first need to set option **output** to AST. Without instructions to the contrary, ANTLR will simply build a flat tree (a linked list) containing pointers to all the input token objects. Upon this basic default mechanism, you will add AST construction operators and AST rewrite rules as described in the following sections. Before going into those specifications, however, you need to learn a little bit about the AST implementation mechanism, which is fairly involved for even a small grammar but is not difficult to understand. The details are important for your overall understanding, and this section provides an in-depth look, but you can initially skim this section and refer to it later. The two sections that follow, on AST operators and rewrite rules, move back to the user level and show you how to annotate grammars in order to build trees.

To explore ANTLR's AST implementation mechanism, consider the following grammar that matches a list of identifiers and integers. Rule r yields a nil-rooted tree with the **ID** and **INT** nodes as children:

trees/List.g

```
grammar List;
options {output=AST;}
r : (ID|INT)+ ;
ID : 'a'..'z'+ ;
INT : '0'..'9'+;
WS : (' '|'\n'|'\r') {$channel=HIDDEN;} ;
```

The following code is a typical test harness that gets the return value data aggregate from rule r, extracts the tree created by r, and prints it:

trees/TestList.java

```
import org.antlr.runtime.*;
import org.antlr.runtime.tree.*;

public class TestList {
    public static void main(String[] args) throws Exception {
        // create the lexer attached to stdin
        ANTLRInputStream input = new ANTLRInputStream(System.in);
        ListLexer lexer = new ListLexer(input);
        // create the buffer of tokens between the lexer and parser
        CommonTokenStream tokens = new CommonTokenStream(lexer);
        // create the parser attached to the token buffer
        ListParser parser = new ListParser(tokens);
        // launch the parser starting at rule r, get return object
        ListParser.r_return result = parser.r();
        // pull out the tree and cast it
        Tree t = (Tree)result.getTree();
        System.out.println(t.toStringTree()); // print out the tree
    }
}
```

All rules return a tree when you specify output=AST. In this case, ANTLR generates the following return value structure for rule r:

```
public static class r_return extends ParserRuleReturnScope {
    Object tree;
    public Object getTree() { return tree; }
}
```

Here is a sample execution:

```
←  $ java TestList
←  abc 34 2 x
←  EOF
⇒  abc 34 2 x
   $
```

ANTLR's basic strategy is straightforward. In this case, the rules are as follows:

1. Create a root pointer for each rule.

2. For each token, create a tree node as a function of the token.

3. Add each tree node to the enclosing rule's current root.

The generated parser accordingly performs the following operations (in pseudocode):

```
define a root pointer for rule, root_0
root_0 = adaptor.nil(); // make a nil root for rule
create a node for abc (element of ID|INT set)
add node as child of root_0
create a node for 34
add node as child of root_0
create a node for 2
add node as child of root_0
create a node for x
add node as child of root_0
return root_0 as r's tree attribute
```

As usual, the best way to figure out exactly what ANTLR is doing is to examine the code it generates. Here is the general structure of the rule's corresponding implementation method:

```
// match rule r and return a r_return object
public r_return r() throws RecognitionException {
►       r_return retval = new r_return(); // create return value struct
►       retval.start = input.LT(1);       // compute $r.start
►       Object root_0 = null;             // define r's root node
        try {
►           root_0 = (Object)adaptor.nil(); // create nil root
            «r-prediction»
            «r-matching-and-tree-construction»
```

```
▶            // rule cleanup next
▶            retval.stop = input.LT(-1);   // compute $r.stop
▶            // set $r.tree to root_0 after postprocessing
▶            // by default, this just converts ^(nil x) to x
▶            retval.tree = (Object)adaptor.rulePostProcessing(root_0);
▶            adaptor.setTokenBoundaries(retval.tree, retval.start, retval.stop);
        }
        catch (RecognitionException re) {
            «error-recovery»
        }
        return retval;
    }
```

The highlighted lines derive from the AST construction mechanism. The code to build tree nodes and add them to the tree is interspersed with the code that matches the set within the (...)+ subrule:

```
    // This code happens every iteration of the subrule
▶   set1=(Token)input.LT(1); // track the input token
    if ( (input.LA(1)>=ID && input.LA(1)<=INT) ) {
        // we found an ID or INT; create node from set1
        // then ask the adapter to add it as a child of
        // rule's root node.
▶       adaptor.addChild(root_0, adaptor.create(set1));
        input.consume();      // move to next input symbol
        errorRecovery=false; // ignore this (just ANTLR error bookkeeping)
    }
    else
        «throw-exception»
    // finished matching the alternative within (...)+
```

After all tree construction for a rule, the rule notifies the adapter that it should perform any necessary postprocessing on the tree before the rule returns it. This gives you a general hook to do whatever processing your trees might need on a per-rule basis. At minimum, the postprocessing needs to convert nil-rooted trees with a single child node to a simple node; that is, the postprocessing must convert ^(nil x) to x. Otherwise, the resulting tree will be filled with superfluous nil nodes. Remember that nil is used only to represent the dummy root node for lists.

Also as part of the final rule tree processing, the parser automatically computes and stores the range of tokens associated with the subtree created for that rule. This information is extremely useful later when generating code. Sometimes you want to replace sections of the input with a translation computed from the tree. To do that, you need to know the corresponding input tokens to replace. For example, consider the expression x + y (including the spaces). The root plus node will store token boundaries 0..4, assuming that the expression is the only input and that it consists of five tokens:

```
0   1    2 3    4        Token index
INT SPACE + SPACE INT    Token sequence
```

The AST nodes will have start and stop token index boundaries, as shown in the following image:

```
        +
      [0..4]
      /   \
     /     \
    x       y
  [0..0]  [4..4]
```

The token range of the root node will include all hidden channel tokens (whitespace in this case) that happen to be between the first and last nonhidden tokens. Also note that, because each node has the token from which it was created as payload, each node knows its corresponding position in the original input stream. So, the + node has a token whose index is 2. These boundaries and indexes allow you to print or replace the associated construct in the original input stream. This assumes that you keep around a buffer of all tokens in input order, which CommonTokenStream does.

The details presented in this section give you a deeper understanding of how ANTLR builds ASTs, but initially you need only a basic understanding that ANTLR uses an adapter to create nodes, hooks nodes together to form trees, and uses nil-rooted trees to represent lists. The following sections move back to the user level and describe how you annotate grammars in order to build the trees you want.

7.4 Constructing ASTs Using Operators

The nice aspect of the automatic AST construction mechanism is that you can just turn it on and it builds a tree, albeit a flat one. With just a little work, however, you can add AST construction operators to have the parser incrementally build the trees you want. These AST operators force you to think about the emergent behavior of a set of operations, but they can be an extremely terse means of specifying AST structure. They work great for some common constructs such as expressions and statements. For other AST structures, though, the rewrite rules described in the next section are more effective.

The operators work like this. First turn on output=AST and assume, by the automatic mechanism, that the parser adds nodes for all tokens to the tree as siblings of the current rule's root. Then, if you do not want the parser to create a node for a particular token, suffix it with the ! operator. If you want certain tokens to become subtree roots (operators or pseudo-operators), suffix the token reference with ^. An example makes all this clear. Consider the following statement rule that has ^ and ! operators in order to build reasonable AST structures:

```
statement
    : // the result of compoundStatement is statement result
      // equivalent to -> compoundStatement
      compoundStatement

      // equivalent to -> ^('assert' $x $y?)
    | 'assert'^ x=expression (':'! y=expression)? ';'!

      // equivalent to -> ^('if' expression $s1 $s2?)
    | 'if'^ expression s1=statement ('else'! s2=statement)?

      // equivalent to -> ^('while' expression statement)
    | 'while'^ expression statement

      // equivalent to -> ^('return' expression?)
    | 'return'^ expression? ';'!
    ;
```

The comments provide the equivalent rewrite rules, which we'll examine in detail later. Generally, the rewrite rules are the clearest. For demonstrating the AST construction operators, though, statements are a good place to start.

The place where AST construction operators really shine is in expression rules. Consider the following rule that matches an integer or sum of integers:

```
expr : INT ('+'^ INT)* ;
```

The rule says that the **INT** nodes are always children and that the '+' node is always a subtree root. The tree becomes one level higher for each iteration of the (...)* subrule. You should look at these as operators that alter the tree during recognition, not tree structure declarations that happen after recognition. As the parser recognizes **INT** tokens, it builds nodes for them and adds them as children of the current root node. The ^ operator takes the node created for the '+' token and makes it the new root, relegating the old root to be a child of the new root.

Operator **Description**

!   Do not include node or subtree (if referencing a rule) in rule's tree. Without any suffix, all elements are added as children of current rule's root.

^   Make node root of subtree created for entire enclosing rule. Height of tree is increased by 1. Next nonsuffixed element's node or subtree becomes the first child of this root node. If the next element has a ^ suffix, then this node becomes the first child of that next element. If the suffixed element is a rule reference, that rule must return a single node, not a subtree. The result must become a root node.

Figure 7.1: AST CONSTRUCTION OPERATORS

Given input 1, rule **expr** builds a single-node tree: INT. Input 1+2 yields ^('+' 1 2), and 1+2+3 yields ^(+ ^(+ 1 2) 3). Graphically, the latter tree looks like this:

After matching 1+2, rule **expr**'s root pointer points to the three-node tree: ^('+' 1 2). After seeing the second plus operator, **expr**'s root pointer will point at a new plus node. The old ^('+' 1 2) tree will be the first child. Then, after seeing the final 3 token, the tree will be complete—the final token will be the second child of the topmost plus operator.

The AST construction operators work great for left-associative operators such as plus and multiply, but what about right-associative operators such as exponentiation? Per Section 11.5, *Arithmetic Expression Grammars*, on page 266, to handle right-associative arithmetic operators, use tail recursion to the enclosing rule. To make the exponential operator a subtree root, use the ^ suffix (do not confuse the input symbol '^', which means exponent in arithmetic expressions, with the ^ AST construction operator; they just happen to be the same symbol):

```
pow :   INT ('^'^ pow)? ;  // right-associative via tail recursion
```

Given input 1^2^3, the parser will build the following AST:

Compare this to the earlier AST built for left-associative operator plus, and input 1+2+3. The operations are effectively swapped as you would expect because the exponent operator is right-associative and should do the 2^3 operation first. The table in Figure 7.1, on the preceding page, summarizes the two AST operators.

The automatic mechanism, in combination with a few AST construction operators, provides a viable and extremely terse means of specifying trees. Except for building ASTs for expressions, however, the AST construction operators are not the best solution. The next section describes a declarative tree construction approach that is more powerful and is usually more obvious than using operators.

7.5 Constructing ASTs with Rewrite Rules

The recommended way to build ASTs is to add *rewrite rules* to your grammar. Rewrite rules are like output alternatives that specify the grammatical, two-dimensional structure of the tree you want to build from the input tokens. The notation is as follows:

New in v3.

```
rule: «alt1» -> «build-this-from-alt1»
    | «alt2» -> «build-this-from-alt2»
    ...
    | «altN» -> «build-this-from-altN»
    ;
```

For example, here is a rule that performs an identity transformation. From the **INT** input token, the parser builds a single-node tree with the **INT** token as payload:

```
e : INT -> INT ;
```

Each rule returns a single AST that you can set zero or more times using the -> operator; generally, you will use the rewrite operator once per rule invocation. The resulting tree is available to invoking rules as a predefined attribute.

For example, here is a rule that invokes **e** and prints the resulting node:

```
r : e {System.out.println($e.tree);} ;
```

While parser grammars specify how to recognize input tokens, rewrite rules are generational grammars that specify how to generate trees. ANTLR figures out how to map input to output grammars automatically. Rules queue up the elements on the left and then use them as input streams to the generational grammar on the right that specifies tree structure.

While designing this new rewrite mechanism,[1] I carefully studied many existing ANTLR v2 grammars to categorize and generalize the kind of input grammar to tree structure transformations programmers were doing. The following subsections describe the operations I found.

Omitting Input Elements

Languages use many input symbols, such as comma, semicolons, colons, curlies, parentheses, and so on, to indicate structure in the input. These symbols are not useful in the AST. The following (unrelated) rules delete superfluous tokens from the AST simply by omitting them from the rewrite specification:

```
stat: 'break' ';' -> 'break' ; // delete by omission

expr: '(' expr ')' -> expr      // omit parentheses
    | INT           -> INT
    ;

a : ID -> ; // return no AST
```

Reordering Input Elements

Sometimes the order of input that humans want to use is not the most convenient processing order for the AST. Reorder elements by specifying a new order in the rewrite rule:

```
/** flip order of ID, type; omit 'var', ':' */
decl : 'var' ID ':' type -> type ID ;
```

Making Input Elements the Root of Others

To specify two-dimensional structure, you must indicate which tokens should become subtree roots. Rewrite rules use ^(...) syntax where the

---

1. I am grateful to Loring Craymer, Monty Zukowski, and John Mitchell (longtime research collaborators) for their help in designing the tree rewrite mechanism.

first element is the root of the remaining (child) elements, as shown in
the following rules:

```
/** Make 'return' the root of expr's result AST */
stat : 'return' expr ';' -> ^('return' expr) ;

/** Use 'var' as root of type, ID; flip over of type, ID */
decl : 'var' ID ':' type -> ^('var' type ID) ;
```

Adding Imaginary Nodes

As discussed in Section 7.1, *Proper AST Structure*, on page 150, you
will create imaginary nodes to represent pseudo-operations such as
"declare variable," "declare method," etc. To create an imaginary node
in the AST, simply refer to its token type, and ANTLR will create a Token
object with that token type and make it the payload of a new tree node:

```
/** Create a tree with imaginary node VARDEF as root and
 * type, ID as children.
 */
decl : type ID ';' -> ^(VARDEF type ID) ;

/** Ensure that there is always an EXPR imaginary node for
 * a loop conditional even when there is no expression.
 */
forLoopConditional
    : expression -> ^(EXPR expression)
    |            -> EXPR // return EXPR root w/o children
    ;
```

An imaginary token reference is a token reference for which there is
no corresponding token reference on the left side of the -> operator.
The imaginary token must be defined elsewhere in a grammar or in the
tokens section.

Collecting Input Elements and Emitting Together

You can collect various input symbols and ASTs created by other rules
to include them as a single list. You can also include a list of repeated
symbols from the input grammar, as shown in the following rules:

```
/** Collect all IDs and create list of ID nodes; omit ',' */
list : ID (',' ID)* -> ID+ ; // create AST with 1 or more IDs

/** Collect the result trees from all formalArg invocations
 * and put into an AST list.
 */
formalArgs
    :  formalArg (',' formalArg)* -> formalArg+
    |
    ;
```

```
/** Collect all IDs and create a tree with 'int' at the root
 *  and all ID nodes as children.
 */
decl : 'int' ID (',' ID)* -> ^('int' ID+) ;

/** Match a complete Java file and build a tree with a UNIT
 *  imaginary root node and package, import, and type definitions
 *  as children.  A package definition is optional in the input
 *  and, therefore, must be optional in the rewrite rule.  In
 *  general, the ''cardinality'' of the rewrite element must match
 *  how many input elements the rule can match.
 */
compilationUnit
    :   packageDef? importDef* typeDef+
        -> ^(UNIT packageDef? importDef* typeDef+)
    ;
```

Duplicating Nodes and Trees

When breaking a single source construct into multiple operations in your AST, you will often need to include pieces of the input in each of the operations. ANTLR will automatically duplicate nodes and trees as necessary, as demonstrated in the following examples:

```
/** Make a flat list consisting of two INT nodes pointing
 *  at the same INT token payload.  The AST nodes are duplicates,
 *  but they refer to the same token.
 */
dup : INT -> INT INT ;

/** Create multiple trees of form ^('int' ID), one for each input
 *  ID.  E.g., "int x,y" yields a list with two trees:
 *  ^(int x) ^(int y)
 *  The 'int' node is automatically duplicated.
 *  Note: to be distinguished from ^('int' ID+), which makes a
 *        single tree with all IDs as children.
 */
decl : 'int' ID (',' ID)* -> ^('int' ID)+ ;

/** Like previous but duplicate tree returned from type */
decl : type ID (',' ID)* -> ^(type ID)+ ;

/** Include a duplicate of modifier if present in input.
 *  Trees look like:
 *      ^(int public x) ^(int public y)
 *  or
 *      ^(int x) ^(int y)
 */
decl : modifier? type ID (',' ID)* -> ^(type modifier? ID)+ ;
```

The advantage of always creating duplicates for elements that you reference multiple times is that there is no possibility of creating cycles in the tree. Recall that a tree must not have children that point upward in the tree.

Otherwise, tree walkers (visitors, tree grammars, and so on) will get stuck in an infinite loop; for example, the AST resulting from t.addChild(t); will prevent a tree walker from terminating. Without automatic duplication, the following rule would be equivalent to t.addChild(t);:

```
a : ID -> ^(ID ID) ; // no cycle
```

ANTLR generates the following code for the rewrite rule:

```
// make dummy nil root for ^(...)
Object root_1 = adaptor.nil();

// make a node created from INT the root
root_1 = adaptor.becomeRoot((Token)list_INT.get(i_0), root_1);

// make another node created from INT as child
adaptor.addChild(root_1, (Token)list_INT.get(i_0));

// add rewrite ^(...) tree to rule result
adaptor.addChild(root_0, root_1);
```

In a rewrite rule, ANTLR duplicates any element with cardinality one (that is, one node or one tree) when referenced more than once or encountered more than once because of an EBNF * or + suffix operator. See Section 7.5, *Rewrite Rule Element Cardinality*, on page 171.

Choosing between Tree Structures at Runtime

Sometimes you do not know which AST structure to create for a particular alternative until runtime. Just list the multiple structures with a semantic predicate in front that indicates the runtime validity of applying the rewrite rule. The predicates are tested in the order specified. The rewrite rule associated with the first true predicate generates the rule's return tree:

```
/** A field or local variable.  At runtime, boolean inMethod
 *  determines which of the two rewrite rules the parser applies.
 */
variableDefinition
    :   modifiers type ID ('=' expression)? ';'
        -> {inMethod}? ^(VARIABLE ID modifier* type expression?)
        ->             ^(FIELD ID modifier* type expression?)
    ;
```

You may specify a default rewrite as the last unpredicated rewrite:

```
a[int which] // pass in parameter indicating which to build
  : ID INT -> {which==1}? ID
          -> {which==2}? INT
          ->                        // yield nothing as else-clause
  ;
```

Referring to Labels in Rewrite Rules

The previous sections enumerated the operations you will likely need when building ASTs and identified, by example, the kinds of rewrite rule elements you can use. The example rewrite rules used token and rule references.

The problem with token and rule references is that they grab all elements on the left side of the -> operator with the same name. What if you want only some of the **ID** references, for example? Using ID+ in the rewrite rule yields a list of all **ID** tokens matched on the left side.

Use labels for more precise control over which input symbols the parser adds to the AST. Imagine that a program in some language is a list of methods where the first method is considered the main method in which execution begins. The AST you create should clearly mark which method is the main method with an imaginary root node; otherwise, you will get a list of undifferentiated methods.

The following rule splits the usual method+ grammar construct into two pieces, method method*, identified with labels so that the rewrite rule can treat the first method separately:

```
prog: main=method others+=method* -> ^(MAIN $main) $others* ;
```

As another example, consider that you might want to encode the expressions in a **for** loop differently in the AST. The following rule illustrates how to refer to two different expressions via labels:

```
forStat
    : 'for' '(' decl? ';' cond=expr? ';' iter=expr? ')' slist
    -> ^( 'for' decl? ^(CONDITION $cond)? ^(ITERATE $iter)? )
    ;
```

You can use labels anywhere you would usually use a token or rule reference.

Creating Nodes with Arbitrary Actions

As a "safety blanket," ANTLR provides a way for you to specify tree nodes via an arbitrary action written in the target language, as shown in the following rule:

```
/** Convert INT into a FLOAT with text = $INT.text + ".0" */
a : INT -> {new CommonTree(new CommonToken(FLOAT,$INT.text+".0"))} ;
```

An action can appear anywhere that a token reference can appear, but you cannot suffix actions with cardinality operators such as + and *.

You can use arbitrary actions to access trees created elsewhere in a grammar. For example, when building class definitions for a Java-like language, the most natural grammar might match modifiers outside the rule that builds the AST for class definitions. The **typeDefinition** rule matches the modifiers and passes the resulting tree to the **classDefinition** rule:

```
typeDefinition
    :   modifiers! classDefinition[$modifiers.tree]
    |   modifiers! interfaceDefinition[$modifiers.tree]
    ;
```

The result AST of the **modifiers** rule is not included in the tree for **typeDefinition** because of the ! operator. The result of **typeDefinition** is, therefore, purely the result of either **classDefinition** or **interfaceDefinition**.

The rewrite rule in **classDefinition** illustrates a number of techniques described by the previous sections. The rule returns a tree rooted by the 'class' token. The children are the class name, the modifiers, the super-class, the potentially multiple interface implementations, the variables, the constructors, and the method definitions:

```
/** Match a class definition and pass in the tree of modifiers
 *  if any.
 */
classDefinition[CommonTree mod]
    :   'class' ID ('extends' sup=typename)?
        ('implements' i+=typename (',' i+=typename)*)?
        '{'
        (   variableDefinition
        |   methodDefinition
        |   ctorDefinition
        )*
        '}'
        -> ^('class' ID {$mod} ^('extends' $sup)? ^('implements' $i+)?
             variableDefinition* ctorDefinition* methodDefinition*
           )
    ;
```

Regardless of the input order of the member definitions, the tree orders them first by variable, then by constructor, and then by method. The action referencing $mod simply inserts that parameter as the second child of the resulting AST. Because you can reference rule elements only within a rewrite rule, you must enclose attribute references such as $mod in the curly braces of an action.

The third child, ^('extends' $sup)?, is a nested subtree whose child is the superclass. If the ('extends' typename)? input clause matches no input, the third child will evaluate to an empty tree. The fourth child similarly represents a nested tree with any interface implementations as children. The subtree evaluates to an empty tree if there were no implementations found on the input stream. The next section describes how EBNF operators such as ? can result in empty trees.

Rewrite Rule Element Cardinality

You can suffix rewrite rule elements with the EBNF subrule operators (?, *, or +) as you have seen, and, for the most part, their semantics are natural and clear. For example, ID+ and atom* obviously generate lists of one or more **ID** nodes and zero or more rule **atom** results, respectively. The parser throws a runtime exception if there is not at least one **ID** token from which to generate a node.

Also, if the parser sees more than one **ID** node during an ID? rewrite, it will also throw a runtime exception. Things get a little more complicated when the suffixed element is within a tree such as ^(VARDEF atom+). That subtree builds a single VARDEF-rooted tree with all **atom** results as children.

What about ('int' ID)+ where the + is now around a group of elements and not the individual **ID** element? This requires a more formal definition of what the EBNF operators do. The best way to think about rewrite rules is that they are the dual of parsing rules. Just imagine the rewrite rule matching input instead of generating output, and things usually make more sense. If you tried to match that closure operation, you would clearly need as many 'int' keywords as identifiers on the input stream.

Similarly, when generating output, ANTLR must create as many 'int' as **ID** nodes, even if it means replicating one or the other to match cardinalities. If the input grammar matched 'int' only once, for example, the AST construction mechanism would duplicate it once for every **ID** found on the input stream.

An Analogy to Explain Rewrite Rule Cardinality

Rewrite rule element cardinalities must match up just like stuffing letters into envelopes and stamping them. If you have one letter, you must have one envelope and one stamp. In general, you must match up the number of letters, envelopes, and stamps. The following rule captures that analogy:

```
/** Match a letter for each envelope and stamp, create trees with
 *  the letter as the root and the envelopes, stamps as children.
 */
pile : (letter envelope stamp)+ -> ^(letter envelope stamp)+ ;
```

Now, if you have only one letter but you want to send it to many people, you must duplicate the letter once for every addressed and stamped envelope:

```
/** Like duplicating one letter to put in multiple envelopes.
 *  The rule generates one tree for every stamped envelope with
 *  the letter node duplicated across them all.
 */
formLetter:letter (envelope stamp)+ -> ^(letter envelope stamp)+ ;
```

A closure operator such as + builds n nodes or trees according to the suffixed element where n is the maximum of the cardinalities of the element or elements within. Revisiting some previous examples, let's identify the cardinality of the elements:

Cardinality means how many of a particular element there are.

```
// cardinality of both type and ID is 1
decl : type ID ';' -> ^(VARDEF type ID) ;

// cardinality of ID is >= 1
list : ID (',' ID)* -> ID+ ;
```

Now consider the case where the + operator suffixes a tree:

```
// cardinality of ID is >= 1
decl : 'int' ID (',' ID)* ';' -> ^(VARDEF ID)+ ;
```

How many times does the + operator loop in the rewrite rule? That is, how many trees does the rule generate? The answer lies in the cardinality of elements referenced within. If all elements have cardinality of 1, then $n=1$, and the rule will generate one tree. If at least one element has cardinality greater than 1, then n is equal to that element's cardinality. All elements with cardinality greater than 1 must have exactly the same cardinality.

When there are some elements with cardinality one and others with cardinality greater than one, the elements with cardinality one are duplicated as the parser creates the tree. In the following rule, the 'int' token has cardinality one and is replicated for every **ID** token found on the input stream:

```
decl : 'int' ID (',' ID)* -> ^('int' ID)+ ;
```

Naturally, when the cardinality of the elements within a suffixed element is zero, the parser does not create a tree at all:

```
// if there is no "int ID" then no tree will be generated
decl : ('int' ID)? -> ^('int' ID)? ;
```

What about imaginary nodes, which always have cardinality one? Do they force the construction of trees even when the real elements within the tree have cardinality zero? No. Trees or subrules suffixed with EBNF operators yield trees only when at least one real element within the tree has cardinality greater than zero. For example, consider the following rule and AST rewrite rule:

```
initValue : expr? -> ^(EXPR expr)? ;
```

Rewrite ^(EXPR expr)? yields no tree when the **expr** on the left side returns no tree (the cardinality is zero). To be clear, ^(EXPR expr?) always yields at least an EXPR node. But, ^(EXPR expr)?, with the suffix on the entire tree, will not yield a tree at all if **expr** matched no input on the left side.

Most of the time the rewrite rules behave as you expect, given that they are the dual of recognition rules. Just keep in mind that the cardinality of the elements within suffixed subrules and trees must always be the same if their cardinality is greater than one. Also, if any element's cardinality is greater than one, the parser replicates any elements with cardinality one.

Rewrite Rules in Subrules

Even when a rewrite rule is not at the outermost level in a rule, it still sets the rule's result AST. For example, the following rule matches **if** statements and uses syntax to drive tree construction. The presence or absence of an **else** clause dictates which rewrite rule in the subrule to execute.

```
ifstat
    : 'if' '(' equalityExpression ')' s1=statement
      ('else' s2=statement -> ^('if' ^(EXPR equalityExpression) $s1 $s2)
      |                    -> ^('if' ^(EXPR equalityExpression) $s1)
      )
    ;
```

Here is another example where you might want to drive AST construction with syntax in a subrule:

```
decl: type
      ( ID '=' INT -> ^(DECL_WITH_INIT type ID INT)
      | ID         -> ^(DECL type ID)
      )
    ;
```

Referencing Previous Rule ASTs in Rewrite Rules

Sometimes you can't build the proper AST in a purely declarative manner. In other words, executing a single rewrite after the parser has matched everything in a rule is insufficient. Sometimes you need to iteratively build up the AST (which is the primary motivation for the automatic AST construction operators described in Section 7.4, *Constructing ASTs Using Operators*, on page 161). To iteratively build an AST, you need to be able to reference the previous value of the current rule's AST. You can reference the previous value by using $r within a rewrite rule where *r* is the enclosing rule. For example, the following rule matches either a single integer or a series of integers added together:

```
expr : (INT -> INT) ('+' i=INT -> ^('+' $expr $i) )* ;
```

The (INT->INT) subrule looks odd but makes sense. It says to match **INT** and then make its AST node the result of **expr**. This sets a result AST in case the (...)* subrule that follows matches nothing. To add another integer to an existing AST, you need to make a new '+' root node that has the previous expression as the left child and the new integer as the right child. The following image portrays the AST that the rewrite rule in the subrule creates for an iteration matching +3. After each iteration, $expr has a new value, and the tree is one level taller.

Input 1 results in a single node tree with token type INT containing 1. Input 1+2 results in the following:

And, input 1+2+3 results in the following:

That grammar with embedded rewrite rules recognizes the same input and generates the same tree as the following version that uses the construction operators:

```
expr : INT ('+'^ INT)* ;
```

The version with operators is much easier to read, but sometimes you'll find embedded rewrite rules easier. Here is a larger example where a looping subrule must reference previous values of the rule's AST incrementally:

```
postfixExpression
    :   (primary->primary) // set return tree to just primary
        (   '(' args=expressionList ')'
            -> ^(CALL $postfixExpression $args)
        |   '[' ie=expression ']'
            -> ^(INDEX $postfixExpression $ie)
        |   '.' p=primary
            -> ^(FIELDACCESS $postfixExpression $p)
        )*
    ;
```

Again, the (primary->primary) subrule matches **primary** and then makes its result tree the result of **postfixExpression** in case nothing is matched in the (...)* subrule. Notice that the last rewrite rule must use a label to specifically target the proper **primary** reference (there are two references to **primary** in the rule).

Deriving Imaginary Nodes from Real Tokens

You will create a lot of imaginary nodes to represent pseudo-operations in your language. A problem with these imaginary nodes is that, because they are not created from real tokens, they have no line and column information or token index pointing into the input stream. This information is useful in a number of situations such as generating error messages from tree walkers. It's also generally nice to know from where in the input stream the parser derived an AST construct.

ANTLR allows you to create imaginary nodes with a constructor-like syntax so you can derive imaginary nodes from existing tokens. The following rule creates an SLIST imaginary node, copying information from the '{' real token:

```
compoundStatement
    : lc='{' statement* '}' -> ^(SLIST[$lc] statement*)
    ;
```

The SLIST node gets the line and column information from the left curly's information.

You can also set the text of an imaginary node to something more appropriate than a left curly by adding a second parameter to the imaginary node constructor: SLIST[$lc,"statements"]. The following table summarizes the possible imaginary node constructors and how they are implemented.

Imaginary Node Constructor	Tree Adapter Invocation
T	adaptor.create(T, "T")
$T[]$	adaptor.create(T, "T")
$T[token\text{-}ref]$	adaptor.create(T, token-ref)
$T[token\text{-}ref, "text"]$	adaptor.create(T, token-ref, "text")

Combining Rewrite Rules and Automatic AST Construction

By default, output=AST in your parser causes each rule to build up a list of the nodes and subtrees created by its elements. Rewrite rules, though, turn off this automatic tree construction mechanism. You are indicating that you want to specify the tree manually. In many cases, though, you might want to combine the automatic mechanism with rewrite rules in the same rule. Or, you might want to have some rules use the automatic mechanism and others use rewrite rules. For example, in the following rule, there is no point in specifying rewrite rules because the automatic mechanism correctly builds a node from the modifier tokens:

```
modifier
    : 'public'
    | 'static'
    | 'abstract'
    ;
```

The same is true for rules that reference other rules:

```
typename
    :   classname
    |   builtInType
    ;
```

The following rule illustrates when you might want to use a rewrite rule in one alternative and the automatic mechanism in another alternative:

```
primary
    :   INT
    |   FLOAT
    |   '(' expression ')' -> expression
    ;
```

In general, the automatic mechanism works well for alternatives with single elements or repeated constructs such as method+.

This chapter described the kinds of tree structures to build for various input constructs,[2] how ANTLR implements tree construction, and how to annotate grammars with rewrite rules and construction operators to build ASTs. In the next chapter, we'll construct a complete parser grammar that builds ASTs for a subset of C and a tree grammar that walks those trees.

---

2. Readers familiar with ANTLR v2 might be curious about building different Java node types depending on the token type or might want to build simple parse trees. Please see the wiki entries on heterogeneous trees at http://www.antlr.org/wiki/pages/viewpage.action?pageId=1763 and parse trees at http://www.antlr.org/wiki/pages/viewpage.action?pageId=1760.

Chapter 8

Tree Grammars

One of the most common questions programmers have when building a translator is, "What do I do with my AST now that I've built it?" Their first reaction is often to use a visitor pattern[1] that essentially does a depth-first walk of the tree, executing an action method at each node. Although easy to understand, this approach is useful only for the simplest of translators. It does not validate tree structure, and actions are isolated "event triggers" that do not have any context information. The actions know only about the current node and know nothing about the surrounding tree structure. For example, visitor actions do not know whether an **ID** node is in a variable definition or an expression.

A good way to think of tree grammars are as executable documentation, formally describing complete tree structure.

The next step is to write a tree walker that manually checks the structure. The walker is aware of context either implicitly by passing information down the tree during the walk or by setting globally visible variables such as instance variables. Rather than build a tree walker by hand, though, you should use a tree grammar just like you do when building a text parser. To execute actions for certain subtrees of interest, just embed actions in your grammar at the right location.

Improved in v3.

ANTLR implements tree parsers with the same mechanism used to parse token streams. When you look at the generated code for a tree parser, it looks almost identical to a token parser. The tree parser expects a one-dimensional stream of nodes with embedded **UP** and **DOWN** imaginary nodes to mark the beginning and end of child lists, as described in Section 3.3, *Evaluating Expressions Encoded in ASTs*, on page 63.

---

1. See http://en.wikipedia.org/wiki/Visitor_pattern.

The CommonTreeNodeStream class will serialize the tree for the tree parser, as shown in the following code template:

```
CommonTreeNodeStream nodes = new CommonTreeNodeStream(tree);
treeGrammarName walker = new treeGrammarName(nodes);
walker.start-symbol();
```

The three sections in this chapter describe the basic approach to writing a tree grammar (by copying and then altering the parser grammar) and then illustrate a complete parser grammar and tree grammar for a simple C-like language.

8.1 Moving from Parser Grammar to Tree Grammar

Once you have a grammar that builds ASTs, you need to build one or more tree grammars to extract information, compute ancillary data structures, or generate a translation. In general, your tree grammar will have the following preamble:

```
tree grammar treeGrammarName;

options {
    tokenVocab=parserGrammarName; // reuse token types
    ASTLabelType=CommonTree; // $label will have type CommonTree
}
...
```

Then it is a matter of describing the trees built by the parser grammar with a tree grammar. AST rewrite rules are actually generational grammars that describe the trees that the parser grammar rule should construct. To build the tree grammar, you can reuse these rewrite rules as tree matching rules. The easiest way to build your tree grammar then is simply to copy and paste your parser grammar into a tree grammar and to remove the original parser grammar components (leaving only the rewrite rules). For example, given the following parser grammar rule:

```
grammar T;
...
decl : 'int' ID (',' ID)* -> ^('int' ID+) ;
```

translate it to this tree grammar:

```
tree grammar T;
...
decl : ^('int' ID+) ;
```

Parser rules that have AST rewrite rules within subrules also translate easily because rewrite rules always set the rule's result tree. The following rule:

```
grammar T;
...
ifstat
    : 'if' '(' equalityExpression ')' s1=stat
      ( 'else' s2=stat -> ^('if' ^(EXPR equalityExpression) $s1 $s2)
      |                -> ^('if' ^(EXPR equalityExpression) $s1)
      )
    ;
```

translates to this:

```
tree grammar T;
...
ifstat
    : ^('if' ^(EXPR equalityExpression) stat stat?)
    ;
```

which merges the two possible tree structures for simplicity. Note that $s1 in the parser grammar becomes the first stat reference in the tree grammar. $s2 becomes the second stat reference if the parser rule matches an else clause.

If the parser rule decides at runtime which tree structure to build using a semantic predicate, there is no problem for the tree grammar. The tree will be either one of those alternatives—just list them. For example, the following grammar:

```
grammar T;
...
variableDefinition
    :   modifiers type ID ('=' expression)? ';'
        -> {inMethod}? ^(VARIABLE ID modifier* type expression?)
        ->             ^(FIELD ID modifier* type expression?)
    ;
```

translates to the following:

```
tree grammar T;
...
variableDefinition
    :   ^(VARIABLE ID modifier* type expression?)
    |   ^(FIELD ID modifier* type expression?)
    ;
```

The AST construction operators are a little trickier, which is why you should use the AST rewrite rules where possible.

The ! operator is usually straightforward to translate because you can simply leave that element out of the tree grammar. For example, in the following rule, the semicolons are not present in the tree grammar:

```
grammar T;
...
stat: forStat
    | expr ';'!
    | block
    | assignStat ';'!
    | ';'!
    ;
```

The tree grammar looks like this:

```
tree grammar T;
...
stat: forStat
    | expr
    | block
    | assignStat
    ;
```

where the final parser rule alternative is absent from the tree grammar because, after removing the semicolon, there are no more elements to match (see the next section for an example rule that contains the ^ operator).

Finally, you can usually copy rules verbatim to the tree grammar that neither have elements modified with AST construction operators nor have rewrite rules. Here are two such rules:

```
tree grammar T;
...
/** Match one or more declaration subtrees */
program
    :   declaration+
    ;

/** Match a single node representing the data type */
type:   'int'
    |   'char'
    |   ID
    ;
```

The best way to learn about tree grammars is by example. The next section illustrates a complete AST-building parser grammar for a simple programming language.

The section following the next section builds a tree grammar to walk those trees and print the variable and function names defined in the input.

8.2 Building a Parser Grammar for the C- Language

This section presents a complete parser grammar with annotations to build ASTs for a small subset of the C programming language that we can call "C-" in honor of the grades I received as an undergraduate.[2]

The next section presents a tree grammar that describes all the possible AST structures emitted from the parser. The tree grammar has a few actions to print variable and function definitions just to be sure that the test rig actually invokes the tree walker.

Where appropriate, this section describes the transformation from parser grammar to tree grammar because that is the best way to build tree grammars for ASTs created by parser grammars.

First, define the language itself. Here is some sample input:

```
trees/CMinus/t.cm
char c;
int x;
int foo(int y, char d) {
  int i;
  for (i=0; i!=3; i=i+1) {
    x=3;
    y=5;
  }
}
```

C- has variable and function definitions and types int and char. Statements are limited to **for**, function calls, assignments, nested code blocks, and the empty statement signified by a semicolon. Expressions are restricted to conditionals, addition, multiplication, and parenthesized expressions.

The combined parser and lexer grammar for C- begins with the **grammar** header, an **options** section to turn on AST construction, and a **tokens**

---

2. See also http://www.codegeneration.net/tiki-read_article.php?articleId=77, which has an ANTLR v2 version of the same parser grammar. This might be useful for those familiar with v2 wanting to upgrade to v3.

section to define the list of imaginary tokens that represent pseudo-operations in C-:

trees/CMinus/CMinus.g

```
/** Recognize and build trees for C-
 * Results in CMinusParser.java, CMinusLexer.java,
 * and the token definition file CMinus.tokens used by
 * the tree grammar to ensure token types are the same.
 */
grammar CMinus;

options {output=AST;} // build trees

tokens {
  VAR;   // variable definition
  FUNC;  // function definition
  ARG;   // formal argument
  SLIST; // statement list
}
```

A C- program is a list of declarations. Declarations can be either variables or functions, as shown in the next chunk of the grammar:

trees/CMinus/CMinus.g

```
program
    :   declaration+
    ;

declaration
    :   variable
    |   function
    ;

variable
    :   type ID ';' -> ^(VAR type ID)
    ;

type:   'int'
    |   'char'
    ;
```

Functions look like this:

trees/CMinus/CMinus.g

```
// E.g., int f(int x, char y) { ... }
function
    :   type ID
        '(' ( formalParameter (',' formalParameter)* )?  ')'
        block
        -> ^(FUNC type ID formalParameter* block)
    ;
```

```
formalParameter
    :   type ID -> ^(ARG type ID)
    ;
```

The parser uses the VAR imaginary node to represent variable declarations and FUNC to represent function declarations. Arguments use ARG nodes. Rule **function** builds trees that look like this:

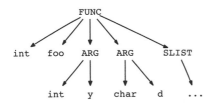

Notice rules **program**, **declaration**, and **type** do not need either AST construction operators or rewrite rules because the default action to build a list of nodes works in each case.

Here are the rules related to statements in C-:

trees/CMinus/CMinus.g

```
block
    :   lc='{' variable* stat* '}'
        -> ^(SLIST[$lc,"SLIST"] variable* stat*)
    ;

stat: forStat
    | expr ';'!
    | block
    | assignStat ';'!
    | ';'!
    ;

forStat
    :   'for' '(' first=assignStat ';' expr ';' inc=assignStat ')' block
        -> ^('for' $first expr $inc block)
    ;

assignStat
    :   ID '=' expr -> ^('=' ID expr)
    ;
```

Statement blocks in curly braces result in an AST rooted with the SLIST imaginary node. The SLIST node is derived from the left curly so that line and column information is copied into the imaginary node for error messages and debugging. The node constructor also changes the text from { to SLIST. Rule **stat** uses the ! AST construction operator to quickly and easily prevent the parser from creating nodes for semicolons. Semicolons make it easier for parsers to recognize statements but are not needed in the tree.

The expression rules use AST construction operators almost exclusively because they are much more terse than rewrite rules:

trees/CMinus/CMinus.g
```
expr:   condExpr ;

condExpr
    :   aexpr ( ('=='^|'!='^) aexpr )?
    ;

aexpr
    :   mexpr ('+'^ mexpr)*
    ;

mexpr
    :   atom ('*'^ atom)*
    ;

atom:   ID
    |   INT
    |   '(' expr ')' -> expr
    ;
```

All nonsuffixed tokens are subtree leaf nodes (operands), and the elements suffixed with ^ are subtree root nodes (operators). The only rule that uses a rewrite is **atom**. The parenthesized expression alternative is much clearer when you say explicitly -> expr rather than putting ! on the left parenthesis and right parenthesis tokens.

There are only three lexical rules, which match identifiers, integers, and whitespace. The whitespace is sent to the parser on a hidden channel and is, therefore, available to the translator. Using skip() instead would throw out the whitespace tokens rather than just hiding them:

trees/CMinus/CMinus.g
```
ID  :   ('a'..'z'|'A'..'Z'|'_') ('a'..'z'|'A'..'Z'|'0'..'9'|'_')* ;

INT :   ('0'..'9')+ ;

WS  :   ( ' ' | '\t' | '\r' | '\n' )+ { $channel = HIDDEN; } ;
```

The following key elements of the test rig create the lexer attached to standard input, create the parser attached to a token stream from the lexer, invoke the start symbol **program**, and print the resulting AST (the full test rig appears in the next section):

```
ANTLRInputStream input = new ANTLRInputStream(System.in);
CMinusLexer lexer = new CMinusLexer(input);
CommonTokenStream tokens = new CommonTokenStream(lexer);
CMinusParser parser = new CMinusParser(tokens);
CMinusParser.program_return r = parser.program();
CommonTree t = (CommonTree)r.getTree();
System.out.println(t.toStringTree());
```

Given the previous input, this test rig emits the following textual version of the AST (formatted and annotated with the corresponding input symbols to be more readable):

```
(VAR char c)                        // char c;
(VAR int x)                         // int x;
(FUNC int foo                       // int foo(...)
  (ARG int y) (ARG char d)          // int y, char d
  (SLIST
    (VAR int i)                     // int i;
    (for (= i 0) (!= i 3) (= i (+ i 1)) // for (int i=0; i!=3; i=i+1)
      (SLIST (= x 3) (= y 5))       // x=3; y=5;
    )
  )
)
```

At this point, we have a complete parser grammar that builds ASTs. Now imagine that we want to find and print all the variable and function definitions with their associated types. One approach would be to simply build a visitor that looks for the VAR and FUNC nodes so conveniently identified by the parser. Then, the visitor action code could pull apart the operands (children) to extract the type and identifier, but that would be manually building a recognizer for ^(VAR type ID) and ^(FUNC type ID ...). A better solution is to describe the AST structure formally with a grammar. Not only does this create nice documentation, but it lets you use a domain-specific language to describe your tree structures rather than arbitrary code. The next section describes how you build a tree grammar by copying and transforming your parser grammar.

8.3 Building a Tree Grammar for the C- Language

Before building the tree grammar, take a step back and think about the relationship between your parser that builds ASTs and the tree parser that walks the ASTs. Your parser grammar describes the one-dimensional structure of the input token stream and defines the (usually infinite) set of valid sentences. You should design your ASTs so that they are a condensed and highly processed representation of the input stream.

Where there can be some tricky constructs in the input language and constructs that represent multiple operations, all subtrees in the AST should represent single operations. These operations should have obvious root node types that clearly differentiate the various subtrees.

For example, both variable and function declarations in the C- language begin with the same sequence, type ID, but in the tree grammar they have unique root nodes, VAR and FUNC, that make them easy to distinguish. So, your tree grammar should match a simpler and two-dimensional version of the same input stream as the parser grammar. Consequently, your tree grammar should look a lot like your parser grammar, as you will see in this section.

Again, begin by examining the input language for your grammar. The following image represents a sample input AST generated for the t.cm file shown in the previous section:

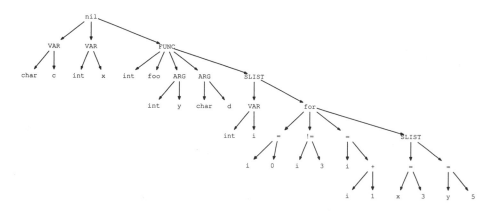

The goal is to generate output such as the following to identify the variables and functions defined in the input.

```
$ java TestCMinus < t.cm
define char c
define int x
define int i
define int foo()
$
```

Because the tree grammar should look very much like the parser grammar, begin by copying the parser grammar from CMinus.g to CMinusWalker.g and then altering the header per Section 8.1, *Moving from Parser Grammar to Tree Grammar*, on page 180:

```
trees/CMinus/CMinusWalker.g
```

```
tree grammar CMinusWalker;

options {
  tokenVocab=CMinus; // import tokens from CMinus.g
  ASTLabelType=CommonTree;
}
```

You do not need the imaginary token definitions in the tree grammar because the tokenVocab=CMinus option imports the token type definitions from the parser grammar, CMinus.g, via the CMinus.tokens file.

In the following declarations area of the grammar, the **program, declaration**, and **type** rules are identical to their counterparts in the parser grammar because they did not use rewrite rules or AST construction operators to create a two-dimensional structure. These rules merely created nodes or lists of nodes, and therefore, the tree grammar matches the same one-dimensional structure. The remaining rules match the trees built by the rules in the parser grammar with the same name:

```
trees/CMinus/CMinusWalker.g
```

```
program
    :   declaration+
    ;

declaration
    :   variable
    |   function
    ;

variable
    :   ^(VAR type ID)
        {System.out.println("define "+$type.text+" "+$ID.text);}
    ;

type:   'int'
    |   'char'
    ;

function
    :   ^(FUNC type ID formalParameter* block)
        {System.out.println("define "+$type.text+" "+$ID.text+"()");}
    ;

formalParameter
    :   ^(ARG type ID)
    ;
```

For the statements area of the grammar, transform the rules from the parser grammar simply by removing the elements to the left of the -> rewrite operator:

trees/CMinus/CMinusWalker.g

```
block
    :    ^(SLIST variable* stat*)
    ;

stat: forStat
    | expr
    | block
    | assignStat
    ;

forStat
    :    ^('for' assignStat expr assignStat block)
    ;

assignStat
    :    ^('=' ID expr)
    ;
```

Rule **stat** has three ! operators, and to transform that parser grammar to a tree grammar, remove the suffixed elements, as shown previously. The empty statement alternative containing just a semicolon disappears from the tree grammar. Once you remove the semicolon reference, nothing is left in that alternative. You do not want to create an empty alternative, which would make statements optional in the tree. They are not optional in the input and should not be optional in the tree grammar. Also of note is that SLIST[$lc,"SLIST"] becomes purely a token type reference, SLIST, in a tree grammar because you are matching, not creating, that node in the tree grammar.

The expressions area of the tree grammar is more interesting. All of the expression rules from the parser grammar collapse into a single recursive rule in the tree grammar. The parser constructs ASTs for expressions that encode the order of operations by their very structure. The tree grammar does not need to repeat the multilevel expression grammar pattern used by parser grammars to deal with different levels of precedence. A tree grammar can just list the possibilities, yielding a much simpler description for expressions than a parser grammar can use. Also notice that the parentheses used for nested expressions in the parser grammar are absent from the tree grammar because those exist only to override precedence in the parser grammar.

Parentheses alter the generated AST to change the order of operations but do not change the kinds of subtree structures found for expressions. Hence, the tree grammar is unaffected:

Collapsing all expression parser rules into a single recursive tree grammar rule is a general grammar design pattern.

trees/CMinus/CMinusWalker.g

```
expr:   ^('==' expr expr)
    |   ^('!=' expr expr)
    |   ^('+' expr expr)
    |   ^('*' expr expr)
    |   ID
    |   INT
    ;
```

Finally, there are no lexer rules in the tree grammar because you are parsing tree nodes, not tokens or characters.

Here is a complete test rig that invokes the parser to create an AST and then creates an instance of the tree parser, CMinusWalker, and invokes its **program** start symbol. The program spits out the text presentation of the AST unless you use the -dot option, which generates DOT[3] format files (that option was used to generate the AST images shown in this chapter).

trees/CMinus/TestCMinus.java

```
// Create input stream from standard input
ANTLRInputStream input = new ANTLRInputStream(System.in);
// Create a lexer attached to that input stream
CMinusLexer lexer = new CMinusLexer(input);
// Create a stream of tokens pulled from the lexer
CommonTokenStream tokens = new CommonTokenStream(lexer);

// Create a parser attached to the token stream
CMinusParser parser = new CMinusParser(tokens);
// Invoke the program rule in get return value
CMinusParser.program_return r = parser.program();
CommonTree t = (CommonTree)r.getTree();

// If -dot option then generate DOT diagram for AST
if ( args.length>0 && args[0].equals("-dot") ) {
    DOTTreeGenerator gen = new DOTTreeGenerator();
    StringTemplate st = gen.toDOT(t);
    System.out.println(st);
}
else {
    System.out.println(t.toStringTree());
}
```

---

3. See http://www.graphviz.org.

```
// Walk resulting tree; create treenode stream first
CommonTreeNodeStream nodes = new CommonTreeNodeStream(t);
// AST nodes have payloads that point into token stream
nodes.setTokenStream(tokens);
// Create a tree Walker attached to the nodes stream
CMinusWalker walker = new CMinusWalker(nodes);
// Invoke the start symbol, rule program
walker.program();
```

To build recognizers from these two grammar files, invoke ANTLR on the two grammar files and then compile:

```
$ java org.antlr.Tool CMinus.g CMinusWalker.g
$ javac TestCMinus.java # compiles the lexer, parser, tree parser too
$
```

The following session shows the output from running the test rig on the t.cm file:

```
$ java TestCMinus < t.cm
(VAR char c) (VAR int x) (FUNC int foo (ARG int y) (ARG char d) ... )
define char c
define int x
define int i
define int foo()
$
```

If your tree grammar is wrong or, for some reason, the input AST is improperly structured, the ANTLR-generated recognizer will emit an error message. For example, if you forgot the second **expr** reference on the != alternative of the **atom**:

```
expr:   ...
    |   ^('!=' expr) // should be ^('!=' expr expr)
    ...
    ;
```

and ran the input into the test rig, you would see the following error message:

```
(VAR char c) (VAR int x) (FUNC int foo (ARG int y) (ARG char d) ... )
CMinusWalker.g:line 5:15 mismatched tree node: 3; expecting type <UP>
```

Improved in v3. The tree parser error messages in v2 were useless.

The ^(!= i 3) subtree does not match the alternative because the alternative is looking for the UP token signifying the end of the child list. The input, on the other hand, correctly has the **INT** node containing 3 before the UP token.

The first part of the error message shows the stack of rules the tree parser had entered (starting from the start symbol) at the time of the error message. This is mainly for programmers to figure out where the problem is, and you can alter these messages to be more user-friendly (that is, have less information); see Chapter 10, *Error Reporting and Recovery*, on page 231.

This chapter provided a sample parser grammar and tree grammar for a small subset of C that prints the list of declarations as a simple translation.[4] It demonstrated that creating a tree grammar is just a matter of copying and transforming the parser grammar. A real application might have multiple copies of the grammar[5] for multiple passes such as symbol definition, symbol resolution, semantic analysis, and finally code generation. In the next chapter, we'll discover how to emit text source code via StringTemplate templates in order to build code generators.

---

4. For a tree grammar that executes some real actions, see the interpreter tutorial at http://www.antlr.org/wiki/display/ANTLR3/Simple+tree-based+interpeter on the wiki.

5. Managing multiple copies of the same grammar but with different actions is an onerous task currently, and discussing the solutions is beyond the scope of this reference guide. I anticipate building tools similar to revision control systems to help programmers deal with multiple tree grammars.

Chapter 9

Generating Structured Text with Templates and Grammars

At the most abstract level, translators map input sentences to output sentences. Translators can be as simple as data extraction programs that count the number of input lines or as complicated as language compilers. The complexity of the translation dictates the architecture of the translator, but no translator can escape the final phase: generating structured text from an internal data structures.[1] The translator component that emits structured text is called the *emitter*.

This chapter shows how to build emitters using ANTLR and the StringTemplate template engine. In particular, we'll see the following:

- Collectively, a group of templates represents a formal emitter specification.

- Templates are easier to build and understand than a collection of print statements in embedded grammar actions.

- Isolating the emitter from the code generation logic allows us to build retargetable code generators and follows good software engineering practice.

- There are two general classes of translators: rewriters and generators.

---

1. Compilers generate text assembly code and then use an assembler to translate to binary. Some translators actually do generate binary output, but they are in the minority.

- Template construction rules let us specify the text to emit for any given grammar rule; these templates rules parallel the AST construction rules described in Section 7.5, *Constructing ASTs with Rewrite Rules*, on page 164.

- StringTemplate has a simple but powerful syntax with a functional language flavor.

- ANTLR and StringTemplate complement each other; translators use ANTLR to recognize input and then use StringTemplate to emit output.

Without a template engine such as StringTemplate, translators must resort to emitting code with print statements. As we'll see in this chapter, using arbitrary code to generate output is not very satisfying. StringTemplate is a separate library, and naturally, we could embed template construction actions in a grammar just like any other action. To make using StringTemplate easier, ANTLR provides special notation that lets us specify output templates among the grammar rules.

To illustrate ANTLR's integration of StringTemplate, this chapter shows how to build a generator and a rewriter. The generator is a Java byte-code generator for the simple calculator language from Chapter 3, *A Quick Tour for the Impatient*, on page 43. The rewriter is a code instrumentor for the subset of C defined in Chapter 7, *Tree Construction*, on page 149. We'll build the code instrumentor first with a simple parser grammar and template construction rules and then solve it with a tree parser grammar that does the same thing. Before diving into the implementations, let's look at why templates provide a good solution, and see how ANTLR integrates StringTemplate.

9.1 Why Templates Are Better Than Print Statements

Emitters built with print statements scattered all over the grammar are more difficult to write, to read, and to retarget. Emitters built with templates, on the other hand, are easier to write and read because you can directly specify the output structure. You do not have to imagine the emergent behavior of each rule to conjure up the output structure. Template-based emitters are easier to maintain because the templates act as executable documentation describing the output structure. Further, by specifying the output structure separately, you can more easily retarget the translator. You can provide a separate group of templates for each language target without having to alter your code generation logic. Indeed, you don't even need to recompile the translator to incorporate a new language target. This section argues for the use of formal template-based emitter specifications by appealing to your software engineering sense.

Consider the abstract behavior of a translator. Each output sentence is a function of input sentence data and computations on that data. For example, a translator's emitter might reference a variable's name and ask, "Is this variable defined and assigned to within the current scope?" An understanding of this behavior does not directly suggest a translator architecture, though. Programmers typically fall back on what they know—arbitrary embedded grammar actions that emit output as a function of the input symbols.

Most emitters are arbitrary, unstructured blobs of code that contain print statements interspersed with generation logic and computations. These emitters violate the important software engineering principle of "separation of concerns." In the terminology of design patterns, such informal emitters violate model-view-controller separation.[2] The collection of emitter output phrases comprises the view. Unfortunately, most emitters entangle the view with the controller (parser or visitor pattern) and often the model (internal data structures). The only exceptions are programming language compilers.

Modern compilers use a specialized emitter called an *instruction generator* such as BURG [FHP92], a tree-walking pattern matcher similar in concept to ANTLR's tree parsers. Instruction generators force a separate, formal output specification that maps intermediate-form subtrees to appropriate instruction sequences. In this way, a compiler can isolate the view from the code generation logic. Retargeting a compiler to a new processor is usually a matter of providing a new set of instruction templates.

Following the lead of compilers, other translators should use formal specifications to describe their output languages. Generated text is structured, not random, and therefore, output sentences conform to a language. It seems reasonable to think about specifying the output structure with a grammar or group of templates.

---

2. For an in-depth discussion, see "Enforcing Strict Model-View Separation in Template Engines" at http://www.cs.usfca.edu/~parrt/papers/mvc.templates.pdf.

To process this high-level specification, you need an "unparser generator" or template engine with the flavor of a generational grammar such as StringTemplate. To encourage the use of separate output specifications, ANTLR integrates StringTemplate by providing template construction rules. These rules let you specify the text to emit for any given grammar rule in a manner that parallels the AST construction rules described in Section 7.5, *Constructing ASTs with Rewrite Rules*, on page 164. Collectively, the templates represent a formal emitter specification similar to the formal specification compilers used to emit machine instructions. By separating the templates from the translation logic, you can trivially swap out one group of templates for another. This means you can usually retarget the translators you build with ANTLR and StringTemplate; that is, the same translator can emit output in more than one language.

New in v3.

ANTLR uses templates to generate the various back ends (such as Java, C, Objective-C, Python, and so on). Each back end has a separate template group. There is not a single print statement in the ANTLR code generator—everything is done with templates. The language target option tells ANTLR which group of templates to load. Building a new ANTLR language target is purely a matter of defining templates and building the runtime library.

Isolating your translator's emitter from the code generation logic and computations make sense from a software engineering point of view. Moreover, ANTLR v3's retargetable emitter proves that you can make it work well in practice. The next section drives the point home by showing you the difference between embedded actions and template construction rules.

9.2 Comparing Embedded Actions to Template Construction Rules

Translating the input matched by a rule without a template engine is painful and error prone. You must embed actions in the rule to translate and then emit or buffer up each rule element. A few example grammars comparing embedded actions with template construction rules makes this abundantly clear.

The Dream Is Alive!

During the development of the ANTLR v1 (PCCTS) and ANTLR v2 code generators, I harbored an extremely uncomfortable feeling. I knew that the undignified blobs of code generation logic and print statements were the wrong approach, but I had no idea how to solve the problem.

Oddly enough, the key idea germinated while building the second incarnation of a big nasty web server called jGuru.com. Tom Burns (jGuru CEO) and I designed StringTemplate in response to the entangled JSP pages used in the first server version. We wanted to physically prevent programmers from embedding logic and computations in HTML pages. In the back of my mind, I mused about turning StringTemplate into a sophisticated code generator.

When designing ANTLR v3, I dreamt of a code generator where each language target was purely a group of templates. Target developers would not have to know anything about the internals of the grammar analysis or code generation logic. StringTemplate evolved to satisfy the requirements of ANTLR v3's retargetable code generator. The dream is now reality. Every single character of output comes from a template, not a print statement. Contrast this with v2 where building a new target amounts to copying an entire Java file (thereby duplicating the generator logic code) and tweaking the print statements. The v2 generators represent 39% of the total lines (roughly 4,000 lines for each language target). In v3, the code generation logic is now only 4,000 lines (8% of the total). Each new language target is about 2,000 lines, a 50% reduction over v2. More important, v3 targets are pure templates, not code, making it much easier and faster to build a robust target.

Consider the following two rules from a Java tree grammar that contain embedded actions to spit Java code back out based upon the input symbols where emit() is essentially a print statement that emits output sensitive to some indentation level:

```
methodHead
    :   IDENT {emit(" "+$IDENT.text+"(");}
        ^( PARAMETERS
            (   p=parameterDef
                {if (there-is-another-parameter) emit(",");}
            )*
        )
        {emit(") ");}
        throwsClause?
    ;


throwsClause
    :   ^( "throws" {emit("throws ");}
            (   identifier
                {if (there-is-another-id) emit(", ");}
            )*
        )
    ;
```

To figure out what these rules generate, you must imagine what the output looks like by "executing" the arbitrary embedded actions in your mind. Embedding all those actions in a grammar is tedious and often makes it hard to read the grammar.

A better approach is to simply specify what the output looks like in the form of templates, which are akin to output grammar rules. The following version of the same rules uses the -> template construction operator to specify templates in double quotes:

```
methodHead
    :   IDENT ^( PARAMETERS ( p+=parameterDef )* ) throwsClause?
        -> template(name={$IDENT.text},
                    args={$p},
                    throws={$throwsClause.st})
            "<name>(<args; separator=\", \">) <throws>"
    ;


throwsClause
    :   ^( "throws" ( ids+=identifier )* )
        -> template(exceptions={$ids})
            "throws <exceptions; separator=\", \">"
    ;
```

Everything inside a template is pure output text except for the expressions enclosed in angle brackets. For most people, seeing a template instead of print statements makes a rule's output much clearer. The template shows the overall structure of the output and has "holes" for computations or data from the input.

Aside from allowing you to specify output constructs in a more declarative and formal fashion, StringTemplate provides a number of great text generation features such as autoindentation. Here is a rule from a Java tree grammar that uses print statements to emit array initializers with the elements indented relative to the curlies that surround them:

```
arrayInitializer
    :   ^( ARRAY_INIT
            {emit("{"); nl(); indent();}
            (   init:initializer
                {if (there-is-another-value) emit(", ");}
            )*
            {undent(); nl(); emit("}");}
        )
    ;
```

where indent() and undent() are methods that increase and decrease the indentation level used by emit(). nl() emits a newline.

Notice that the actions must take care of indentation manually. StringTemplate, on the other hand, automatically tracks and generates indentation. The following version of **arrayInitializer** generates the same output with the array initialization values indented two spaces (relative to the curlies) automatically:

```
arrayInitializer
    :   ^( ARRAY_INIT (v+=initializer)* )
        -> template(values={$v})
        <<
        {
          <values; separator=", ">
        }
        >>
    ;
```

This section illustrates the convenience of using templates to specify output. The next section describes the StringTemplate template engine in more detail. You'll learn more about what goes inside the templates.

9.3 A Brief Introduction to StringTemplate

StringTemplate[3] is a sophisticated template engine, and you should familiarize yourself with it by referring to its documentation[4] before you build a translator, but this section explains its basic operation. You will learn enough to understand the templates used in the large examples in Section 9.6, *A Java Bytecode Generator Using a Tree Grammar and Templates*, on page 208, Section 9.7, *Rewriting the Token Buffer In-Place*, on page 217, and Section 9.8, *Rewriting the Token Buffer with Tree Grammars*, on page 223. You should at least skim this section before proceeding to the examples.

Templates are strings or "documents" with holes that you can fill in with template expressions that are a function of *attributes*. You can think of attributes as the parameters passed to a template (but don't confuse template attributes with the grammar attributes described in Chapter 6, *Attributes and Actions*, on page 117). StringTemplate breaks up your template into chunks of text and attribute expressions, which are by default enclosed in angle brackets: <«*attribute-expression*»>. String-Template ignores everything outside attribute expressions, treating them as just text to spit out.

StringTemplate is not a system or server—it is just a library with two primary classes of interest: StringTemplate and StringTemplateGroup. You can directly create a template in code, you can load a template from a file, and you can load a single file with many templates (a template group file). Here is the core of a "Hello World" example that defines a template, sets its sole attribute (name), and prints it:

```
import org.antlr.stringtemplate.*;
...
StringTemplate hello = new StringTemplate("Hello <name>");
hello.setAttribute("name", "World");
System.out.println(hello.toString());
```

The output is Hello World. StringTemplate calls toString() on each object to render it to text. In this case, the name attribute holds a String already.

If an attribute is multivalued, such as an instance of a list, or if you set attribute name multiple times, the expression emits the elements one after the other.

---

3. See http://www.stringtemplate.org.
4. See http://www.antlr.org/wiki/display/ST/StringTemplate+3.0+Documentation.

For example, the following change to the earlier code sample sets the name attribute to an array:

```
...
String[] names = {"Jim", "Kay", "Sriram"};
hello.setAttribute("name", names);
System.out.println(hello.toString());
```

The output is Hello JimKaySriram, but if you change the template definition to include a separator string, you can emit better-looking output:

```
StringTemplate hello =
    new StringTemplate("Hello <name; separator=\", \">");
```

Now, the output is Hello Jim, Kay, Sriram.

One final operation that you will see is *template application*. Applying a template to an attribute or multivalued attribute using the : operator is essentially a map operation. A map operation passes the elements in the attribute one at a time to the template as if it were a method. The following example applies an anonymous template to a list of numbers (anonymous templates are enclosed in curly brackets). The n variable defined between the left curly and the | operator is a parameter for the anonymous template. n is the iterated value moving through the numbers.

```
<numbers:{ n | sum += <n>; }>
```

Assuming the numbers attribute held the values 11, 29, and 5 (in a list, array, or anything else multivalued), then the template would emit the following when evaluated:

```
sum += 11; sum += 29; sum += 5;
```

Rather than having to create instances of templates in actions manually, grammars can use template construction rules, as demonstrated in the next section.

9.4 The ANTLR StringTemplate Interface

Grammars that set option output=template can use the -> operator to specify the enclosing rule's template return value. The basic syntax mirrors AST construction rules:

```
rule: «alt1» -> «alt1-template»
    | «alt2» -> «alt2-template»
    ...
    | «altN» -> «altN-template»
    ;
```

Each rule's template specification creates a template using the following syntax (for the common case):

```
... -> template-name(«attribute-assignment-list»)
```

The resulting recognizer looks up *template-name* in the StringTemplate-Group that you pass in from your invoking program via setTemplateLib(). A StringTemplateGroup is a group of templates and acts like a dictionary that maps template names to template definitions. The attribute assignment list is the interface between the parsing element values and the attributes used by the template. ANTLR translates the assignment list to a series of setAttribute() calls. For example, attribute assignment a={«expr»} translates to the following where retval.st is the template return value for the rule:

```
retval.st.setAttribute("a", «expr»);
```

As a more concrete example, consider the following grammar that matches simple assignments and generates an equivalent assignment using the Pascal := assignment operator:

templates/T.g
```
grammar T;
options {output=template;}
s : ID '=' INT ';' -> assign(x={$ID.text},y={$INT.text}) ;
ID: 'a'..'z'+ ;
INT:'0'..'9'+ ;
WS :(' '|'\t'|'\n'|'\r') {skip();} ;
```

Rule **s** matches a simple assignment statement and then creates an instance of template **assign**, setting its x and y attributes to the text of the identifier and integer, respectively. Here is a group file that defines template **assign**:

templates/T.stg
```
group T;
assign(x,y) ::= "<x> := <y>;"
```

The following code is a simple test rig that loads the StringTemplate group from a file (T.stg), instantiates the parser, invokes rule **s**, gets the result template, and prints it:

templates/Test.java
```
import org.antlr.runtime.*;
import org.antlr.stringtemplate.*;
import java.io.*;
```

```
public class Test {
    public static void main(String[] args) throws Exception {
        // load in T.stg template group, put in templates variable
        FileReader groupFileR = new FileReader("T.stg");
        StringTemplateGroup templates =
            new StringTemplateGroup(groupFileR);
        groupFileR.close();

        // PARSE INPUT AND COMPUTE TEMPLATE
        ANTLRInputStream input = new ANTLRInputStream(System.in);
        TLexer lexer = new TLexer(input);      // create lexer
        CommonTokenStream tokens = new CommonTokenStream(lexer);
        TParser parser = new TParser(tokens); // create parser
        parser.setTemplateLib(templates); // give parser templates
        TParser.s_return r = parser.s();       // parse rule s
        StringTemplate output = r.getTemplate();
        System.out.println(output.toString());// emit translation
    }
}
```

The test program accepts an assignment from standard input and emits
the translation to standard output:

```
⇐    $ java Test
⇐    x=101;
⇐    EOF
⇒    x := 101;
     $
```

Most of the time you will place your templates in another file (a
StringTemplateGroup file[5]) to separate your parser from your output
rules. This separation makes it easy to retarget your translator because
you can simply swap out one group of templates for another to generate different output. For simple translators, however, you might want
to specify templates in-line among the rules instead. In-line templates
use notation like this:

```
... -> template(«attribute-assignment-list») "in-line-template"
```

or like this:

```
... -> template(«attribute-assignment-list»)
<<
«in-line-template-spanning-multiple-lines»
>>
```

---

5. See http://www.antlr.org/wiki/display/ST/Group+Files.

You can also use an arbitrary action that evaluates to a template as the template specification:

```
... -> {«arbitrary-template-expression»}
```

Now that you have some understanding of what templates look like and how to use them in a grammar, you're about ready to tackle some real examples. The first example generates Java bytecodes for simple arithmetic expressions. The second example instruments C code to track function calls and variable assignments. On the surface, the two applications appear to be similar because they both use templates to specify the output. What they do with the templates, however, is very different. The Java bytecode generator combines template results computed from input phrases into an overall template. In contrast, the C instrumentor gets away with just tweaking the input. For example, when it sees an assignment statement, the translator can simply append an instrumentation call. Rebuilding the whole C file complete with whitespace and comments is much more difficult. Before diving into the examples, let's examine the two fundamental translator categories they represent.

9.5 Rewriters vs. Generators

A translator's input to output relationship classifies it into one of two overall categories in the translation taxonomy: either the output looks very much like the input, or it does not, which says a lot about the most natural implementation, as we'll see in a moment. Examples abound for each category.

In the first category, the output looks very much like the input, and the translator is usually just tweaking the input or, when reading source code, instrumenting it for debugging, code coverage, or profiling purposes. I would include in this category translators that keep the same output structure and data elements but that do a fair bit of augmentation. A wiki-to-HTML translator is a good example of this. Let's call this the *rewriter* category.

Generally speaking, the more different the output is from the input, the more difficult it is to build the translator.

In the second category, the output looks very different from the input. The translator might condense the input into a report such as a set of source code metrics or might generate Javadoc comments from Java source code. Compilers and other tools in this category such as ANTLR generate an equivalent version of the input but a version that looks totally different because it has been highly processed and reorganized.

In other cases, the output is similar to the input, but the relative order of the elements is different in the output. For example, translating from a language where declaration order doesn't matter to a language where it does means that the translator must topologically sort the declarations according to their referential dependencies (declarations that refer to type T must occur after the declaration for T). Because the majority of the text emitted by translators in this category is not directly present in the input or has been significantly rebuilt, let's call this category the *generator* category.

The translation category often dictates which general approach to use:

- *Rewriters*. I recommend modifying input constructs in-place, meaning rewriting sections of the input buffer during translation. At the end of translation, you can simply print the modified buffer to get the desired output. ANTLR provides an excellent token buffer called TokenRewriteStream that is specifically designed to efficiently handle multiple in-place insertions, deletions, and replacements.

- *Generators*. This category generates and then buffers up bits of translated input that it subsequently organizes into larger and larger chunks, leading to the final chunk representing the complete output.

For both rewriters and generators, you'll use grammars to direct the translation. You'll embed actions and template construction rules (using operator ->) to perform computations and create pieces of the output. Rewriters will directly replace portions of the original input buffer with these output pieces, whereas generators will combine output pieces to form the overall output without touching the input buffer. Your translator might even have multiple grammars because, for complicated translations, you might need to break the problem down into multiple phases to make the translator easier to build and maintain. This means creating an AST intermediate form and making multiple passes over the AST to gather information and possibly to alter the AST.

How do you know whether you need multiple grammars (one parser grammar and multiple tree grammars) or whether you can get away with just a single parser grammar? Answering this question before attempting to build the actual translator requires a good deal of experience.

Generally speaking, though, you can usually get away with a single parser grammar if your translator can generate all output pieces without needing information from further ahead in the input stream and without needing information from another input file. For example, you can generate Javadoc comments just by looking at the method itself, and you can compute word and line counts by looking at the current and previous lines. On the other hand, compilers for object-oriented languages typically allow forward references and references to classes and methods in other files. The possibility of forward references alone is sufficient to require multiple passes, necessitating an intermediate form such as an AST and tree grammars.

The remainder of this chapter provides a Java bytecode generator as an example in the generator category and a code instrumentor as an example in the rewriter category. Let's begin with the generator category because the rewriter category is just a special case of a generator.

9.6 Building a Java Bytecode Generator Using a Tree Grammar and Templates

In Chapter 3, *A Quick Tour for the Impatient*, on page 43, we saw how to build an interpreter for some simple arithmetic expressions. This section illustrates how to build a Java bytecode generator for those same expressions.

As before, the input to the translator is a series of expressions and assignments. The output is a Java bytecode sequence in bytecode assembler format. Then Jasmin[6] can translate the text-based bytecode assembly program to a binary Java .class file. Once you have the .class file, you can directly execute expressions via the Java virtual machine. In a sense, the generator is a Java compiler for an extremely limited subset of Java. Naturally, a real compiler would be vastly more complicated, and I am not suggesting that you build compilers this way—generating Java bytecodes is merely an interesting and educational demonstration of template construction.

Before exploring how to build the generator, you need to know something about Java bytecodes and the underlying stack machine.

---

6. See http://jasmin.sourceforge.net.

Java Bytecodes Needed for Expressions

The executable instructions you will use for the translator are limited to the following:

Bytecode Instruction	Description
ldc *integer-constant*	Push constant onto stack.
imul	Multiply top two integers on stack and leave result on the stack. Stack depth is one less than before the instruction. Executes push(pop*pop).
iadd	Add top two integers on stack and leave result on the stack. Stack depth is one less than before the instruction. Executes push(pop+pop).
isub	Subtract top two integers on stack and leave result on the stack. Stack depth is one less than before the instruction. Executes b=pop; a=pop; push(a-b).
istore *local-var-num*	Store top of stack in local variable and pop that element off the stack. Stack depth is one less than before the instruction.
iload *local-var-num*	Push local variable onto stack. Stack depth is one more than before the instruction.

The Java bytecode generator accepts input:

`templates/generator/1pass/input`

```
3+4*5
```

and generates the following bytecodes:

```
ldc 3   ; push integer 3
ldc 4   ; push 4
ldc 5   ; push 5
imul    ; pop 2 elements, multiply; leave 4*5 on stack
iadd    ; pop 2 elements, 3 and (4*5), add, leave on stack
```

What about storing and retrieving local variables? This input:

`templates/generator/1pass/input2`

```
a=3+4
a
```

results in the following bytecodes:

templates/generator/1pass/input2.j

```
; code translated from input stream
; compute 3+4
ldc 3
ldc 4
iadd
istore 1 ; a=3+4
; compute a
iload 1 ; a
```

The Java virtual machine places local variables and method parameters on the stack. The bytecodes must allocate space for both at the start of each method. Also, the method must have space for the operands pushed onto the stack by the instructions. The proper way to compute stack space needed by a method is too much to go into here. The generator simply estimates how much operand stack space it will need according to the number of operator instructions.

All Java code must exist within a method, and all methods must exist within a class. The generator must emit the bytecode equivalent of this:

```
public class Calc {
    public static void main(String[]) {
        System.out.println(«executable-bytecodes-from-expression»);
    }
}
```

Unfortunately, the overall bytecode infrastructure just to wrap the bytecode in a main() method is fairly heavy. For example, given input 3+4*5, the generator must emit the following complete assembly file:

templates/generator/1pass/input.j

```
; public class Calc extends Object { ...}
.class public Calc
.super java/lang/Object

; public Calc() { super(); } // calls java.lang.Object()
.method public <init>()V
    aload_0
    invokenonvirtual java/lang/Object/<init>()V
    return
.end method

; main(): Expr.g will generate bytecode in this method
.method public static main([Ljava/lang/String;)V
    .limit stack 4 ; how much stack space do we need?
    .limit locals 1 ; how many locals do we need?
```

```
      getstatic java/lang/System/out Ljava/io/PrintStream;
      ; code translated from input stream
►     ; compute 3+4*5
►     ldc 3
►     ldc 4
►     ldc 5
►     imul
►     iadd
      ; print result on top of stack
      invokevirtual java/io/PrintStream/println(I)V
      return
.end method
```

The generator modifies or emits the highlighted lines. The getstatic and invokevirtual bytecodes implement the System.out.println(*expr*) statement:

```
; get System.out on stack
getstatic java/lang/System/out Ljava/io/PrintStream;
«compute-expr-leaving-on-stack»
; invoke println on System.out (object 1 below top of stack)
invokevirtual java/io/PrintStream/println(I)V
```

To execute the generated code, you must first run the Jasmin assembler, which converts bytecode file input.j into Calc.class. Calc is the class definition surrounding the expression bytecodes. Installing Jasmin is easy. Just download and unzip the ZIP file. The key file is jasmin-2.3/jasmin.jar, which you can add to your CLASSPATH or just reference directly on the command line. Here is a sample session that "executes" the earlier input.j file using Jasmin and then the Java interpreter:

```
$ java -jar /usr/local/jasmin-2.3/jasmin.jar input.j
Generated: Calc.class
$ java Calc
23
$
```

That big file of bytecodes looks complicated to generate, but if you break it down into the individual pieces, the overall generator is straightforward. Each rule maps an input sentence phrase to an output template. Combining the templates results in the output assembly file. The following section shows how to implement the translator.

Generating Bytecode Templates with a Tree Grammar

This section shows you how to build a Java bytecode generator for a simple calculator language. The implementation uses the parser and tree grammars given in Chapter 3, *A Quick Tour for the Impatient*, on page 43. The parser, **Expr**, creates ASTs and fills a symbol table with variable definitions. A second pass, specified with tree grammar **Gen**, constructs templates for the various subtrees. There is a template construction for just about every rule in a generator category translator. Generators must literally generate output for even the simplest input constructs such as comma-separated lists.

Generating templates behaves just like generating trees using rewrite rules.Each rule implicitly returns a template or tree, and the -> rewrite operator declares the output structure.

Grammar **Expr** is the same as the tree construction grammar given in Chapter 3, *A Quick Tour for the Impatient*, on page 43, except for the actions tracking the number of operations and computing the locals symbol table. Here is the grammar header that contains the infrastructure instance variables:

templates/generator/2pass/Expr.g

```
/** Create AST and compute ID -> local variable number map */
grammar Expr;
options {
    output=AST;
    ASTLabelType=CommonTree; // type of $stat.tree ref etc...
}

@header {
import java.util.HashMap;
}

@members {
int numOps = 0; // track operations for stack size purposes
HashMap locals = new HashMap(); // map ID to local var number
/* Count local variables, but don't use 0, which in this case
 * is the String[] args parameter of the main method.
 */
int localVarNum = 1;
}
```

The **prog** and **stat** rules create trees with AST rewrite rules as before:

templates/generator/2pass/Expr.g

```
prog:   stat+ ;

stat:   expr NEWLINE         -> expr
    |   ID '=' expr NEWLINE
        {
        if ( locals.get($ID.text)==null ) {
            locals.put($ID.text, new Integer(localVarNum++));
        }
        }
        -> ^('=' ID expr)
    |   NEWLINE              ->
    ;
```

Do You Ever Need to Return a List of Templates?

Some of you will see rules such as this:

```
prog : stat+ ;
```

and question why **prog** should not return a list of templates. Remember that for translators in the generator category, you must literally specify what to emit for every input construct even if it is just a list of input elements. The proper generated output for **prog** is in fact a template that represents a list of statements. For example, you might use something akin to this:

```
prog : (s+=stat)+ -> template(stats={$s}) "<stats>"
```

Upon an assignment statement, though, the recognizer must track implicit local variable definitions by using the locals HashMap. Each variable in a list of input expressions receives a unique local variable number.

The expression rules are as before except for the addition of code to track the number of operations (to estimate stack size):

templates/generator/2pass/Expr.g

```
expr:   multExpr (('+'^|'-'^) multExpr {numOps++;})*
    ;

multExpr
    :   atom ('*'^ atom {numOps++;})*
    ;

atom:   INT
    |   ID
    |   '('! expr ')'!
    ;
```

Once you have a parser grammar that builds the appropriate trees and computes the number of operations and locals map, you can pass that information to the tree grammar. The tree grammar will create a template for each subtree in order to emit bytecodes. Start rule **prog**'s template return value represents the template for the entire assembly file. The grammar itself is identical to the **Eval** tree grammar from Chapter 3, *A Quick Tour for the Impatient*, on page 43, but of course the actions are different.

Here is the start of the **Gen** tree grammar:

templates/generator/2pass/Gen.g

```
tree grammar Gen;

options {
    tokenVocab=Expr; // use the vocabulary from the parser
    ASTLabelType=CommonTree; // what kind of trees are we walking?
    output=template; // generate templates
}

@header {
import java.util.HashMap;
}

@members {
/** Points at locals table built by the parser */
HashMap locals;
}
```

The test rig pulls necessary data out of the parser after parsing is complete and passes it to the tree grammar via **prog** rule parameters:

templates/generator/2pass/Gen.g

```
/** Match entire tree representing the arithmetic expressions. Pass in
 *  the number of operations and the locals table that the parser computed.
 *  Number of elements on stack is roughly number of operations + 1 and
 *  add one for the address of the System.out object. Number of locals =
 *  number of locals + parameters plus 'this' if non-static method.
 */
prog[int numOps, HashMap locals]
@init {
this.locals = locals; // point at map created in parser
}
    :   (s+=stat)+ -> jasminFile(instructions={$s},
                                 maxStackDepth={numOps+1+1},
                                 maxLocals={locals.size()+1})
    ;
```

The **stat** rule creates an instance of template **exprStat** or **assign**, depending on which alternative matches:

templates/generator/2pass/Gen.g

```
stat:   expr -> exprStat(v={$expr.st}, descr={$expr.text})
    |   ^('=' ID expr)
        -> assign(id={$ID.text},
                  descr={$text},
                  varNum={locals.get($ID.text)},
                  v={$expr.st})
    ;
```

The template specifications compute template attributes from grammar attributes and members such as locals.

Here are the templates used by rule **stat**:

`templates/generator/2pass/ByteCode.stg`

```
assign(varNum,v,descr,id) ::= <<
; compute <descr>
<v>
istore <varNum> ; <id>
>>

exprStat(v, descr) ::= <<
; compute <descr>
<v>
>>
```

All the expression-related rules in the parser grammar collapse into a single **expr** rule in the tree grammar:

`templates/generator/2pass/Gen.g`

```
expr returns [int value]
    :   ^('+' a=expr b=expr) -> add(a={$a.st},b={$b.st})
    |   ^('-' a=expr b=expr) -> sub(a={$a.st},b={$b.st})
    |   ^('*' a=expr b=expr) -> mult(a={$a.st},b={$b.st})
    |   INT -> int(v={$INT.text})
    |   ID  -> var(id={$ID.text}, varNum={locals.get($ID.text)})
    ;
```

Each subtree results in a different template instance; here are the template definitions used by rule **expr**:

`templates/generator/2pass/ByteCode.stg`

```
add(a,b) ::= <<
<a>
<b>
iadd
>>

sub(a,b) ::= <<
<a>
<b>
isub
>>

mult(a,b) ::= <<
<a>
<b>
imul
>>

int(v) ::= "ldc <v>"

var(id, varNum) ::= "iload <varNum> ; <id>"
```

The operation templates do the obvious: push both operands and then do the operation.

Finally, here is a test rig with in-line comments to explain the various operations:

templates/generator/2pass/Test.java

```java
import org.antlr.runtime.*;
import org.antlr.runtime.tree.*;
import org.antlr.stringtemplate.*;
import java.io.*;

public class Test {
    public static void main(String[] args) throws Exception {
        // load the group file ByteCode.stg, put in templates var
        FileReader groupFileR = new FileReader("ByteCode.stg");
        StringTemplateGroup templates =
            new StringTemplateGroup(groupFileR);
        groupFileR.close();

        // PARSE INPUT AND BUILD AST
        ANTLRInputStream input = new ANTLRInputStream(System.in);
        ExprLexer lexer = new ExprLexer(input);     // create lexer
        // create a buffer of tokens pulled from the lexer
        CommonTokenStream tokens = new CommonTokenStream(lexer);
        ExprParser parser = new ExprParser(tokens); // create parser
        ExprParser.prog_return r = parser.prog();   // parse rule prog

        // WALK TREE
        // get the tree from the return structure for rule prog
        CommonTree t = (CommonTree)r.getTree();
        // create a stream of tree nodes from AST built by parser
        CommonTreeNodeStream nodes = new CommonTreeNodeStream(t);
        // tell it where it can find the token objects
        nodes.setTokenStream(tokens);
        Gen walker = new Gen(nodes); // create the tree Walker
        walker.setTemplateLib(templates); // where to find templates
        // invoke rule prog, passing in information from parser
        Gen.prog_return r2 = walker.prog(parser.numOps, parser.locals);

        // EMIT BYTE CODES
        // get template from return values struct
        StringTemplate output = (StringTemplate)r2.getTemplate();
        System.out.println(output.toString()); // render full template
    }
}
```

The one key piece that is different from a usual parser and tree parser test rig is that, in order to access the text for a tree, you must tell the tree node stream where it can find the token stream:

```
CommonTokenStream tokens = new CommonTokenStream(lexer);
...
CommonTreeNodeStream nodes = new CommonTreeNodeStream(t);
nodes.setTokenStream(tokens);
```

References such as $expr.text in rule **stat** in the tree parser make no sense unless it knows where to find the stream of token objects. Recall that $expr.text provides the text matched by the parser rule that created this subtree.

In this section, you learned how to generate output by adding template construction rules to a tree grammar. This generator category translator emits an output phrase for every input phrase. In the following two sections, you'll learn how to rewrite pieces of the input instead of generating an entirely new output file. You'll again use template construction rules, but this time the templates will replace input phrases.

9.7 Rewriting the Token Buffer In-Place

Traditionally, one of the most difficult tasks in language translation has been to read in some source code and write out a slightly altered version, all while preserving whitespace and comments. This is hard because translators typically throw out whitespace and comments since the parser has to ignore them. Somehow you must get the parser to ignore those tokens without throwing them away and without losing their original place in the input stream.

A further hassle involves the mechanism used to emit the tweaked source code. As you saw earlier, adding a bunch of print statements to your grammar is not a very good solution. Even using templates and the generator strategy, you have to specify a lot of unnecessary template construction rules. The generated recognizer performs a lot of unnecessary work. If the output is identical to the input most of the time, adding template construction actions to each rule is highly inefficient and error prone. You need a specification whose size is commensurate with the amount of work done by the translator.

In this section and the next, you'll see two different solutions to a source code rewriting problem, one using a parser and the next using a parser and tree parser combination. The task is to instrument simplified C source code with code snippets that track function calls and variable assignments. The translator must pass through whitespace and comments unmolested.

For example, it must rewrite this input:

templates/rewriter/1pass/input

```
int x;
/* A simple function foo */
void foo() {
    int y;
    y = 1;
    /* start */ g(34,y); /* end of line comment */
    x = h(/* inside */);
}
```

to be the following:

templates/rewriter/1pass/output

```
int x;
/* A simple function foo */
void foo() {
    int y;
    y = 1; write_to("y",y);
    /* start */ g(34,y); call("g"); /* end of line comment */
    x = eval("h",h(/* inside */)); write_to("x",x);
}
```

where call() tracks "procedure" calls, eval tracks function calls, and write_to() tracks variable assignments. The rule that translates function calls will have to use context to know whether the invocation is part of an assignment or is an isolated "procedure" (function without a return value) statement.

The way you'll solve this code instrumentation problem is with ANTLR's *rewrite mode* (see Section 5.6, *rewrite Option*, on page 110). This mode automatically copies the input to the output except where you have specified translations using template rewrite rules. In other words, no matter how big your grammar is, if you need to translate only one input phrase, you will probably need to specify only one template rewrite rule.

The "magic" behind ANTLR's rewrite mode is a fiendishly clever little token buffer called TokenRewriteStream that supports insert, delete, and replace operations. As recognition progresses, actions in your grammar or template rewrite rules can issue instructions to the token stream that are queued up as commands. The stream does not actually execute the commands until you invoke toString(), which avoids any physical modification of the token buffer. As toString() walks the buffer emitting each token's text, it looks for commands to be executed at that particular token index.

How ANTLR Differs from Perl and awk for Rewriting

Those familiar with common text-processing tools such as Perl or the Unix utility awk (or even sed) might disagree with me that tweaking source code is difficult while preserving whitespace and comments. Those tools are, in fact, specifically designed for translation, but lexical, not grammatical, translation. They are good at recognizing and translating structures that you can identify with regular expressions but not so good at recognizing grammatical structure, while ANTLR is. You can look at it like ANTLR is designed to handle "heavy lifting" translation tasks, but Perl and sed are better for simple tasks.

That is not to say that you can't amaze your family and friends with awk. For example, here's a Unix one-liner that generates Java class hierarchy diagrams in DOT (graphviz) format using only the Unix utilities cat, grep, and awk (try it—it's amazing!):

```
# pulls out superclass and class as $5 and $3:
# public class A extends B . . .
# only works for public classes and usual formatting
# Run the output into dot tool
cat *.java | grep 'public class' $1 | \
    awk 'BEGIN {print "digraph foo {";} \
        {print $5 "->" $3;} \
        END {print "}"}'
```

Although this is impressive, it is not perfect because it cannot handle class definitions on multiple lines and so on. More important, the strategy is not scalable because these tools do not have grammatical context like ANTLR does. Consider how you would alter the command so that it ignored inner classes. You would have to add a context variable that says "I am in a class definition already," which would require knowing when class definitions begin and end. Computing that requires that you track open and close curlies, which means ignoring them inside multiline comments and strings; eventually you will conclude that using a formal grammar is your best solution. Complicated translators built without the benefit of a grammar are usually hard to write, read, and maintain.

If the command is a replace operation, for example, toString() simply emits the replacement text instead of the original token (or token range). Because the operations are done lazily at toString() execution time, commands do not scramble the token indexes. An insert operation at token index i does not change the index values for tokens $i+1..n-1$. Also, because operations never actually alter the buffer, you can always get back the original token stream, and you can easily simulate transactions to roll back any changes. You can also have multiple command queues to get multiple rewrites from a single pass over the input such as generating both a C file and its header file (see the TokenRewriteStream Javadoc for an example).

To recognize the small subset of C, you will use a variation of the **CMinus** grammar from Section 8.2, *Building a Parser Grammar for the C-Language*, on page 183 (this variation adds function calls and removes a few statements). The grammar starts with the options to generate templates and turn on rewrite mode:

templates/rewriter/1pass/CMinus.g

```
grammar CMinus;
options {output=template; rewrite=true;}
```

The declarations are the same:

templates/rewriter/1pass/CMinus.g

```
program
    :   declaration+
    ;

declaration
    :   variable
    |   function
    ;

variable
    :   type ID ';'
    ;

function
    :   type ID '(' ( formalParameter (',' formalParameter)* )? ')' block
    ;

formalParameter
    :   type ID
    ;

type:   'int'
    |   'void'
    ;
```

The translator must rewrite assignments. The alternative that matches assignments in rule **stat** must, therefore, have a template rewrite rule:

templates/rewriter/1pass/CMinus.g

```
stat
scope {
boolean isAssign;
}
    :    expr ';'
    |    block
    |    ID '=' {$stat::isAssign=true;} expr ';'
         -> template(id={$ID.text},assign={$text})
            "<assign> write_to(\"<id>\",<id>);"
    |    ';'
    ;


block
    :    '{' variable* stat* '}'
    ;
```

Because this application is going from C to C and the number of templates is very small, it is OK to in-line the templates rather than referencing templates stored in a group file as the bytecode generator example did. The assignment rewrite just emits the original assignment (available as $text, the text matched for the entire rule) and then makes a call to write_to() with the name of the variable written to. Rule **stat** tracks whether it is in the process of recognizing an assignment. Rule **stat**'s dynamic scope makes that context information available to the rules it invokes directly or indirectly.

The **expr** rule must translate function calls in two different ways, depending on whether the expression is the right side of an assignment or an isolated procedure call in an expression statement:

templates/rewriter/1pass/CMinus.g

```
expr:   ID
    |   INT
    |   ID '(' ( expr (',' expr)* )? ')'
        -> {$stat::isAssign}? template(id={$ID.text},e={$text})
           "eval(\"<id>\",<e>)"  // rewrite ...=f(3) as eval("f",f(3))
        -> template(id={$ID.text},e={$text})
           "<e>; call(\"<id>\")" // rewrite ...f(3) as f(3); call("f")
    |   '(' expr ')'
    ;
```

As with AST rewrite rules, you can prefix rewrites with semantic predicates that indicate which of the rewrite rules to apply. Both templates spit the expression back out verbatim but with surrounding instrumentation code. Note that the text for the function call, available as

$text, will include any whitespace and comments matched in between the first and last real (nonhidden) tokens encountered by rule **expr**. The translator can use the usual token definitions:

templates/rewriter/1pass/CMinus.g

```
ID  :   ('a'..'z'|'A'..'Z'|'_') ('a'..'z'|'A'..'Z'|'0'..'9'|'_')*
    ;

INT :   ('0'..'9')+
    ;

CMT :   '/*' (options {greedy=false;} : .)* '*/' {$channel = HIDDEN;} ;

WS  :   ( ' ' | '\t' | '\r' | '\n' )+ {$channel = HIDDEN;}
    ;
```

The only thing to highlight in the token rules is that they must pass the whitespace and comments tokens to the parser on a hidden channel rather than throwing them out (with skip()). This is an excellent solution because, in order to tweak two constructs, only two rules of the grammar need template specifications. Perl aficionados might ask why you need all the other grammar rules. Can't you just look for function call patterns that match and translate constructs like g(34,y)? The unfortunate answer is no. The expressions within the argument list can be arbitrarily complex, and the regular expressions of Perl cannot match nested parentheses, brackets, and so on, that might appear inside the argument list. Avoiding code in comments and strings further complicates the issue. Just to drive the point home, if you change the problem slightly so that the translator should track only global variable access, not local variables and parameters, you will need a symbol table and context to properly solve the problem. The best you can do in general is to use a complete grammar with a rewrite mode that minimizes programmer effort and maximizes translator efficiency. For completeness, here is the core of a test rig:

templates/rewriter/1pass/Test.java

```
ANTLRInputStream input = new ANTLRInputStream(System.in);
CMinusLexer lexer = new CMinusLexer(input);
// rewrite=true only works with TokenRewriteStream
// not CommonTokenStream!
TokenRewriteStream tokens = new TokenRewriteStream(lexer);
CMinusParser parser = new CMinusParser(tokens);
parser.program();
System.out.println(tokens.toString()); // emit rewritten source
```

The next section solves the same problem using a two-pass parser and tree parser combination.

9.8 Rewriting the Token Buffer with Tree Grammars

Complicated translators need to use a multipass approach. In this situation, the parser grammar merely builds ASTs that one or more tree grammars examine. A final tree grammar pass must perform the rewriting instead of the parser grammar. Fortunately, tree grammars can generate templates just as easily as parser grammars because tree grammars also have access to the TokenRewriteStream object (via the TreeNodeStream).

This section solves the same source code instrumentation problem as the previous section but uses the parser grammar to build ASTs. We'll then walk the trees with a tree parser to perform the rewrites using the TokenRewriteStream. Let's start by building the AST for your simple subset of C. Here is the parser grammar again from Section 8.2, *Building a Parser Grammar for the C- Language*, on page 183 for your convenience:

templates/rewriter/2pass/CMinus.g

```
grammar CMinus;
options {output=AST;}

tokens {
  VAR;   // variable definition
  FUNC;  // function definition
  ARG;   // formal argument
  SLIST; // statement list
  CALL;  // function call
}
```

templates/rewriter/2pass/CMinus.g

```
program
    :    declaration+
    ;

declaration
    :    variable
    |    function
    ;

variable
    :    type ID ';' -> ^(VAR type ID)
    ;

function
    :    type ID '(' ( formalParameter (',' formalParameter)* )? ')' block
         -> ^(FUNC type ID formalParameter* block)
    ;
```

```
formalParameter
    :   type ID -> ^(ARG type ID)
    ;

type:   'int'
    |   'void'
    ;
```

This variation of the grammar has a simplified **stat** rule—the **for** statement is gone:

templates/rewriter/2pass/CMinus.g

```
block
    :   lc='{' variable* stat* '}'
        -> ^(SLIST[$lc,"SLIST"] variable* stat*)
    ;

stat
    :   expr ';'!
    |   block
    |   ID '=' expr ';' -> ^('=' ID expr)
    |   ';'!
    ;
```

Rule **expr** has an additional alternative to match function calls and generate ASTs with the CALL imaginary node:

templates/rewriter/2pass/CMinus.g

```
expr:   ID
    |   INT
    |   ID '(' ( expr (',' expr)* )? ')' -> ^(CALL ID expr*)
    |   '(' expr ')' -> expr
    ;
```

Here is the relevant piece of the test rig that launches the parser to build an AST:

templates/rewriter/2pass/Test.java

```java
// PARSE INPUT AND BUILD AST
ANTLRInputStream input = new ANTLRInputStream(System.in);
CMinusLexer lexer = new CMinusLexer(input);        // create lexer
// create a buffer of tokens pulled from the lexer
// Must use TokenRewriteStream not CommonTokenStream!
TokenRewriteStream tokens = new TokenRewriteStream(lexer);
CMinusParser parser = new CMinusParser(tokens);    // create parser
CMinusParser.program_return r = parser.program(); // parse program
```

Once you have a parser that builds valid ASTs, you can build the tree grammar that alters the token buffer. The template rewrite rules to tweak assignments and function calls are identical to the rewrite rules in the parser grammar from the last section. You can simply move them from the parser to the tree parser at the equivalent grammar locations. The tree grammar starts out very much like the tree grammar above in Section 9.6, *Generating Bytecode Templates with a Tree Grammar*, on page 211 with the addition of the rewrite=true option:

```
templates/rewriter/2pass/Gen.g
```

```
tree grammar Gen;

options {
  tokenVocab=CMinus; // import tokens from CMinus.g
  ASTLabelType=CommonTree;
  output=template;
  rewrite=true;
}
```

The tree matching rules for declarations do not have any template rewrite rules because the translator does not need to tweak those phrases:[7]

```
templates/rewriter/2pass/Gen.g
```

```
program
    :   declaration+
    ;

declaration
    :   variable
    |   function
    ;

variable
    :   ^(VAR type ID)
    ;

function
    :   ^(FUNC type ID formalParameter* block)
    ;

formalParameter
    :   ^(ARG type ID)
    ;

type:   'int'
    |   'void'
    ;
```

---

7. Unlike the parser grammar solution, you might be able to get away with just the tree grammar rules that specify rewrite templates. The AST is a highly processed version of the token stream, so it is much easier to identify constructs of interest. Future research should yield a way to avoid having to specify superfluous tree grammar rules for rewriting applications.

Rule **stat** defines the dynamic scope with isAssign like the parser grammar did. **stat** also specifies a template that rewrites the text from which the parser created the AST. In other words, parser grammar rule **stat** builds an assignment AST with token '=' at the root. **stat** records the token range it matches in its result AST's root node. For input x=3;, the root of the AST would contain token index range $i..i+3$ where i is the index of the x. Rule **stat** in the tree grammar then also knows this token range just by asking the root of the AST it matches. This is how template construction rewrite rules in a tree grammar know which tokens to replace in the input stream.

templates/rewriter/2pass/Gen.g

```
block
    :    ^(SLIST variable* stat*)
    ;

stat
scope {
boolean isAssign;
}
    :    expr
    |    block
    |    ^('=' ID {$stat::isAssign=true;} expr)
         -> template(id={$ID.text},assign={$text})
            "<assign> write_to(\"<id>\",<id>);"
    ;
```

A word of caution: if an alternative matches a list instead of a single subtree, ANTLR will not give you the right result for $text. That attribute expression is defined as the text for the first subtree a rule matches. This might seem a little odd, but it works well in practice.

Rule **expr** performs the same translation based upon context as did the solution in the previous section:

templates/rewriter/2pass/Gen.g

```
expr:   ID
    |   INT
    |   ^(CALL ID expr*)
        -> {$stat::isAssign}? template(id={$ID.text},e={$text})
           "eval(\"<id>\",<e>)"
        -> template(id={$ID.text},e={$text})
           "<e> call(\"<id>\")"
    ;
```

Here is the final piece of the test rig that walks the tree, rewrites the token buffer, and finally emits the altered token buffer:

templates/rewriter/2pass/Test.java

```
// WALK TREE AND REWRITE TOKEN BUFFER
// get the tree from the return structure for rule prog
CommonTree t = (CommonTree)r.getTree();
// create a stream of tree nodes from AST built by parser
CommonTreeNodeStream nodes = new CommonTreeNodeStream(t);
// tell it where it can find the token objects
nodes.setTokenStream(tokens);
Gen gen = new Gen(nodes);
gen.program(); // invoke rule program
System.out.println(tokens.toString()); // emit tweaked token buffer
```

At this point, you've seen one generator and two rewriter category examples. You know how to use template construction rules in both a parser grammar and a tree grammar. The type of grammar to use depends on the complexity of a translator. More complicated translators need multiple passes and, consequently, create templates in tree grammars.

For the most part, the examples given in this chapter avoid constructing templates with actions and do not set template attributes manually. Sometimes, however, the translation is complicated enough that you want to use arbitrary actions to create or modify templates. The next section describes the special symbols related to templates that you can use in actions as shorthand notation.

9.9 References to Template Expressions within Actions

In some rare cases, you might need to build templates and set their attributes in actions rather than using the template rewrite rules. For your convenience in this situation, ANTLR provides some template shorthand notation for use in embedded actions. All template-related special symbols start with % to distinguish them from normal attribute notation that uses $.

Consider the following grammar that uses a template rewrite rule:

```
s : ID '=' INT ';' -> assign(x={$ID.text},y={$INT.text})
  ;
```

Syntax	Description
%foo(a={},b={},...)	Template construction syntax. Create instance of template **foo**, setting attribute arguments a, b, ...
%({«nameExpr»})(a={},...)	Indirect template constructor reference. *nameExpr* evaluates to a String name that indicates which template to instantiate. Otherwise, it is identical to the other template construction syntax.
%x.y = «z»;	Set template attribute y of template x to z. Languages such as Python without semicolon statement terminators must still use them here. The code generator is free to remove them during code generation.
%{«expr»}.y = «z»;	Set template attribute y of StringTemplate typed expression *expr* to expression z.
%{«stringExpr»}	Create an anonymous template from String *stringExpr*.

Figure 9.1: TEMPLATE SHORTHAND NOTATION AVAILABLE IN GRAMMAR ACTIONS

You can get the same functionality using an action almost as tersely:

```
s : ID '=' INT ';' {$st = %assign(x={$ID.text},y={$INT.text});}
  ;
```

Or, you can create the template and then manually set the attributes using the attribute assignment notation:

```
s : ID '=' INT ';'
    {
    $st = %assign();     // set $st to instance of assign
    %{$st}.x=$ID.text;   // set attribute x of $st
    %{$st}.y=$INT.text;
    }
  ;
```

ANTLR translates that action to the following:

```
retval.st = templateLib.getInstanceOf("assign");
(retval.st).setAttribute("x",ID3.getText());
(retval.st).setAttribute("y",INT4.getText());
```

The table in Figure 9.1, on the preceding page summarizes the template shorthand notation available to you in embedded actions.

This chapter demonstrated that using StringTemplate templates in conjunction with ANTLR grammars is a great way to build both generators and rewriters. ANTLR v3's new rewrite mode is especially effective for those applications that need to tweak the input slightly but otherwise pass most of it through to the output.

The next chapter discusses an important part of any professional translator: error reporting and recovery.

Chapter 10

Error Reporting and Recovery

The quality of a language application's error messages and recovery strategy often makes the difference between a professional application and an amateurish application. Error recovery is the process of recovering from a syntax error by altering the input stream or consuming symbols until the parser can restart in a known state. Many hand-built and many non-*LL*-based recognizers emit less than optimal error messages, whereas ANTLR-generated recognizers automatically emit very good error messages and recover intelligently, as shown in this chapter. ANTLR's error handling facility is even useful during development.

During the development cycle, you will have a lot of mistakes in your grammar. The resulting parser will not recognize all valid sentences until you finish and debug your grammar. In the meantime, informative error messages help you track down grammar problems. Once you have a correct grammar, you then have to deal with ungrammatical sentences entered by users or even ungrammatical sentences generated by other programs gone awry.

In both situations, the manner in which your parser responds to ungrammatical input is an important productivity consideration. In other words, a parser that responds with "Eh?" and bails out upon the first syntax error is not very useful during development or for the people who have to use the resulting parser. For example, some SQL engines can only tell you the general vicinity where an error occurred rather than exactly what is wrong and where, making query development a trial-and-error process.

Developers using ANTLR get a good error reporting facility and a sophisticated error recovery strategy for free. ANTLR automatically generates recognizers that emit rich error messages upon syntax error and successfully resynchronize much of the time. The recognizers even avoid generating more than a single error message for each syntax error.

New in v3.

This chapter describes the automatic error reporting and recovery strategy used by ANTLR-generated recognizers and shows how to alter the default mechanism to suit your particular needs.

10.1 A Parade of Errors

The best way to describe ANTLR's error recovery strategy is to show you how ANTLR-generated recognizers respond to the most common syntax errors: mismatched token, no viable alternative, and early exit from an EBNF (...)+ subrule loop. Consider the following grammar for simple statements and expressions, which we'll use as the core for the examples in this section and the remainder of the chapter:

errors/E.g

```
grammar E;

prog:    stat+ ;

stat:    expr ';'
         {System.out.println("found expr: "+$stat.text);}
    |    ID '=' expr ';'
         {System.out.println("found assign: "+$stat.text);}
    ;

expr:    multExpr (('+'|'-') multExpr)*
    ;

multExpr
    :    atom ('*' atom)*
    ;

atom:    INT
    |    '(' expr ')'
    ;

ID  :    ('a'..'z'|'A'..'Z')+ ;
INT :    '0'..'9'+ ;
WS  :    (' '|'\t'|'\n'|'\r')+ {skip();} ;
```

And here is the usual test rig that invokes rule **prog**:

errors/TestE.java

```
import org.antlr.runtime.*;

public class TestE {
    public static void main(String[] args) throws Exception {
        ANTLRInputStream input = new ANTLRInputStream(System.in);
        ELexer lexer = new ELexer(input);
        CommonTokenStream tokens = new CommonTokenStream(lexer);
        EParser parser = new EParser(tokens);
        parser.prog();
    }
}
```

First run some valid input into the parser to figure out what the normal behavior is:

```
⇐    $ java TestE
⇐    (3);
⇐    Eof
⇒    found expr: (3);
     $
```

Upon either expression statement or assignment statement, the translator prints a message indicating the text matched for rule **stat**. In this case, (3); is an expression, not an assignment, as shown in the output.

Now, leaving off the final), the parser detects a mismatched token because rule **atom** was looking for the right parenthesis to match the left parenthesis:

```
⇐    $ java TestE
⇐    (3;
⇐    Eof
⇒    line 1:2 mismatched input ';' expecting ')'
     found expr: (3;
     $
```

The line 1:2 component of the error message indicates that the error occurred on the first line and at the third character position in that line (indexed from zero, hence, index 2).

Generating that error message is straightforward, but how does the parser successfully match the ; and execute the print action in the first alternative of rule **stat** after getting a syntax error all the way down in **atom**? How did the parser successfully recover from that mismatched token to continue as if nothing happened? This error recovery feature is called *single token insertion* because the parser pretends to insert the missing) and keep going. We'll examine the mechanism in Section 10.7, *Recovery by Single Symbol Insertion*, on page 248. Notice that with multiple expressions, the parser successfully continues and matches the second alternative without error:

```
⇐   $ java TestE
⇐   (3;
⇐   1+2;
⇐   Eof
⇒   line 1:2 mismatched input ';' expecting ')'
    found expr: (3;
    found expr: 1+2;
    $
```

ANTLR also avoids generating cascading error messages if possible. That is, recognizers try to emit a single error message for each syntax error. In the following sample run, the first expression has two errors: the missing) and the missing ;. The parser normally emits only the first error message, suppressing the second message that has the [SPURIOUS] prefix:

```
⇐   $ java TestE
⇐   (3
⇐   a=1;
⇐   Eof
⇒   line 2:0 mismatched input 'a' expecting ')'
    [SPURIOUS] line 2:0 mismatched input 'a' expecting ';'
    found expr: (3
    found assign: a=1;
    $
```

Another common syntax error occurs when the parser is at a decision point and the current lookahead is not consistent with any of the alternatives of that rule or subrule. For example, the decision in rule **atom** must choose between an integer and the start of a parenthesized expression. Input 1+; is missing the second operand, and rule **atom** would see ; instead, causing a "no viable alternative exception:"

```
⇐   $ java TestE
⇐   1+;
⇐   Eof
⇒   line 1:2 no viable alternative at input ';'
    found expr: 1+;
    $
```

The parser successfully recovers by scanning ahead to look for a symbol that can follow a reference to **atom** or a rule that has invoked **atom**. In this case, the ; is a viable symbol following a reference to **atom** (and therefore **expr**). The parser consumes no tokens and simply exits from **atom** knowing that it is probably correctly resynchronized.

> ### Back When You Could Almost Parse C++
>
> In the early 1990s, I was consulting at NeXT and was helping Sumana Srinivasan build a C++ code browser using ANTLR v1 (ANTLR is still used in NeXTStep, er, Mac OS X today). The manager, Steve Naroff, insisted that the ANTLR-generated parser provide the same high-quality error messages as his hand-built C parser did. Because of this, I introduced the notion of parser exception handling (the analog of the familiar programming exception handling) and created a simple single-token deletion mechanism. Ironically, the ANTLR-generated C++ recognizer emitted better messages in some circumstances than the hand-built parser because ANTLR never got tired of computing token sets and generating error recovery code—humans, on the other hand, often get sick of this tedious job.

You will also run into early subrule exit exceptions where a one-or-more (...)+ subrule matched no input. For example, if you send in an empty input stream, the parser has nothing to match in the stat+ loop:

```
$ java TestE
EOF
line 0:-1 required (..)+ loop did not match anything at input '<EOF>'
$
```

The line and character position information for EOF is meaningless; hence, you see the odd 0:-1 position information.

This section gave you a taste of ANTLR's default error reporting and recovery capabilities (see Section 10.7, *Automatic Error Recovery Strategy*, on page 246 for details about the automatic error recovery mechanism). The next few sections describe how you can alter the standard error messages to help with grammar debugging and to provide better messages for your users.

10.2 Enriching Error Messages during Debugging

By default, recognizers emit error messages that are most useful to users of your software. The messages include information only about what was found and what was expected such as in the following:

```
line 10:22 mismatched input INT expecting ID
```

Unfortunately, your grammar has probably 200 references to token **ID**. Where in the grammar was the parser when it found the **INT** instead of the **ID**? You can use the debugger in ANTLRWorks to set a breakpoint upon exception and then just look to see where in the grammar the parser is. Sometimes, though, sending text error messages to the console can be more convenient because you do not have to start the debugger.

With a little bit of work, you can override the standard error reporting mechanism to include information about the rule invocation stack. The invocation stack is the nested list of rules entered by the parser at any given moment, that is, the stack trace. You can also add more information about the mismatched token. For no viable alternative errors, you can do even more. For example, the following run illustrates a rich, no viable alternative error message that is much more useful for debugging grammars than the default:

```
⇐    $ java TestE2
⇐    1+;
⇐    EOF
⇒    line 1:2 [prog, stat, expr, multExpr, atom] no viable alternative,
     token=[@2,2:2=';',<7>,1:2] (decision=5 state 0)
     decision=<<35:1: atom : ( INT | '(' expr ')' );>>
     found expr: 1+;
     $
```

The message includes a rule invocation stack trace where the last rule mentioned is the rule the parser was in when it encountered the syntax error. The error includes a detailed report on the token itself that includes the token index, a character index range into the input stream, the token type, and the line and character position within the line. Finally, for no viable alternative exceptions such as this, the message includes information about the decision in a grammar: the decision number, the state within the decision's lookahead DFA, and a chunk of the grammar that describes the decision. To use the decision and state information, turn on ANTLR option -dfa, which will generate DOT (graphviz) descriptions you can display. Filenames are encoded with the grammar name and the decision number, so, for example, the DOT file for decision 5 of grammar **E** is E_dec-5.dot and looks like the following:

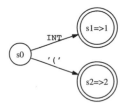

The state 0 mentioned in the error message is s0 in the diagram. In this case, the parser had a lookahead of ; that clearly does not match either alternative emanating from s0; hence, you have the no viable alternative exception.

To get these rich error messages, override two methods from BaseRecognizer, displayRecognitionError() and getTokenErrorDisplay(), where the grammar itself stays the same:

`errors/E2.g`

```
grammar E2;

@members {
public String getErrorMessage(RecognitionException e,
                              String[] tokenNames)
{
    List stack = getRuleInvocationStack(e, this.getClass().getName());
    String msg = null;
    if ( e instanceof NoViableAltException ) {
      NoViableAltException nvae = (NoViableAltException)e;
      msg = " no viable alt; token="+e.token+
          " (decision="+nvae.decisionNumber+
          " state "+nvae.stateNumber+")"+
          " decision=<<"+nvae.grammarDecisionDescription+">>";
    }
    else {
        msg = super.getErrorMessage(e, tokenNames);
    }
    return stack+" "+msg;
}
public String getTokenErrorDisplay(Token t) {
    return t.toString();
}
}
```

The next section describes how to improve error messages for your users rather than for yourself during debugging.

10.3 Altering Recognizer Error Messages

This section describes the information available to you when generating error messages and provides an example that illustrates how to enrich error messages with context information from the grammar.For each problem that can occur during sentence recognition, the recognizer creates an exception object derived from RecognitionException.

RecognitionException

The superclass of all exceptions thrown by an ANTLR-generated recognizer. It tracks the input stream; the index of the symbol (character, token, or tree node) the recognizer was looking at when the error occurred; the erroneous symbol pointer (int, Token, or Object); the line; and the character position within that line.

MismatchedTokenException

Indicates that the parser was looking for a particular symbol that it did not find at the current input position. In addition to the usual fields, this object tracks the expected token type (or character code).

MismatchedTreeNodeException

Indicates that the tree parser was looking for a node with a particular token type and did not find it. This is the analog of a mismatched token exception for a token stream parser. It tracks the expected token type.

NoViableAltException

The recognizer came to a decision point, but the lookahead was not consistent with any of the alternatives. It tracks the decision number and state number within the lookahead DFA where the problem occurred and also stores a chunk of the grammar from which ANTLR generated the decision.

EarlyExitException

The recognizer came to a (..)+ EBNF subrule that must match an alternative at least once, but the subrule did not match anything. It tracks the decision number but not the state number because it is obviously not in the middle of the lookahead DFA; the whole thing was skipped.

FailedPredicateException

A validating semantic predicates evaluated to false. It tracks the name of the rule in which the predicate failed as well as the text of the predicate itself from your grammar.

MismatchedRangeException

The recognizer tried to match a range of symbols, usually characters, but could not. It tracks the minimum and maximum element in the range.

MismatchedSetException

The recognizer attempted to match a set of symbols but could not. It tracks the set of elements in which the recognizer was interested.

MismatchedNotSetException

The recognizer attempted to match the inverse of a set (using the ~ operator) but could not.

Figure 10.1: ANTLR RECOGNITION EXCEPTIONS

These exception objects contain information about what was found on the input stream, what was expected, and sometimes information about the location in the grammar associated with the erroneous parser state.

To avoid forcing English-only error messages and to generally make things as flexible as possible, the recognizer does not create exception objects with string messages. Instead, it tracks the information necessary to generate an error.

Then the various reporting methods in BaseRecognizer generate a localized error message, or you can override them. Do not expect the exception getMessage() methods to return anything. The table in Figure 10.1, on the facing page, summarizes the exception classes and the information they contain.

Improved in v3.

Beyond the information in these exception objects, you can collect any useful information you want via actions in the grammar and then use it to provide better error messages for your users.

One of the most useful enhancements to error messages is to include information about the kind of abstract construct the parser was recognizing when it encountered an error. For example, instead of just saying "missing **ID**," it is better to say "missing **ID** in expression." You could use the literal rule name such as "multExpr," but that is usually meaningless to users.

You can think of this as a *paraphrase* mechanism because you are representing a collection of grammar rules with a short description. What you want is a map from all rules associated with a particular abstract language construct (that is, declarations, statements, and expressions) to a user-friendly string such as "expression."

*In v2, there was a **paraphrase** option that automated this.*

The easiest way to implement a paraphrase mechanism is to push a string onto a stack when you enter a rule that represents an abstract construct in a language and then pop the value off when leaving the rule. Do not push a paraphrase string for all rules. Just push a paraphrase for the top-level rule such as **expr**, but not **multExpr** or **atom**.

First, define a stack of paraphrases and override getErrorMessage() to include the paraphrase at the end:

`errors/P.g`

```
/** This grammar demonstrates creating a "paraphrase" error reporting option. */
grammar P;

@members {
Stack paraphrases = new Stack();
public String getErrorMessage(RecognitionException e,
                              String[] tokenNames)
{
    String msg = super.getErrorMessage(e, tokenNames);
    if ( paraphrases.size()>0 ) {
        String paraphrase = (String)paraphrases.peek();
        msg = msg+" "+paraphrase;
    }
    return msg;
}
}
```

Then, at the start of each rule that relates to an abstract concept in your language, push and pop a paraphrased grammar location that will be used in the error reporting:

`errors/P.g`

```
prog:   stat+ ;

stat
@init  { paraphrases.push("in statement"); }
@after { paraphrases.pop(); }
    :   expr ';'
        {System.out.println("found expr: "+$stat.text);}
    |   ID '=' expr ';'
        {System.out.println("found assign: "+$stat.text);}
    ;

expr
@init  { paraphrases.push("in expression"); }
@after { paraphrases.pop(); }
    :   multExpr (('+'|'-') multExpr)*
    ;

multExpr
    :   atom ('*' atom)*
    ;

atom:   INT
    |   '(' expr ')'
    ;
```

Here are three sample runs to illustrate the improved error messages for the same invalid input used in previous sections:

```
⇐  $ java TestP
⇐  (3;
⇐  EOF
⇒  line 1:2 mismatched input ';' expecting ')' in expression
   found expr: (3;
⇐  $ java TestP
⇐  1+;
⇐  EOF
⇒  line 1:2 no viable alternative at input ';' in expression
   found expr: 1+;
⇐  $ java TestP
⇐  a;
⇐  EOF
⇒  line 1:1 mismatched input ';' expecting '=' in statement
   $
```

Recall that the parser detects the first error in **atom** but emits "in expression" rather than the less useful "in atom" (the user does not know what an atom is). All rules invoked from **expr** will use that paraphrase. The last run did not execute the embedded action because the parser could not recover using single symbol deletion or insertion and it therefore had to bail out of rule **stat**.

What if you want the parser to bail out upon the first syntax error without ever trying to recover? The next section describes how to make the parser exit immediately upon the first syntax error.

10.4 Exiting the Recognizer upon First Error

Sometimes for invalid input you simply want to report an error and exit without trying to recover and continue parsing. Examples include unrecognized network protocol messages and expressions in spreadsheets.

Most likely, your embedded actions will not be valid given the erroneous input, so you might as well just report an error and ask the user to fix the problem.

To make your recognizer (parser or tree parser) exit immediately upon recognition error, you must override two methods, mismatch() and recoverFromMismatchSet(), and alter how the parser responds to thrown exceptions.

errors/Bail.g

```
grammar Bail;

@members {
protected void mismatch(IntStream input, int ttype, BitSet follow)
    throws RecognitionException
{
    throw new MismatchedTokenException(ttype, input);
}
public void recoverFromMismatchedSet(IntStream input,
                                     RecognitionException e,
                                     BitSet follow)

    throws RecognitionException
{
    throw e;
}
}

// Alter code generation so catch-clauses get replace with
// this action.
@rulecatch {
catch (RecognitionException e) {
    throw e;
}
}
```

As usual, the remainder of the grammar is the same. Here is a sample run using the typical test rig:

```
⇐    $ java TestBail
⇐    (3;
⇐    1+2;
⇐    EOF
⇒    Exception in thread "main" MismatchedTokenException(7!=13)
            at BailParser.mismatch(BailParser.java:29)
            at org.antlr.runtime.BaseRecognizer.match(BaseRecognizer.java:92)
            at BailParser.atom(BailParser.java:307)
            at BailParser.multExpr(BailParser.java:226)
            at BailParser.expr(BailParser.java:163)
            at BailParser.stat(BailParser.java:117)
            at BailParser.prog(BailParser.java:57)
            at TestBail.main(TestBail.java:9)
```

The parser throws an exception rather than recovering, and Java displays the uncaught exception emanating from the main program.

The **rulecatch** action changes the default code ANTLR generates at the end of each rule's method. In this case, it will change this code:

```
catch (RecognitionException re) {
    reportError(re);
    recover(input,re);
}
```

to the code in the **rulecatch** action:

```
catch (RecognitionException e) {
    throw e;
}
```

Note that because ANTLR traps exceptions only under RecognitionException, your parser will exit if you throw an exception that is not under this hierarchy such as a RuntimeException.

You have control over whether a recognizer throws an exception and what to do if it does. This even allows you to do context-sensitive error recovery by putting a conditional in the **rulecatch** action. In this way, some rules in your grammar could do automatic recovery where it makes sense, leaving the other rules to bail out of the parser.

The **rulecatch** alters the default code generation for all rules, but sometimes you want to alter exception handling for just one rule; the following section describes how to use individual exception handlers.

10.5 Manually Specifying Exception Handlers

You can trap any exception you want in any rule of your grammar by specifying manual exception handlers after the semicolon at the end of the rule. You can trap any Java exception. The basic idea is to force all errors to throw an exception and then catch the exception where you think it is appropriate. Given the same **rulecatch** action and method overrides from Bail.g in the previous section, here is how to catch all recognition exceptions in rule **stat**:

errors/Exc.g

```
stat:   expr ';'
        {System.out.println("found expr: "+$stat.text);}
    |   ID '=' expr ';'
        {System.out.println("found assign: "+$stat.text);}
    ;
    catch [RecognitionException re] {
        reportError(re);
        consumeUntil(input, SEMI); // throw away all until ';'
        input.consume(); // eat the ';'
    }
```

The exception action reports the errors as usual but manually recovers by just killing everything until the semicolon. Also, the grammar needs a **tokens** specification so that the exception action can refer to the **SEMI** token type:

```
tokens { SEMI=';' }
```

Here are some sample runs:

```
⇐  $ java TestExc
⇐  (3;
⇐  a=1;
⇐  EOF
⇒  line 1:2 mismatched input ';' expecting ')'
   found assign: a=1;
⇐  $ java TestExc
⇐  3+;
⇐  a=1;
⇐  EOF
⇒  line 1:2 no viable alternative at input ';'
   found assign: a=1;
   $
```

This strategy does not do as well as ANTLR's default because it gobbles input more aggressively. In the following run, the mismatched token for the expression 3 forces the exception handler to consume until it sees a semicolon, effectively tossing out the second line of input:

```
⇐  $ java TestExc
⇐  3
⇐  a=1;
⇐  x=2;
⇐  EOF
⇒  line 2:0 mismatched input 'a' expecting SEMI
   found assign: x=2;
   $
```

The default mechanism would recover properly and match the first assignment correctly, but this example illustrates how to specify your own exceptions.

10.6 Errors in Lexers and Tree Parsers

So far this chapter has focused primarily on parsers, but errors can occur in lexers and tree parsers as well, of course. For example, returning to the original **E** grammar from the beginning of this chapter, entering an invalid character such as & results in a no viable alternative exception:

```
⇐  $ java TestE
⇐  &3;
⇐  EOF
⇒  line 1:0 no viable alternative at character '&'
   found expr: 3;
   $
```

The only difference is that the error message says "character" instead of "input." In between tokens, lexers recover by blindly killing the offending character and looking for another token. Once the lexer has recovered, it is free to send the next token to the parser. You can see that the parser finds a valid expression after the offending character and prints the expression, 3;, as usual.

Within a token definition rule, however, mismatched character errors can also occur, which are analogous to mismatched token errors. For example, if you forget to terminate a string, the lexer might consume until the end of file and would emit something like the following error:

```
line 129:0 mismatched character '<EOF>' expecting '"'
```

Turning to tree parsers now, recall that they are really just parsers that read streams of nodes instead of streams of tokens. Recall the expression evaluator from Chapter 3, *A Quick Tour for the Impatient*, on page 43. Imagine that, while developing a grammar, you forget to "delete" parentheses in rule **atom** (that is, you forgot to add the ! operators):

errors/Expr.g
```
atom:    INT
    |    ID
    |    '(' expr ')' // should have ! ops or use "-> expr"
    ;
```

Now if you rebuild and run with sample input a=(3), the parser will no longer build a proper tree. It will leave in the parenthesis tokens, which will cause syntax errors in the tree parser. The following session illustrates the error message emitted by the tree parser:

```
⇐  $ java org.antlr.Tool Expr.g Eval.g
⇐  $ javac TestEval.java # compiles all files
⇐  $ java TestEval
⇐  a=(3)
⇐  EOF
⇒  (= a ( 3 ))  // note the extra ( and ) around '3'
   Eval.g: node from line 1:2 no viable alternative at input '('
   3
   $
```

Tree parsers have slightly different error headers (the "*tree-grammar-name*: node from" prefix) to indicate that a tree parser emitted the error rather than a normal parser. Tree parsers emit error messages with the grammar name because the message is always intended for the programmer—a malformed tree is the programmer's fault, not the user's.

Naturally for development, you can augment these messages to indicate where in the grammar the tree parser had a problem just like with parser grammars. You can even print the offending subtree because the RecognitionException object contains the appropriate node pointer.

10.7 Automatic Error Recovery Strategy

ANTLR's error recovery mechanism is based upon Niklaus Wirth's early ideas in *Algorithms + Data Structures = Programs* [Wir78] (as well as Rodney Topor's *A Note on Error Recovery in Recursive Descent Parsers* [Top82]) but also includes Josef Grosch's good ideas from his CoCo parser generator (*Efficient and Comfortable Error Recovery in Recursive Descent Parsers* [Gro90]). Essentially, recognizers perform single-symbol insertion and deletion upon mismatched symbol errors (as described in a moment) if possible. If not, recognizers gobble up symbols until the lookahead is a member of the *resynchronization set* and then exit the rule. The resynchronization set is the set of input symbols that can legally follow references to the current rule and references to any invoking rules up the call chain. Similarly, if the recognizer cannot choose any of the alternatives from the start of a rule, the recognizer again uses the gobble-and-exit strategy.

This "consume until symbol in resynchronization set" strategy makes sense because the recognizer knows there is something wrong with the input that should match for the current rule. It decides to throw out tokens until the lookahead is consistent with something that should match after the recognizer exits from the rule. For example, if there is a syntax error within an assignment statement, it makes a great deal of sense to throw out tokens until the parser sees a semicolon or other statement terminator.

Another idea from Grosch that ANTLR implements is to emit only a single message per syntax error to prevent spurious, cascading errors. Through the use of a simple boolean variable, set upon syntax error, the recognizer can avoid emitting further errors until the recognizer

> ### Language Theory Humor
>
> Apparently, the great Niklaus Wirth* had an excellent sense of humor. He used to joke that in Europe people called him by "reference" (properly pronouncing his name "Ni-klaus Virt") and that in America people called him by "value" (pronouncing his name "Nickle-less Worth").
>
> At the Compiler Construction 1994 conference, Kristen Nygaard[†] (inventor of Simula) told a story about how, while teaching a language theory course, he commented that "Strong typing is fascism," referring to his preference for languages that are loose with types. A student came up to him afterward and asked why typing hard on the keyboard was fascism.
>
> *. See http://en.wikipedia.org/wiki/Niklaus_Wirth.
> †. See http://en.wikipedia.org/wiki/Kristen_Nygaard.

successfully matches a symbol and resets the variable. See field error-Recovery in BaseRecognizer. The following three sections describe ANTLR's automatic error recovery system in more detail.

Recovery by Single Symbol Deletion

Consider erroneous expression (3));. The parser responds with this:

```
⇐   $ java TestE
⇐   (3));
⇐   EOF
⇒   line 1:3 mismatched input ')' expecting ';'
    found expr: (3));
    $
```

Even though there is an extra right parenthesis, the parser is able to continue, implicitly deleting the extra symbol. Instead of giving up on the rule, the parser can examine the next symbol of lookahead to see whether that symbol is the one it wanted to find. If the next symbol is exactly what it was looking for, the parser assumes the current symbol is a junk token, executes a consume() call, and continues. If the parser fails to resynchronize by deleting a symbol, it attempts to insert a symbol instead.

Recovery by Single Symbol Insertion

Consider the erroneous input (3; discussed at the start of this chapter. The parser continued parsing and executed the embedded action even though it complained that it was expecting ')' but it found ';':

```
⇐   $ java TestE
⇐   (3;
⇐   EOF
⇒   line 1:2 mismatched input ';' expecting ')'
    found expr: (3;
    $
```

The parser first tries single-token deletion but finds that the next symbol of lookahead, EOF, is not what it was looking for—deleting it and continuing would be wrong. Instead, it tries the opposite: is the current token consistent with what could come after the expected token? In this case, the parser expects to see a semicolon next, which is in fact the current token. In this case, the parser can assume that the user simply forgot the expected token and can continue, implicitly inserting the missing token.

If single-symbol deletion and insertion both fail, the parser has no choice but to attempt to resynchronize using the aggressive strategy described in the next section.

Recovery by Scanning for Following Symbols

When within-rule error recovery fails or upon a no viable alternative situation, the best recovery strategy is to consume tokens until the parser sees a token in the set of tokens that can legally follow the current rule. These following symbols are those that appear after a reference to the current rule or any rule invocation that led to the current rule. That set of tokens is called the *resynchronization set*.

It is worthwhile going through an example to understand how ANTLR recovers via resynchronization sets. Consider the following grammar and imagine that, at each rule invocation, the parser pushes the set of tokens that could follow that rule invocation onto a stack:

```
s : '[' b ']'
  | '(' b ')'
  ;
b : c '^' INT ;
c : ID
  | INT
  ;
```

Here are the following sets: ']' follows the first reference to **b** in **s**, ')' follows the reference to **b** in the second alternative, and '^' follows the reference to **c** in **b**.

With the erroneous input [], the call chain is as follows: **s** calls **b** calls **c**. In **c**, the parser discovers that the lookahead, ']', is not consistent with either alternative of **c**. The following table summarizes the call stack and associated resynchronization set context for each rule invocation.

Call Depth	Resynchronization Set	In Rule
0	EOF	main()
1	EOF	**s**
2	']'	**b**
3	'^'	**c**

The complete resynchronization set for the current rule is the union of all resynchronization sets walking up the call chain. Rule **c**'s resynchronization set is therefore { '^', ']', EOF }. To resynchronize, the parser consumes tokens until it finds that the lookahead is consistent with the resynchronization set. In this case, lookahead ']' starts out as a member of the resynchronization set, and the parser won't actually consume any symbols.

After resynchronization, the parser exits rule **c** and returns to rule **b** but immediately discovers that it does not have the '^' symbol. The process repeats itself, and the parser consumes tokens until it finds something in the resynchronization set for rule **b**, which is { ']', EOF }. Again, the parser does not consume anything and exits **b**, returning to the first alternative of rule **s**. Now, the parser finds exactly what it is looking for, successfully matching the ']'. The parser is now properly resynchronized.

Those familiar with language theory will wonder whether the resynchronization set for rule **c** is just *FOLLOW*(c), the set of all viable symbols that can follow references to **c** in some context. It is not that simple, unfortunately, and the resynchronization sets must be computed dynamically to get the set of symbols that can follow the rule in a particular context rather than in all contexts.[1] *FOLLOW*(b) is { ')', ']' }, which includes all symbols that can follow references to **b** in both contexts

---

1. In the generated source code, the partial resynchronization sets look like FOLLOW_b_in_s7. Every rule invocation is surrounded by something like pushFollow(FOLLOW_expr_in_expr334); expr(); _fsp--;. This code pushes the exact set of symbols that can follow the rule reference.

(alternatives one and two of **s**). Clearly, though at runtime, the parser can call **b** from only one location at a time. Note that $FOLLOW(c)$ is '^', and if the parser resynchronized to that token instead of the resynchronization set, it would consume until the end of file because there is no '^' on the input stream.

ANTLR provides good error reporting for both the developer and the users of the deployed language application. Further, ANTLR's automatic error recovery mechanism resynchronizes recognizers very well, again yielding an excellent experience for your users.

This chapter concludes Part II of the book, which focused on explaining the various syntax and semantics of ANTLR grammars. Part III of this book explains and illustrates ANTLR's sophisticated new *LL(*)* parsing strategy and the use of semantic and syntactic predicates.

Part III

Understanding Predicated-*LL(*)* Grammars

Chapter 11

LL(*) Parsing

The chapters in the third part of this book represent a thorough study of ANTLR's predicated-*LL(*)* parsing mechanism. Unfortunately, this topic is not easy and typically requires an advanced parsing background to fully understand. The discussion is as clear and easy to follow as possible, but you'll still have to read some sections multiple times, which is typical of any dense technical material. This reference book includes such an advanced discussion because it is simply not available anywhere else, and ultimately, you'll want a deep understanding of exactly how ANTLR recognizers work. You'll be able to resolve grammar analysis warnings more easily, build simpler grammars, and tackle more challenging language problems. You don't need these chapters to get started using ANTLR, but you should read them when you run into grammar analysis errors or have trouble designing a grammar for a tricky language construct.

This chapter defines ANTLR's *LL(*)* parsing, describes how it works, and characterizes the kinds of grammars that are *LL(*)* conformant. More important, this chapter emphasizes grammars that are not *LL(*)* and tells you how to deal with them. When ANTLR accepts your grammar, you will not notice ANTLR's underlying parsing strategy—it is only when you get a warning that you need to know more about how *LL(*)* works. Although *LL(*)* increases the fundamental power of ANTLR's parsing strategy beyond *LL(k)*'s fixed lookahead parsing, sometimes you will need more power than even *LL(*)* can provide. The three chapters on predicated-*LL(*)* parsing following this chapter discuss how to handle non-*LL(*)* grammars for context-sensitive, ambiguous, and other problematic languages.

Let's begin the discussion of *LL(*)* by covering the difference between a grammar and the program that recognizes sentences in the language described by that grammar.

11.1 The Relationship between Grammars and Recognizers

Building a grammar means creating a specification that not only conforms to a particular parser generator's grammar metalanguage (per Chapter 4, *ANTLR Grammars*, on page 71) but that also conforms to its underlying parsing strategy. The stronger the parsing strategy, the more grammars that the parser generator will accept, thus making it easier to describe your language with a natural, easy-to-read grammar.

Ideally a parser generator would accept any grammar, but there are two reasons why such parser generators are not commonly used. First, parsing strategies that accept any grammar are usually less efficient and more difficult to understand.[1] Second, some syntactically valid grammars are ambiguous in that the grammar can match the same input following multiple paths through the grammar, which makes it difficult for actions to interpret or translate the input. Should the parser execute actions found along all paths or just one? If along just one path, which one? Computers only deal well with deterministic languages: languages that have exactly one meaning for each statement. It has been the focus of my research for more than fifteen years to make parsing as powerful as possible without allowing ambiguous grammars or sacrificing accessibility, simplicity, and efficiency—ANTLR is constrained by what most programmers can and will use.

ANTLR v3 introduces a new parsing strategy called *LL(*) parsing*[2] that is much more powerful than traditional *LL(k)*-based parsers, which are limited to a finite amount of lookahead, *k*. *LL(*)*, in contrast, allows the lookahead to roam arbitrarily far ahead, relieving you of the responsibility of specifying *k*. *LL(*)* does not alter the recursive-descent parsing strategy itself at all—it just enhances an *LL* decision's predictive capabilities, which we'll explore in a moment. You will find that building grammars for ANTLR v3 is much easier than for ANTLR v2 or any other

---

1. Generalized *LR* (*GLR*) parsing [Tom87] is the latest parsing technology that handles any context-free grammar.
2. The *LL(*)* term was coined by Sriram Srinivasan, a friend who helped me think through this new parsing strategy. See http://www.antlr.org/blog/antlr3/lookahead.tml for more information about the *LL(*)* algorithm.

LL-based parser generator. For example, *LL(*)* lets you build grammars the way you want and then automatically does left-factoring to generate efficient decisions. *LL(*)* is also much more flexible in terms of attributes and actions than bottom-up *LR*-based tools, such as YACC and its derivatives,[3] yet has as much or more parsing power.

Another great aspect of ANTLR is that it unifies the notions of lexing, parsing, and tree parsing. It doesn't matter whether you are parsing a stream of characters, tokens, or tree nodes: ANTLR uses the same recognition strategy. The generated recognizers even derive from the same base class, BaseRecognizer. This implies that lexers have the power of context-free grammars rather than simple regular expressions[4]—you can match recursive structures such as nested comments inside the lexer. Discussions of *LL(*)* apply equally well to any ANTLR grammar. Before detailing how *LL(*)* works, let's zero in on the weaknesses of *LL(k)* that provided the impetus for the development of *LL(*)*.

11.2 Why You Need *LL(*)*

Natural grammars are sometimes not *LL(k)*. For example, the following easy-to-read grammar specifies the syntax of both abstract and concrete methods:

```
method
    : type ID '(' args ')' ';'           // E.g., "int f(int x,int y);"
    | type ID '(' args ')' '{' body '}' // E.g., "int f() {...}"
    ;
type: 'void' | 'int' ;
args: arg (',' arg)* ; // E.g., "int x, int y, int z, ..."
arg : 'int' ID ;
body: ... ;
```

The grammar is valid in the general sense because the rules follow the syntax of the ANTLR metalanguage and because the grammar is unambiguous (the grammar cannot match the same sentence in more than

---

3. *LR*-based parsers can use only synthesized attributes, analogous to return values, whereas *LL*-based parsers can pass inherited attributes (parameters) to rules and use synthesized attributes. Further, introducing an action into an *LR* grammar can cause a grammar nondeterminism, which cannot happen in an *LL* grammar.

4. Regular expressions are essentially grammars that cannot invoke other rules. These expressions are said to match the "regular" languages, which are a subset of the context-free languages matched by context-free grammars. See Section 2.2, *The Requirements for Generating Complex Language*, on page 21 and Section 4.1, *Describing Languages with Formal Grammars*, on page 72 for more about context-free grammars.

one way). According to the requirements of *LL(k)* parsing technology, however, the grammar is not *LL(k)* for any *fixed* value of *k*. From the left edge of **method**'s alternatives, the amount of lookahead necessary to see the distinguishing input symbol, ';' or '{', is unbounded because the incoming method definition can have an arbitrary number of arguments. At runtime, though, "arbitrary" does not imply "infinite," and the required lookahead is usually from five to ten symbols for this decision. You will see in a moment that *LL(*)* takes advantage of this practical limit to generate efficient parsing decisions that, in theory, could require infinite lookahead.

The traditional way to resolve this *LL(k)* conflict is to left-factor offending rule **method** into an equivalent *LL(k)*-conformant rule. *Left-factoring* means to combine two or more alternatives into a single alternative by merging their common left prefix:

```
method
    :    type ID '(' args ')' (';' | '{' body '}')
    ;
```

Unfortunately, this version is less readable. Worse, in the presence of embedded actions, it can be difficult to merge alternatives. You have to delay actions until after the recognizer sees ';' or '{'.

Consider another natural grammar that matches class and interface definitions:

```
def : modifier* classDef      // E.g., public class T {...}
    | modifier* interfaceDef // E.g., interface U {...}
    ;
```

Again, you could refactor the rule, but it is not always possible and leads to unnatural grammars:

```
def : modifiers* (classDef|interfaceDef) ;
```

When building grammars for really difficult languages such as C++, engineers often leave the grammar in a natural condition and then add semantic predicates (see Chapter 13, *Semantic Predicates*, on page 309) to manually scan ahead looking for the distinguishing symbol:

```
def : {findAhead(CLASS_TOKEN)}?     modifier* classDef
    | {findAhead(INTERFACE_TOKEN)}? modifier* interfaceDef
    ;
```

where findAhead() is a loop that scans ahead in the input stream looking for a particular token. This solution works but requires manual coding and is sometimes difficult to get right.

In this case, for example, the findAhead() method must stop when it sees a '{', lest it look past the current type declaration to the next declaration beyond. The next two sections describe how ANTLR automatically generates a similar lookahead mechanism that is correct and efficient.

11.3 Toward *LL(*)* from *LL(k)*

Building a parser generator is easy except for the static grammar analysis that computes the lookahead sets needed to make parsing decisions. For BNF grammars, grammars with just rule and token references, the code generation templates are straightforward. References to rule r become method calls, $r()$;. References to token T become match(T);. match() checks that the current input symbol is T and moves to the next symbol. Rule definitions themselves are a little more complicated; an arbitrary rule r definition with multiple alternatives translates to this:

```
void r() {
  if ( «lookahead-consistent-with-alt1» ) { «code-for-alt-1»; }
  else if ( «lookahead-consistent-with-alt2» ) { «code-for-alt-2»; }
  ...
  else error;
}
```

The series of **if** expressions represents the parsing decision for **r**. Therefore, the power of these expressions dictates the strength of your parser. When building such recursive-descent parsers (see Section 2.7, *Recognizing Computer Language Sentences*, on page 31) by hand, you are free to use any expression you want, but a parser generator must divine these expressions from the grammar. The smarter the grammar analysis algorithm, the more powerful the expressions it can generate.

Until the ANTLR v1.0 release fifteen years ago, all practical parser generators were limited to one symbol of lookahead (k=1). Top-down parser generators were therefore limited to *LL(1)*, which is pretty weak. For example, the following simple grammar is not *LL(1)* because rule **stat**'s parsing decision cannot distinguish between its two alternatives looking only at the first symbol, **ID**:

```
stat : ID '=' expr
     | ID ':' stat
     ;
```

Rule **stat** is, however, *LL(2)*. By looking two symbols ahead, the parsing decision can see either the '=' or the ':'. ANTLR v1.0 could generate Java code like the following to implement rule **stat** using *k=2*:

```
void stat() {
  if ( LA(1)==ID&&LA(2)==EQUALS ) { // PREDICT
    match(ID);                      // MATCH
    match(EQUALS);
    expr();
  }
  else if ( LA(1)==ID&&LA(2)==COLON ) { // PREDICT
    match(ID);                      // MATCh
    match(COLON);
    stat();
  }
  else «error»;
}
```

Method LA() evaluates to the **int** token type of the token at the specified lookahead depth. As is often the case, it is not the sequence of lookahead symbols that distinguishes alternatives—it is a token (or tokens) at a particular lookahead depth that matters. Here, the first token **ID** does not help distinguish between the alternatives because it is common to both. Consider the following alternative implementation that focuses on the second symbol of lookahead:

```
void stat() {
  // PREDICTION CODE; yield an alternative number
  int alt=0;
  if ( LA(1)==ID ) {
    if ( LA(2)==EQUALS ) alt=1;      // predict alternative 1
    else if ( LA(2)==COLON ) alt=2;  // predict alternative 2
  }
  // MATCH PREDICTED ALTERNATIVE
  switch (alt) {
    case 1 : // match alternative 1
      match(ID);
      match(EQUALS);
      expr();
      break;
    case 2 : // match alternative 2
      match(ID);
      match(COLON);
      stat();
      break;
    default : «error»;
  }
}
```

This implementation style factors out the parsing decision to the front of the rule, which now yields an alternative number. The rest of the rule is just a **switch** on the predicted alternative number. In this style, the true form of the parsing decision becomes clear, as illustrated in the following DFA:

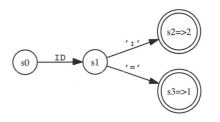

This DFA encodes that lookahead sequence ID '=' predicts alternative one by traversing states s0, s1, s3. s3 is an accept state that indicates the predicted alternative. The DFA encodes one other lookahead sequence, ID ':', that predicts alternative two by traversing states s0, s1, s2.

Lookahead decisions that use fixed lookahead, such as *LL(k)* decisions, always have *acyclic DFA*.[5] The next section describes the *cyclic DFA* *LL(*)* uses to support arbitrary lookahead.[6]

11.4 *LL(*)* and Automatic Arbitrary Regular Lookahead

LL(*) extends *LL(k)* by allowing cyclic DFA, DFA with loops, that can scan arbitrarily far ahead looking for input sequences that distinguish alternatives. Using the maze analogy, *LL(*)*'s arbitrary lookahead is like bringing a trained monkey along that can race ahead at each maze fork. If two paths emanating from a fork have the same initial words, you can send the monkey down both paths looking for a few of the future words in your passphrase. One of the most obvious benefits of *LL(*)* is that you do not have to specify the lookahead depth as you do with *LL(k)*—ANTLR simply figures out the minimum lookahead necessary to distinguish between alternatives. In the maze, *LL(k)* decision makers do not have trained monkeys and have limited information. They can see only the next *k* words along the paths emanating from a fork.

---

5. An acyclic DFA is one that matches a finite set of input sequences because there are no loops to match repeated, arbitrarily long sequences. While traversing an acyclic DFA, you can never revisit a state.
6. Cyclic DFA allows states to transition to previously visited states.

Reconsider the non-*LL(k)* **class** or **interface** definition grammar shown in the previous section:

```
def : modifier* classDef
    | modifier* interfaceDef
    ;
```

Using ANTLRWorks, you can look at the DFA created for a decision by right-clicking a rule or subrule and selecting Show Decision DFA.

A cyclic DFA can easily skip ahead past the modifiers to the **class** or **interface** keyword beyond, as illustrated by the following DFA:

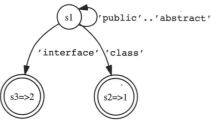

In this case, a simple **while** loop implements rule **def**'s prediction DFA:

```
void def() {
  int alt=0;
  while (LA(1) in modifier) consume(); // scan past modifiers
  if ( LA(1)==CLASS ) alt=1;          // 'class'?
  else if ( LA(1)==INTERFACE ) alt=2;  // 'interface'?
  switch (alt) {
    case 1 : ...
    case 2 : ...
    default : error;
  }
}
```

Just as with the earlier *LL(2)* solution, the initial **modifier** symbols do not help distinguish between the alternatives. The loop (trained monkey) simply scans past those tokens to the important token that follows. Notice that the decision DFA looks like a left-factored version of rule **def**.

It is important to point out that ANTLR is not approximating the entire grammar with a DFA. DFAs, which are equivalent to regular expressions, are not as powerful as context-free grammars (see Section 2.2, *The Requirements for Generating Complex Language*, on page 21). ANTLR is using the DFAs only to distinguish between alternatives. In the earlier example, ANTLR creates a DFA that stops matching at the **class** or **interface** keyword. ANTLR does not build a DFA that matches the entire **classDef** rule or **interfaceDef** rule. Once **def** predicts which alternative will succeed, it can begin parsing like any normal *LL* parser. As another example, here is the DFA for the grammar in Section 11.2,

Why You Need LL(*), on page 255 that predicts abstract vs. concrete methods:

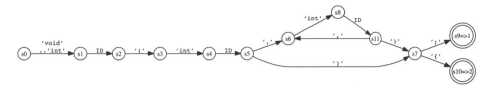

This DFA matches the start of a method definition, splits for the optional arguments, and then pinches back to state s7. s7 then splits upon either the ';' or the '{' to distinguish between abstract and concrete methods. State s9 predicts alternative one ("s9=>1"), and state s10 predicts alternative two. Input void foo(int i); predicts alternative one by following this path: s0, s1, s2, s3, s4, s5, s7, s9. Input void foo(int i) {... predicts alternative two by following this path: s0, s1, s2, s3, s4, s5, s7, s10. Because the starting portion of these two inputs is identical, the state sequence is identical until the DFA reaches the critical s7 state.

Sometimes these DFAs become complicated, but ultimately they simply yield a predicted alternative number as in the previous example. DFAs scan past common left prefixes looking for distinguishing symbols. The following rule for a Java-like language has a subrule that matches the variables and method definitions within an **interface**:

```
interfaceDef
    :   'interface' ID ('extends' classname)?
        '{'
        (   variableDefinition
        |   methodDefinition
        )*
        '}'
    ;
```

The DFA for the embedded subrule, shown in Figure 11.1, on page 263, has some interesting characteristics. The details are not that important—the DFA merely illustrates that ANTLR sometimes needs to build a large DFA while looking for the few symbols that will differentiate alternatives. The accept states s18 and s19 are the most interesting states because the cloud of other states pinches back together into s16 and then splits on the single symbol that distinguishes between variable and method definitions. The complicated cyclic states before that just scan past tokens, as defined in the grammar, until the semicolon or left curly.

Also note that upon seeing the right curly the DFA immediately predicts the third alternative via states s0 and s1, which is the implied exit branch of the (...)* loop. State s1 is an accept state that predicts alternative 3. This DFA illustrates a case where a recognizer uses various lookahead depths even within the same decision. The DFA uses more-or-less lookahead for optimal efficiency, depending on what it finds on the input stream.

A decision is *LL(*)* if a DFA exists that recognizes the decision's exact lookahead language and has the following:

LL(*) degenerates to LL(k) for a fixed k if your grammar is LL(k). If it is not LL(k), ANTLR searches further ahead in a grammar to find tokens that will help it make choices.

- No unreachable states

- No dangling states, that is, states that cannot reach an accept state

- At least one accept state for each alternative

Each alternative has a lookahead language, and if the lookahead languages are disjoint for a decision, then the decision is *LL(*)*. It is like building a regular expression to describe what input predicts each alternative and then verifying that there is no overlap between the input matched by the regular expressions.

At this point, the reader might ask, "Isn't this just backtracking?" No. An *LL(5)* parser, for example, uses a maximum of five lookahead symbols and is considered to have linear complexity, albeit with a bigger constant in front than an *LL(1)* parser. Similarly, if an *LL(*)* parser can guarantee in practice that it will never look ahead more than five symbols, is it not effectively the same as *LL(5)*? Further, *LL(*)* is scanning ahead with a DFA, not backtracking with the full parser. It is the difference between having a trained monkey in the maze racing ahead looking for a few symbols and you having to laboriously backtrack through each path emanating from a fork. The lookahead DFAs are smaller and faster because they are not descending into deep rule invocation chains. Each transition of the DFA matches a symbol, whereas a backtracking parser might make twenty method calls without matching a single symbol. The DFAs are efficiently coded and automatically throttle down when less lookahead is needed. ANTLR is also not sucking actions into lookahead DFAs. DFAs automatically avoid action execution during *LL(*)* prediction. Backtracking parsers, on the other hand, must turn off actions or figure out how to unroll them.

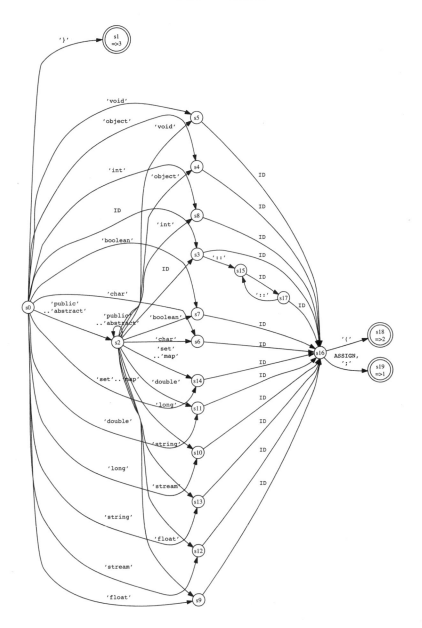

Figure 11.1: VARIABLE VS. METHOD PREDICTION DFA THAT ILLUSTRATES A COMPLICATED CLOUD OF CYCLIC STATES THAT PINCHES BACK TO A SINGLE STATE, s16, TO DISTINGUISH BETWEEN VARIABLE AND METHOD DEFINITIONS

Now that you know a little bit about *LL(*)* parsing decisions, it is time to focus on non-*LL(*)* decisions because, in practice, that is when you care about the underlying parsing strategy. It is only when ANTLR fails to generate a deterministic *LL(*)* decision that you need to figure out why ANTLR could not handle the decision. The next section explains what can go wrong in detail.

11.5 Ambiguities and Nondeterminisms

When analyzing a grammar warning or error from ANTLR, your task is to impersonate ANTLR's grammar analysis algorithm and try to figure out why the decision has a problem. There are two general categories of issues. In the first category, you have specified a decision that either is fundamentally incompatible with top-down recursive-descent parsing or is non-*LL(*)* because the lookahead language is not regular (cannot be described with a regular expression). This category always involves recursive rules within the grammar. In the second category, ANTLR has no problem building a DFA, but at least one input sequence can be matched by more than one alternative within a decision. This category therefore deals with recognizer nondeterminism, an inability to decide which path to take. The following sections describe the issues in each category in detail.

LL-Incompatible Decisions

Some grammars just simply do not make sense regardless of the parsing tool. For example, here is a rule that can match only an infinite sequence, which is obviously incompatible with a finite computer:

```
a : A a ;
```

The sequence of rule invocations, the *derivation*, for this rule looks like the following:

```
a => A a
a => A A a
a => A A A a
...
```

where each occurrence of **a** on the right side is replaced with A a per the definition of **a**. Rule **a** matches a token **A** followed by another reference to **a**, which in turn can be a token **A** followed by another reference to **a**, *ad nauseam*.

This grammar is equivalent to the following Java code:

```
void a() {
    match(A);
    a();
}
```

Clearly, this will never terminate, and you will get a stack overflow exception. As a general rule, grammar rules with recursive alternatives must also include an alternative that is not recursive even if that alternative is an empty alternative. The following rewrite of the grammar is probably more what is intended anyway:

```
a : A a
  |
  ;
```

This grammar matches A*, and naturally, you should simply use this EBNF construct in your grammar rather than tail recursion:[7]

```
a : A* ;
```

The two grammars are equivalent, but the tail-recursive version is less efficient and less clear. A* clearly indicates repetition, whereas the programmer must imagine the tail recursion's emergent behavior to figure out what the grammar developer intends.

Left-Recursive Grammars

What if the recursion is on the left edge of an alternative or reachable from the left edge without consuming an input symbol? Such a rule is said to be *left recursive*. Left recursion is a perfectly acceptable grammar for some parser generators, but not for ANTLR. Consider the reverse of the previous tail recursive grammar that matches the same language:

```
a : a A
  |
  ;
```

The derivation for AAA looks like this where the final reference to **a** on the right side is replaced with the empty alternative:

```
a => a A
a => a A A
a => a A A A
a => A A A
```

---

7. A rule that uses tail recursion calls itself, or another rule that ultimately calls that rule, at the end of an alternative. A rule that invokes itself loops via recursion.

Unfortunately, although a valid grammar construct in general, an *LL*-based top-down parser cannot deal with left-recursion. ANTLR reports the following:

```
error(210): The following sets of rules are mutually left-recursive [a]
```

Be aware that left-recursion might not be direct and might involve a chain of multiple rules:

```
a : b A
  |
  ;
b : c ;
c : a ;
```

ANTLR reports the following:

```
error(210): The following sets of rules are mutually
            left-recursive [a, c, b]
```

Arithmetic Expression Grammars

In my view, left-recursion is pretty unnatural (EBNF looping constructs are easier to understand) except in one case: specifying the structure of arithmetic expressions. In this case, bottom-up parser generators allow a much more natural grammar than top-down parser generators, and you will encounter this if you are trying to convert a grammar from, say, YACC to ANTLR. The grammar usually looks something like this:

```
// non-LL yacc grammar
%left  '+'
%left  '*' // higher precedence than '+'
expr:   expr '+' expr
    |   expr '*' expr
  ...
    |   ID
    |   INT
    ;
```

This might seem natural if you ignore that the grammar is left-recursive. Without the precedence %left specifier, this grammar would be ambiguous, and bottom-up parser generators require that you specify the priority of those operators (as described in every compiler book ever written). In a top-down parser generator, you must explicitly encode the priorities of the operators by using different rules. The following *LL*-compatible grammar matches the same language, but with explicit priorities:

```
expr:   mult ('+' mult)* ;
mult:   atom ('*' atom)* ;
```

```
atom:   ID
    |   INT
    ;
```

The way to think about this grammar is from the highest level downward. In rule **expr**, think of the references to **mult** as simply metatokens separated by the '+' operator. View 3*4+5*6 as the addition of two metatokens as if the expression were (3*4)+(5*6). Here is the parse tree as generated by ANTLRWorks' interpreter:

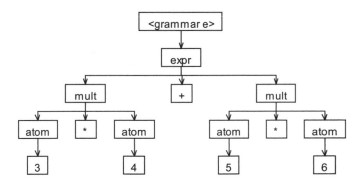

The deeper the nesting level, the higher the precedence of the operator matched in that rule. The loop subrules, (...)*, match the addition of repeated multiplicative metatokens such as 3*4+5+7.

Top-down parsers naturally associate operators left to right so that the earlier operators are matched correctly using a natural grammar. But, what about operators that are right-associative such as the exponentiation operator? In this case, you must use tail recursion to get the associativity right:

Even if you do not understand exactly how the precedence and associativity works, you can blindly accept these examples as grammar design patterns during the learning process.

```
expr:   mult ('+' mult)* ; // left-associative via (...)*
mult:   pow ('*' pow)* ;
pow :   atom ('^' pow)? ;   // right-associative via tail recursion
atom:   ID
    |   INT
    ;
```

The grammar derives input 2*3^4^5 as follows:

```
expr => mult
expr => pow * pow
expr => 2 * pow
expr => 2 * atom ^ pow
expr => 2 * 3 ^ pow
expr => 2 * 3 ^ atom ^ pow
expr => 2 * 3 ^ 4 ^ pow
expr => 2 * 3 ^ 4 ^ 5
```

The parse tree is as follows:

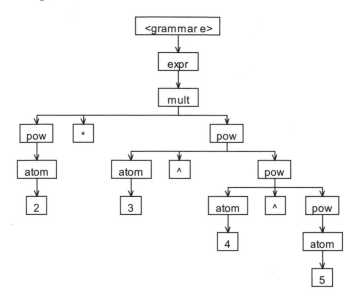

The first exponent operator has a complete subtree (also containing an exponent operator) as a right operand; consequently, the second exponent is evaluated first. Expression tree nodes must evaluate their children before they can perform the operation. This means the second exponent operator executes before the first, providing the necessary right associativity.

Non-*LL(*)* Decisions

Rule recursion can also cause trouble even when the rule references are not left-recursive. Although *LL(*)* DFA construction takes the parsing rule invocation stack into consideration, the resulting DFA will not have a stack. Instead, the DFA must use sequences of states. Consider the following grammar that allows zero or more labels on the front of each statement. Because the reference to rule **label** is common to both alternatives, ANTLR must try to see past it to the **ID** or 'return' token in order to distinguish between the alternatives.

```
grammar stat;

s : label ID '=' expr
  | label 'return' expr
  ;
label
  : ID ':' label // uses tail recursion to loop
  |
  ;
```

ANTLR reports two problems:

```
error(211): stat.g:3:5: [fatal] rule s has non-LL(*) decision due to
recursive rule invocations reachable from alts 1,2.  Resolve by
left-factoring or using syntactic predicates or using
backtrack=true option.
warning(200): stat.g:3:5: Decision can match input such as
"ID ':' ID ':'" using multiple alternatives: 1, 2
```

The first issue is that, without a stack, a DFA predictor cannot properly recognize the language as described by rule **label** because of the tail recursion. The second issue is derived from the fact that ANTLR tried to create a DFA anyway but had to give up after recursing a few times.[8] An easy fix for this grammar makes it trivially *LL(*)*:

```
grammar stat;

s : label ID '=' expr
  | label 'return' expr
  ;
label
  : (ID ':')*
  ;
```

The language is the same, but rule **label** expresses its repetitious nature with an EBNF construct rather than tail recursion. Figure 11.2, on the following page, shows the DFA for the decision in rule **s**. The EBNF looping construct maps to a cycle in the DFA between s1 and s4 and is clearer than tail recursion because you are explicitly expressing your intention to loop.

Generally, it is not possible to remove recursion because recursion is indispensable for describing self-similar language constructs such as nested parentheses (see Section 2.2, *The Requirements for Generating Complex Language*, on page 21). Imagine a simple language with expressions followed by '%' (modulo) or '!' (factorial):

```
se: e '%'
  | e '!'
  ;
e : '(' e ')'
  | ID
  ;
```

---

8. To be precise, ANTLR's analysis algorithm will follow recursive rule indications until it hits constant MAX_SAME_RULE_INVOCATIONS_PER_NFA_CONFIG_STACK in NFAContext. You can set this threshold using the -Xm option. After hitting the threshold, ANTLR will have created a DFA containing a state reachable upon ID:ID: that predicts both alternatives one and two of rule **s**. This nondeterminism results in the warning. Note that there might be other states with problems in the DFA, but ANTLR tries to merge related warnings.

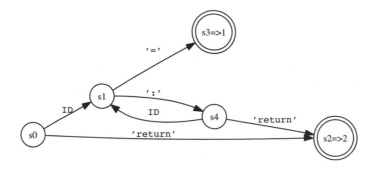

Figure 11.2: DFA PREDICTING ALTERNATIVES IN RULE s MATCHING (ID ':')*

Not only can rule **e** match infinitely long sequences, the sequences must be properly nested, parenthesized expressions. There is no way to describe this construct without recursion (hence, a regular expression is insufficient). ANTLR will generate a DFA that favors alternative one in rule **se** unless it knows for sure that alternative two will succeed, such as when the input is ID!. ANTLR builds the DFA shown in Figure 11.3, on the facing page, and warns this:

```
warning(200): e2.g:3:5: Decision can match input such as
"'(' '('" using multiple alternatives: 1, 2
```

The DFA does, however, correctly predict alternatives for input sequences not requiring deep recursive invocation of rule **e** such as v and (v).

Without left-factoring rule **se**, the only way to resolve this non-*LL(*)* decision is to allow ANTLR to backtrack over the reference to rule **e**, as discussed later in Chapter 14, *Syntactic Predicates*, on page 323. In this grammar, a parser could technically scan ahead looking for the '%' or '!', but in general this approach will not work. What if '%' were a valid binary operator as well as a suffix unary operator as shown? The only way to distinguish between the binary and unary suffix operators would be to properly match the expressions as part of the lookahead. Scanning ahead with a simple loop looking for the suffix operators amounts to a much weaker strategy than actually recognizing the expressions.

In some cases, however, ANTLR can deal with recursion as long as only one of the alternatives is recursive. The following grammar is *LL(*)* as

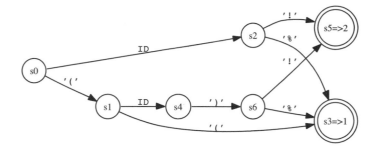

Figure 11.3: DFA PREDICTING ALTERNATIVES IN RULE SE

long as the internal recursion overflow constant (specified by -Xm) is sufficiently large; the default value is 4, meaning the analysis engine can recurse four times before hitting the threshold:

```
grammar t;
a : L a R
  | L L X
  ;
```

The analysis sees that L begins both alternatives and looks past it in both alternatives to see whether there is something that follows that will distinguish the two. In the first alternative, therefore, the analysis must enter rule a again. The first symbol that it can see upon reentry is L. Hence, the algorithm must continue again past that L recursively into rule a hoping for a lookahead symbol that will distinguish the two alternatives. Ultimately, the algorithm sees the X in the second alternative, which allows it to distinguish the two alternatives. Clearly, though, if the second alternative were recursive as well, this process would never terminate without a threshold. ANTLR generates the following DFA where state path s0, s1, s2, s3 predicts alternative two:

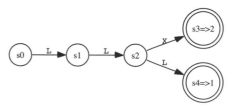

To illustrate what happens when you hit the recursion overflow threshold, consider the following invocation of ANTLR on the same grammar. The command-line option restricts the analysis engine so that it can recurse to **a** exactly once:

```
$ java org.antlr.Tool -Xm 1 t.g
ANTLR Parser Generator  Version 3.0  1989-2007
warning(206): t.g:2:5: Alternative 1: after matching input such as
L L decision cannot predict what comes next due to recursion
overflow to a from a
warning(201): t.g:2:5: The following alternatives are unreachable: 2
```

Because of the restriction that the analysis cannot recurse more than once, the analysis cannot enter **a** a second time when computing lookahead for the first alternative. It can't see past **L L** to another **L**. One more recursive examination of **a** would allow the analysis to distinguish the first alternative's lookahead from the **L L X** lookahead of the second. The recursion overflow threshold restricts only the maximum recursion depth, not the simple stack size of invoked rules, so it is not very restrictive.[9]

Nondeterministic Decisions

Once you get used to *LL* top-down parsers, you will not make many recursion mistakes. Most of your grammar problems will stem from *nondeterminisms*: the parser can go down two or more different paths given the same lookahead language.

Each lookahead sequence must uniquely predict an alternative. Just like in a maze with words written on the floor, if the next few words in your passphrase appear on the floor down both paths of a fork in the maze, you will not know which path to take to reach the exit. This section illustrates many of the common nondeterminisms you will encounter.

Most nondeterminisms arise because of ambiguities; all grammar ambiguities result in parser nondeterminisms, but some nondeterminisms are not related to ambiguities, as you will see in a moment.

---

9. The m=4 threshold makes sense because the Java grammar did not work with m=1 but did work with m=4. Recursion is sometimes needed to resolve some fixed lookahead decisions. Note: m=0 implies the algorithm cannot ever jump to another rule during analysis (stack size 0), m=1 implies you can make as many calls as you want as long as they are not recursive, and m=2 implies that you are able to recurse exactly once (that is, enter a rule twice from the same place).

> ### Tracking Down Nondeterminisms
>
> When tracking down nondeterminisms, the key is asking yourself how the grammar can match the indicated lookahead sequence in more than one way. ANTLRWorks was designed to be particularly good at helping you understand nondeterminisms, so this is easier than it used to be. With a little bit of experience, you will get good at figuring out what is wrong.
>
> Once you discover exactly how the grammar can match a lookahead sequence in more than one way, you must generally alter the grammar so that ANTLR sees exactly one path. If you do not resolve a nondeterminism, ANTLR will always resolve it for you by simply choosing the alternative specified first in a decision.

Here is an obvious ambiguity:

```
r : ID {...}
  | ID {...}
  ;
```

to which ANTLR responds as follows:

```
warning(200): t.g:3:5: Decision can match input such as
"ID" using multiple alternatives: 1, 2
As a result, alternative(s) 2 were disabled for that input
warning(201): t.g:3:5: The following alternatives are unreachable: 2
```

Clearly, ANTLR could match **ID** by entering either alternative. To resolve the issue, ANTLR turns off alternative two for that input, which causes the unreachable alternative warning. After removing **ID**, no tokens predict the second alternative; hence, it is unreachable. Figure 11.4, on the following page, illustrates how ANTLRWorks highlights the two paths (emphasized with thick lines here). You can trace the nondeterministic paths by using the cursor keys in ANTLRWorks.

Such an obvious syntactic ambiguity is not as crazy as you might think. In C++, for example, a typecast can look the same as a function call:

```
e : ID '(' exprList ')' // function-style typecast; E.g., "T(x)"
  | ID '(' exprList ')' // function call; E.g., "foo(32)"
  ;
```

The reality is that the syntax is inherently ambiguous—there is no amount of grammar shuffling that will overcome an ambiguity in the language syntax definition.

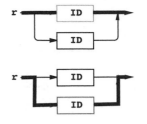

Figure 11.4: ANTLRWorks highlighting both paths predicted by **ID**

In the case of C++, however, knowledge about the **ID**'s type from the symbol table (that is, whether it is a type name or function name) neatly resolves the issue. Use a semantic predicate to consult the symbol table per Chapter 13, *Semantic Predicates*, on page 309.

Consider a more subtle ambiguity problem. Imagine you want to build a language with optional semicolons following statements (such as Python), but where semicolons can also be a statements:

```
grammar t;
slist
    :   ( stat ';'? )+
    ;
stat:   ID '=' expr
    |   ';'
    ;
```

The optional ';'? subrule in rule **slist** cannot decide whether to match ';' immediately or to bypass the subrule and reenter **stat** to match it as a proper, stand-alone statement. ANTLR reports this:

```
warning(200): t.g:3:11: Decision can match input such as
"';'" using multiple alternatives: 1, 2
As a result, alternative(s) 2 were disabled for that input
```

ANTLRWorks highlights both paths in the syntax diagram shown in Figure 11.5, on the facing page.

The solution is to either make semicolons required or make them only statements. Semicolons should not be both statement terminators and statements as shown previously. Naturally, a good language designer would simply fix the language. With the grammar as is, though, ANTLR automatically resolves the nondeterminism *greedily* (see Section 4.3, *Extended BNF Subrules*, on page 83 for information about the **greedy**

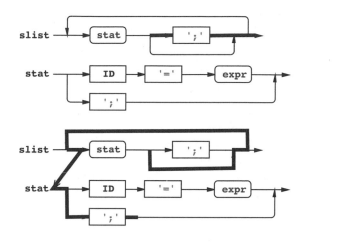

Figure 11.5: SYNTAX DIAGRAMS FOR SLIST AND STAT

option). In other words, ANTLR resolves the issue in favor of matching semicolons immediately following a statement if one exists. A greedy decision is one that decides to match all possible input as soon as possible, rather than delegating the match to a future part of the grammar. Input x=1; ; would match the first ';' in the optional ';'? subrule and the second as a statement in rule **stat**.

The most common form of this ambiguity, and one whose automatic resolution is handled naturally by ANTLR, is the **if-then-else** ambiguity:

```
grammar t;
stat:    'if' expr 'then' stat ('else' stat)?
    |    ID '=' expr ';'
    ;

warning(200): <t.g>:2:29: Decision can match input such as
"'else'" using multiple alternatives: 1, 2
As a result, alternative(s) 2 were disabled for that input
warning(201): <t.g>21:29: The following alternatives are unreachable: 2
```

The issue is similar to the optional semicolon in that ANTLR cannot decide whether to match 'else' immediately or bypass the subrule and match it to a previous 'if'. In other words, how should ANTLR interpret the following input?

```
if done then
if alreadySaved then x=2;
else x=3;
```

Should else x=3; bind to the second and most recent **if** or to the first one? The grammar allows both. Language designers have decided that it's most natural to bind to the most recent **if** (greedily), which is fortunately the way ANTLR automatically resolves ambiguities. ANTLR generates a warning, but you can safely ignore it.[10]

Sometimes the explicit alternatives (nonexit branches of an EBNF construct) within a decision are ambiguous. Consider the following grammar for a Java-like language that can have nested code blocks in statements and also a code block at the class level that acts like a default constructor (Java uses these for default constructors for anonymous inner classes):

```
classDef
    :   'class' ID '{' decl* '}'
    ;
slist:  decl
    |   stat
    ;
decl:   field
    |   method
    |   block // default ctor code block
    ;
stat:   block // usual statement nested code block
    |   'return' expr ';'
    ;
block:  '{' slist '}'
    ;
```

Rule **slist** has a problem in that both alternatives eventually reach rule **block**, making the decision totally ambiguous for code blocks. Should ANTLR match a code block by entering rule **decl** or by entering **stat**? This matters because you are likely to have very different actions depending on the code block's context.

In this case, the grammar is loosely written because **decl** should recognize a code block only at the class level, not at the statement level. Any code block within a statement should be interpreted simply as a nested code block, not a constructor.

Tightening up the grammar to use context information makes it clearer and removes the ambiguity:

---

10. At some point ANTLR will let you silence warnings for decisions that ANTLR properly resolves.

```
classDef
    :   'class' ID '{' member* '}'
    ;
member
    :   decl
    |   block // default ctor code block
    ;
slist:  decl
    |   stat
    ;
decl:   field
    |   method
    ;
...
```

The addition of **member** makes it clear that the grammar should interpret a code block matched within the class definition differently than a code block matched via **slist**.

Sometimes a grammar is ambiguous but is the most natural and correct way to express the language. In the following grammar (pulled from the larger Java grammar at http://www.antlr.org), rule **castExpression** indicates that only typecasts based upon primitive type names such as **int** can prefix expressions that have '+' or '-'. Expressions such as (Book)+3 make no sense, and it is correct to make such cases illegal using the syntax of the language. Rule **castExpression** is a natural way to express the restriction, but it is ambiguous.

```
unaryExpression
    :   '+' unaryExpression
    |   '-' unaryExpression
    |   unaryExpressionNotPlusMinus
    ;
unaryExpressionNotPlusMinus
    :   '~' unaryExpression
    |   castExpression
    |   primary
    ;
castExpression
    :   '(' primitiveType ')' unaryExpression
    |   '(' type ')' unaryExpressionNotPlusMinus
    ;
```

primitiveType and **type** are defined as follows:

```
primitiveType
    :   'int'
    |   'float'
    ;
type:   (primitiveType|ID)  ('[' ']')*
    ;
```

The problem is that rule **type** is a superset of **primitiveType**, so both **cast-Expression** alternatives can match (int)34, for example. Without making a variant of **type**, there is no way to fix this ambiguity using pure *LL(*)*. A satisfying solution, however, involves syntactic predicates whereby you can simply tell ANTLR to try the two alternatives. ANTLR chooses the first alternative that succeeds (see Chapter 14, *Syntactic Predicates*, on page 323):

```
castExpression
// backtrack=true means to just try out the alternatives. If
// the first alternative fails, attempt the second alternative.
options {backtrack=true;}
    :    '(' primitiveType ')' unaryExpression
    |    '(' type ')' unaryExpressionNotPlusMinus
    ;
```

For completeness, it is worth mentioning one of the rare situations in which ANTLR reports a nondeterminism (as opposed to a recursion issue) that is not related to a grammar ambiguity. It turns out that when people say "*LL*," they actually mean "*SLL*" (*strongLL*). The *strong* term implies stronger constraints so that *SLL(k)* is weaker than *LL(k)* for $k>1$ (surprisingly, they are identical in strength for $k=1$). ANTLR and all other *LL*-based parser generators accept SLL grammars (grammars for which an *SLL* parser can be built). Using the proper terminology, you can say that the following grammar is *LL(2)*, but it is not *SLL(2)*:[11]

```
grammar t;
s : X r A B
  | Y r B
  ;
r : A
  |
  ;
```

Rule **r** cannot decide what to do upon lookahead sequence AB. The parser can match A in **r** and then return to the second alternative of **s**, matching B following the reference to **r**. Alternatively, the parser can choose the empty alternative in **r**, returning to the first alternative of **s** to match AB. The problem is that ANTLR has no idea which alternative of **s** will be invoking **r**. It must consider all possible rule invocation sites when building lookahead DFAs for rule **r**. ANTLR reports this:

```
warning(200): <t.g>:5:5: Decision can match input such as
"A A..B" using multiple alternatives: 1, 2
As a result, alternative(s) 2 were disabled for that input
```

---

11. Following convention, this book uses *LL* even though *SLL* is more proper.

This message is correct for SLL(*), but it is a weakness in the parsing strategy, due to a lack of context, rather than a grammar ambiguity as described previously. Naturally, you could trivially rewrite the grammar, duplicating rule r, or ANTLR could generate different methods for r depending on the context. This transformation from LL to SLL is always possible but in the worst case results in exponentially large grammars and parsers.

ANTLR resolves nondeterminisms by predicting the first of multiple alternatives that can match the same lookahead sequence. It removes that lookahead sequence from the prediction set of the other alternatives. If ANTLR must remove all lookahead sequences that predict a particular alternative, then ANTLR warns you that the alternative is unreachable.

In previous versions, ANTLR presented you with all possible lookahead sequences for each nondeterminism. In v3, ANTLR displays a short *Improved in v3.* lookahead sequence from the nondeterministic paths within the lookahead DFA to make it easier for you to find the troublesome paths. ANTLRWorks highlights these paths for you in the syntax diagram and is a great grammar debugging aid.

In summary, all grammar ambiguities lead to parser nondeterminisms, but some nondeterminisms arise because of a weakness in the parsing algorithm. In these cases, you should consider altering the grammar rather than assuming that ANTLR will resolve things properly.

Lexer Grammar Ambiguities

Ambiguities result in nondeterministic lexers just like they do in parsers, but lexers have a special case not present in parsers. Recall that ANTLR builds an implicit **nextToken** rule that has all non-**fragment** tokens as alternatives. ANTLR builds a DFA that, at runtime, decides which token is coming down the input stream and then jumps to that token rule. Again, the **nextToken** prediction DFA examines only as much lookahead as necessary to decide which token rule to jump to.

As with the parser, the lexer sometimes has some fundamentally ambiguous constructs that ANTLR handles naturally. Consider the following grammar that defines a keyword and an identifier:

```
BEGIN : 'begin' ;
ID : 'a'..'z'+ ;
```

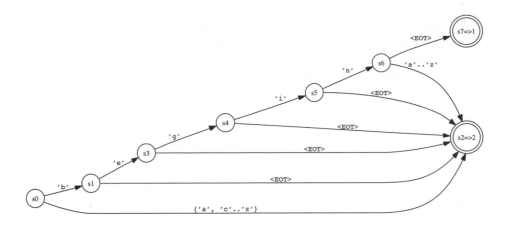

Figure 11.6: LEXER RULE PREDICTION DFA FOR KEYWORD RULES **BEGIN** VS. **ID**

The implicitly constructed **nextToken** rule is as follows:

```
nextToken
    :   BEGIN
    |   ID
    ;
```

Rule **nextToken**'s two alternatives are ambiguous upon 'begin' because rule **BEGIN** is a special case of rule **ID** (keywords are also lexically identifiers). This is such a common situation that ANTLR does not emit warnings about these ambiguities. Just like in the parser, ANTLR resolves the ambiguity by favoring the rule specified first in the grammar. Figure 11.6 shows the DFA that correctly predicts **BEGIN** vs. **ID**. The EOT (end of token) DFA edge label means "anything else," so input beg⸆" (with a space character afterward) predicts the second alternative (rule **ID**) via s0, s1, s3, s4, s2 since the space character is not i.

It is not always the case that specifying superset rules is OK. Using the following two rules is a common mistake:

```
INT : DIGIT+ ;
DIGIT : '0'..'9' ; // needs to be fragment
```

ANTLR reports this:

```
warning(208): t.g:2:1: The following token definitions are
                       unreachable: DIGIT
```

The prediction DFA must choose which rule to match upon saying a single-digit such as 4. When one rule directly references another rule on the left edge, the referenced rule must usually be a **fragment** rule. In this case, clearly **DIGIT** is only a helper rule, and the parser is not expecting to see a **DIGIT** token. Make **DIGIT** a fragment rule:

```
INT : DIGIT+ ;
fragment
DIGIT : '0'..'9' ;
```

Another form of this same issue appears in the following grammar:

```
NUMBER : INT | FLOAT ;
INT : '0'..'9'+ ;
FLOAT : '0'..'9'+ ('.' '0'..'9'*)? ; // simplified
```

Both integers and floating-point numbers match, but they both match via token **NUMBER**. Rules **INT** and **FLOAT** are unreachable. In this case, however, the problem relates to the boundary between lexer and parser rules. You should restrict lexer rules to matching single lexical constructs whereas rule **NUMBER** is one of two different lexical constructs. That indicates you should draw the line between lexer and parser rules differently, as follows, where rule **number** is now a parser rule and correctly indicates a set of tokens representing numbers:

```
number : INT | FLOAT ; // a parser rule
INT : '0'..'9'+ ;
FLOAT : '0'..'9'+ ('.' '0'..'9'*)? ; // simplified
```

The wildcard . operator is often ambiguous with every other rule but can be very useful as an else clause rule if you use it last:

```
BEGIN : 'begin' ;
ID : 'a'..'z'+ ;
OTHER: . ; // match any other single character
```

Rule **OTHER** matches any single character that is not an **ID**. Be careful not to use .+ as a greedy subrule all by itself without anything following it. Such a subrule consumes all characters until the end of file. If you put a grammar element after the .+ loop, it will consume only until it finds that element.

Tree Grammar Ambiguities

Tree grammar ambiguity warnings sometimes reference two implicitly defined tokens: **UP** and **DOWN**. ANTLR parses trees the same way it parses token streams by serializing trees into streams of nodes. The special imaginary tokens indicate the beginning and end of a child list. Consider the following tree grammar rule where both alternatives can match the same input tree node sequence, assuming **type** matches matches 'int':

```
a : ^(DECL 'int' ID)
  | ^(DECL type ID)
  ;
```

Both alternatives can match a tree with the following structure and token types:

The associated tree node stream for that tree is as follows:

```
DECL DOWN 'int' ID UP
```

ANTLR reports this:

```
warning(200): u.g:3:5: Decision can match input such as
"DECL Token.DOWN 'int' ID Token.UP" using multiple alternatives: 1, 2
As a result, alternative(s) 2 were disabled for that input
```

After resolving grammar ambiguities, you can begin testing your grammar for correctness. Unfortunately, a lack of grammar nondeterminisms does not mean that the resulting parser will behave as you want or expect. Checking your grammar for correctness can highlight a number of other problems: Why is this grammar improperly matching a particular input? Why is there a syntax error given this input? Or even, why is there no syntax error given this ungrammatical input? ANTLRWorks' debugger is the best tool for answering these questions. ANTLRWorks has breakpoints and single-step facilities that allow you to stop the parser when it reaches an input construct of interest rather than merely breaking at a grammar location. ANTLRWorks' debugger can even move backward in the parse after a syntax error to examine the events leading up to it. ANTLRWorks' interpreter is also useful for figuring out how a particular input sequence matches.

This chapter described why you need *LL(*)* and how it works. It also explained grammar ambiguities and recognizer nondeterminisms by example. Used in conjunction with the semantic and syntactic predicates described in the next three chapters, *LL(*)* is close to the most powerful parsing algorithm that the average programmer will find accessible. The next chapter demonstrates how *LL(*)* augmented with predicates can resolve some difficult language recognition problems.

Chapter 12

Using Semantic and Syntactic Predicates

LL(*) is a powerful extension to *LL(k)* that makes it much easier to write natural grammars and build grammars for difficult languages. The previous chapter explained how *LL(*)* uses DFAs to scan arbitrarily far ahead looking for input symbols and sequences that distinguish alternatives. *LL(k)*, on the other hand, can see only fixed k symbols ahead. Even though *LL(*)* is much better than *LL(k)*, it still has its weaknesses, particularly when it comes to recursive rules. This chapter illustrates how to use two powerful constructs, *syntactic* and *semantic predicates*, that boost the power of *LL(*)* to the point where it is essentially indistinguishable from recognizers you could build by hand. Predicates alter the parse based upon runtime information. As we'll see in this chapter, predicates help do the following:

- Distinguish syntactically identical language constructs such as type names vs. variable or method names

- Resolve *LL(*)* recognizer nondeterminisms; that is, overcome weaknesses in *LL(*)*

- Resolve grammar ambiguities derived from true language ambiguities by prioritizing alternatives

- Formally encode semantic, syntactic, and other contextual constraints written loosely in English

Predicated-*LL(*)* recognizers readily match almost any context-free grammar and can even deal with context-sensitive language constructs.

ANTLR pioneered the use of predicates in practical parser generators, and you will find it easier to build natural grammars in ANTLR than in other parser generators—at least when it comes to embedding arbitrary actions, supporting context-sensitive parsing, and resolving ambiguous constructs.

Many real language problems require predicated parsers, but there is essentially nothing written about the practical use of predicated parsing. Worse, predicates can be a fairly complicated subject because they are most useful for difficult language implementation problems. For these reasons, it is worth devoting a significant portion of this book to predicated parsing. The discussion is broken into three chapters: how to use predicated parsing to solve real language recognition problems followed by more formal treatments of semantic and syntactic predicates in Chapter 13, *Semantic Predicates*, on page 309 and Chapter 14, *Syntactic Predicates*, on page 323. The last two chapters explain all the variations, hazards, and details concerning predicates, whereas this chapter emphasizes the application of predicates. You should read this chapter first to get the most out of the two subsequent chapters.

This chapter presents a number of situations in which pure *LL(*)* parsing provides an unsatisfactory solution or is even completely insufficient without semantic or syntactic predicates. Let's begin by examining the different kinds of semantic predicates and how they can resolve syntactic ambiguities.

12.1 Resolving Syntactic Ambiguities with Semantic Predicates

Some languages are just plain nasty to parse such as C++ and Ruby, because of context-sensitive constructs. Context-sensitive constructs are constructs that translators cannot interpret without relying on knowledge about surrounding statements. The unfortunate truth is that we cannot build a correct context-free grammar for many languages (see Section 4.1, *Describing Languages with Formal Grammars*, on page 72). We need the ability to drive recognition with runtime information such as symbol table information. Using semantic predicates to alter the parse is analogous to referring to a notebook (such as a symbol table) while navigating the maze. The notebook might contain information about where you've walked in the maze and how the maze matched previous words in the passphrase. The following sections illustrate solutions to a number of difficult language recognition problems that typically flummox everyone except language tool experts.

First let's demonstrate that some problems are hard to describe with a pure context-free grammar (that is, a grammar without semantic predicates).

The Three Semantic Predicate Variations

The semantics of a language refer, loosely, to everything beyond syntax. Another way to look at it is that you specify syntax with a grammar and semantics with embedded actions. Semantics can mean everything from the relationship between input symbols to the interpretation of statements. Although you can sometimes use the grammar to enforce certain semantic rules, most of the time you'll need *semantic predicates* to encode semantic constraints and other language "rules."

Consider the problem of matching an element at most four times. Surprisingly, this is difficult to specify with syntax rules. Using a pure context-free grammar (in other words, without semantic actions or predicates), you must delineate the possible combinations:

```
data:   BYTE BYTE BYTE BYTE
    |   BYTE BYTE BYTE
    |   BYTE BYTE
    |   BYTE
    ;
```

When four becomes a larger number, the delineation solution quickly breaks down. An easier solution is to match as many **BYTE** tokens as there are on the input stream and then, in an action, verify that there are not too many:

```
data:   ( b+=BYTE )+ {if ( $b.size()>4 ) «error»;}
    ;
```

Or, you can use the formal equivalent provided by ANTLR called a *validating semantic predicate*. A validating semantic predicate looks like an action followed by a question mark:

```
data:   ( b+=BYTE )+ {$b.size()<=4}?
    ;
```

Validating semantic predicates are boolean expressions that the recognizer evaluates at runtime. If the expression is false, the semantic predicate fails, and the recognizer throws a FailedPredicateException.

In other cases, no context-free grammar notation exists to specify what you want because an alternative must be gated in or out depending on runtime information. No amount of static grammar analysis will help.

For example, certain languages have extensions that must be turned on or off depending on a command-line switch. For example, Java has **enum** and **assert**; GCC has C extensions. Naturally, the recognizer could allow all extensions and then use an action to emit a syntax error if it sees a disallowed extension. Instead, ANTLR provides a more formal solution called a *gated semantic predicate* (see Section 13.2, *Gated Semantic Predicates Switching Rules Dynamically*, on page 317). Gated semantic predicates look like {...}?=> and enclose a boolean expression that is evaluated at runtime. The gated semantic predicates dictate whether the recognizer can choose that alternative. When false, the alternative is invisible to the recognizer. The following rule fragment is from the statement rule in a Java grammar. The gated semantic predicate uses the boolean variable allowAssert to turn the **assert** statement on and off dynamically.

New in v3.

```
stat:   ifStat
    |   {allowAssert}?=> assertStat
    ...
    ;
```

As another example, reconsider the earlier example matching four **BYTE**. If you want a syntax error rather than a FailedPredicateException, you can use a gated semantic predicate:

```
data
@init {int n=1;} // n becomes a local variable
    :   ( {n<=4}?=> BYTE {n++;} )+ // enter loop only if n<=4
    ;
```

The **BYTE** alternative becomes invisible after the parser has seen four **BYTE** tokens. ANTLR generates the following code for the (...)+ subrule:

```
do {
    int alt1=2;
    int LA1_0 = input.LA(1);
    // predict alternative one if lookahead is consistent with
    // first (and only) alternative of loop and if gated predicate
    // is true.
    if ( (LA1_0==BYTE) && (n<=4)) { // evaluate gated predicate
        alt1=1;
    }
    switch (alt1) {
        ...
    }
} while (true);
```

The gated semantic predicate is part of the decision expression that decides whether to enter an alternative one. There are plenty of real-world examples such as SQL and its vendor variations where you would like to dynamically turn on and off subsets of the language. In this way, you can create one large static grammar and then use gated semantic predicates to selectively turn on and off subsets.

The final variant of the semantic predicate is called a *disambiguating semantic predicate* and looks like {«*expression*»}?. Disambiguating semantic predicates are predicates that *LL(*)* recognizers include in prediction decisions just like gated semantic predicates. The difference is that decisions use disambiguating semantic predicates only when syntax alone is insufficient to distinguish between alternatives. In two general situations, disambiguating semantic predicates really help: when a property of a token must dictate how the parser interprets it and when a surrounding construct or some arbitrary boolean expression must alter how the parser matches the current construct. The following sections illustrate how to use disambiguating semantic predicates.

Keywords as Variables

Consider those twisted languages, written by social deviants, that allow keywords to be used as variables like this: if if call call; or call if;. The context dictates whether an identifier is a keyword or a variable. At the beginning of a statement, if is a keyword, but it is a variable in an expression. One possible solution is to treat all identifiers as variables except in the specific cases where you know an identifier must be a keyword. Because context-free grammars cannot test the attributes of a token, you must use semantic predicates to check that the text of an identifier matches a keyword. In the following grammar, the disambiguating semantic predicates indicate the semantic validity of matching an identifier as a keyword:

predicates/keywords/Pred.g

```
prog: stat+ ;

/** ANTLR pulls predicates from keyIF and keyCALL into
 *  decision for this rule.
 */
stat: keyIF expr stat
    | keyCALL ID ';'
    | ';'
    ;
```

```
expr: ID
    ;

/** An ID whose text is "if" */
keyIF : {input.LT(1).getText().equals("if")}? ID ;

/** An ID whose text is "call" */
keyCALL : {input.LT(1).getText().equals("call")}? ID ;
```

In a mechanism unique to ANTLR, the semantic predicates in rules **keyIF** and **keyCALL** are *hoisted* out of their native rules into the decision for rule **stat**. More specifically, the lookahead prediction DFA shown in Figure 12.1, on the facing page incorporates semantic predicates when it finds that syntax alone is insufficient to distinguish between alternatives.

Notice that the DFA will evaluate the predicates only upon ambiguous sequence ID ID ;. Input ID ID ID, for example, can be an **if** statement only because it is too long to be a **call** statement. The DFA predicts alternative one without evaluating a predicate. For this grammar, the decision needs to know only its grammatical context ("start of statement") and the next token's text attribute.

Sometimes, however, a decision needs context information about how the parser interpreted previous statements. Typically these previous statements are variable, method, or type definitions. The next section shows how to resolve a syntactic ambiguity in the Ruby language with its optional method call parentheses.

Ruby Array Reference vs. Method Call

The Ruby language is nice, but it has some syntactic ambiguities. For example, a[i] can be either an array reference or a method call with an array return value. The proper interpretation depends on how the program previously defines a.[1] The following Ruby code fragment uses a as an array; hence, a[i] is an array reference:

```
a = [20,30]
puts a[1]
```

---

1. The situation is made worse by the lack of static typing in Ruby because you must look backward in the source code for a prior assignment to a even if it's inside a nested conditional. a [i] with a space after the variable name could even mean that [i] (a list with i in it) is a parameter if a is a method.

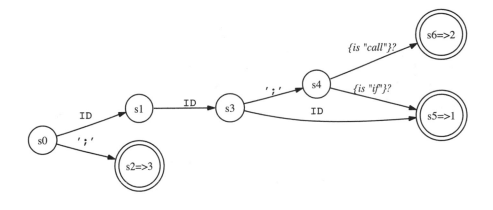

Figure 12.1: Prediction DFA for rule STAT that distinguishes between IF and CALL statements when keywords can be variables

If a is defined as a method, then a[1] represents a method call (call the method and then index into the array that it returns):

```
def a
  return [20,30]
end
puts a[1]
```

In both cases, Ruby prints "30" to the console. At runtime, it is not ambiguous because the [] (array reference) message is sent to whatever object a is. But, imagine you want to perform static analysis of Ruby source code and print all the method references. A simplified grammar demonstrating this notation is as follows:

predicates/ruby/Ruby.g

```
grammar Ruby;

expr:   atom ('+' atom)* // E.g., "a[i]+foo[i]"
    ;

atom:   arrayIndex
    |   methodCall ('[' INT ']')? // E.g., "foo[i]" or "foo(3,4)[i]"
    ;

arrayIndex
    :   ID '[' INT ']' // E.g., "a[i]"
    ;

methodCall
    :   ID ( '(' expr (',' expr)* ')' )? // E.g., "foo" or "foo(3,4)"
    ;
//...
```

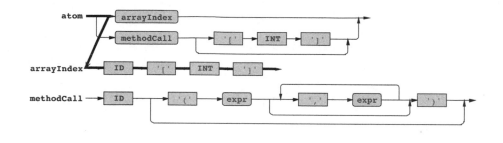

Figure 12.2: SYNTAX DIAGRAM ILLUSTRATING THE PATH ANTLR CHOOSES FOR AMBIGUOUS INPUT ID [INT]

ANTLR reports this:

```
$ java org.antlr.Tool Ruby.g
ANTLR Parser Generator  Version 3.0   1989-2007
warning(200): Ruby.g:6:9: Decision can match input such as
"ID '[' INT ']'" using multiple alternatives: 1, 2
As a result, alternative(s) 2 were disabled for that input
```

The syntax for an array index and the syntax for the method invocation without parentheses are syntactically identical, so you cannot tell the difference just by looking at the syntax. Rule **atom** is nondeterministic because of the ambiguity. Figure 12.2 illustrates the path that the recognizer will take. Figure 12.3, on the facing page illustrates the path that is syntactically ambiguous with the first alternative and that the recognizer will not take.

Adding semantic predicates resolves this ambiguity nicely where isArray() and isMethod() look up their token arguments in a symbol table that records how variables are used:

```
arrayIndex
    :   {isArray(input.LT(1))}? ID '[' INT ']'
    ;

methodCall
    :   {isMethod(input.LT(1))}? ID ('(' expr (',' expr)* ')')?
    ;
```

During a parse, the two semantic predicates test to see whether the next symbol is an array variable or a method.

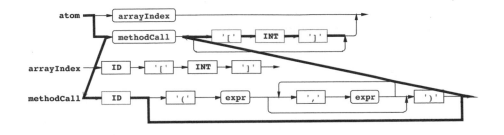

Figure 12.3: SYNTAX DIAGRAM ILLUSTRATING THE PATH ANTLR DOES NOT CHOOSE FOR AMBIGUOUS INPUT ID [INT]

Here is the lookahead prediction DFA for rule **atom** that illustrates how the parser incorporates the semantic predicates:

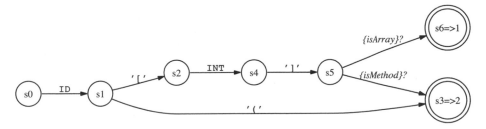

Notice that upon ID '(', the decision immediately predicts alternative two (via s0, s1, s3) because that input can begin only a method call.

This Ruby example illustrated how you can distinguish between two alternatives. The next section uses an example from C to show how semantic predicates can alter a looping subrule's exit test.

C Type Names vs. Variables

C is another language whose grammar needs a semantic predicate. The **typedef** keyword introduces new types that are available later in the program:

```
typedef int I;
I a; // define a as an int
```

C also allows some rather strange-looking declaration-modifier orderings such as the following:

```
int register unsigned g;
I register i;
```

The easiest way to encode this in a grammar is simply to loop around the various declaration modifiers and types even if some combinations are not semantically valid:

`static register int` i;

Using a pure context-free grammar, the only other way to deal with this would be to try to delineate all possible combinations. That is tedious and awkward because you would be trying to enforce semantics with syntax. The more appropriate way to draw the line between syntax and semantics for C is to allow the parser to match an arbitrary modifier list and have the compiler's semantic phase examine the list for nonsensical combinations. The simplified and partial grammar for a C declaration looks like this:

```
declaration
    :   declaration_specifiers declarator? ';' // E.g., "int x;"
    ;

declarator
    :   '*' declarator // E.g., "*p", "**p"
    |   ID
    ;

declaration_specifiers
    :   (   storage_class_specifier // E.g., "register"
        |   type_specifier
        |   type_qualifier          // E.g., "const", "volatile"
        )+
    ;

type_specifier
    : 'void'
    | 'int'
    | ...
    | 'unsigned'
    | struct_or_union_specifier // E.g., "struct {...}", "struct a"
    | type_id
    ;

type_id
    :   ID
    ;
```

The problem is that the looping subrule in **declarator_specifiers** and rule **declarator** can both begin with an **ID** token. Upon **ID**, the subrule loop does not know whether to continue matching or to exit and match the identifier in **declarator**. Now, we know as humans that x y; syntactically must be a variable declaration and, hence, that x must be a user-defined type. Unfortunately, the (. . .)+ loop has no idea how many times it has gone around. The definition of the EBNF construct simply does not incorporate the notion of history. Syntax cannot resolve the recognizer nondeterminism.

Semantic predicates provide a much simpler solution. You can use the natural grammar with a small amount of semantic testing to tell ANTLR when an identifier is a type name:

```
type_id
    :    {isTypeName(input.LT(1).getText())}? ID
    ;
```

The predicate is hoisted into the prediction DFA for the (...)+ subrule in **declaration_specifiers**:

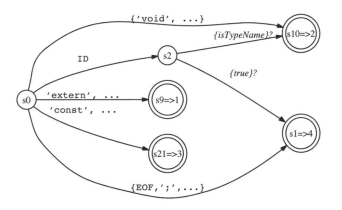

Upon **ID**, the DFA reaches s2 and predicts alternative two (**type_id**) if the identifier is defined as a type name. Otherwise, the DFA fixes alternative four, which is the loop exit branch. In other words, the loop exits when it sees an identifier that is not a type because this must be a variable or method name (the declarator).

To make this semantic predicate work, other parts of the grammar must add type names to a symbol table upon **typedef**. Unfortunately, tracking C symbols properly is a bit involved, particularly using ANTLR's fancy dynamic scopes, as shown next. You can skip to the next section on C++ if you don't care about those details. The point related to semantic predicates has already been made.

To make life easier when passing information between rules, your solution can use dynamic scopes, as described in Section 6.5, *Dynamic Attribute Scopes for Interrule Communication*, on page 135. You'll need a global dynamic scope to track type names because multiple rules will share the same stack of scopes (rules **translation_unit**, **function_definition**, **struct_or_union_specifier**, and **compound_statement**):

```
scope Symbols {
    Set types; // track types only for example
}
```

In this way, the rules that represent C scopes use ANTLR specification scope Symbols; to share the same stack of scopes. For example, here is **translation_unit**:

```
translation_unit
scope Symbols; // entire file is a scope; pushes new scope
@init {
  $Symbols::types = new HashSet(); // init new scope
}
    : external_declaration+
    ;
```

Because of the distance between the **typedef** keyword and the actual **ID** token recognition in rule **declarator**, you must pass information from the **declaration** rule all the way down to **declarator**. The easiest way to do that is to declare a rule-level dynamic scope with a boolean that indicates whether the current declaration is a **typedef**:

```
declaration
scope {
  boolean isTypedef;
}
@init {
  $declaration::isTypedef = false;
}
    : {$declaration::isTypedef=true;} // special case, look for typedef
      'typedef' declaration_specifiers declarator ';'
    | declaration_specifiers declarator? ';'
    ;
```

Any rule, such as **declarator** ultimately invoked from **declaration**, can access the boolean via $declaration::isTypedef:

```
declarator
    : '*' declarator // E.g., "*p", "**p"
    | ID
      {
      // if we're called from declaration and it's a typedef.
      // $declaration.size() is 0 if declaration is not currently
      // being evaluated.
```

```
        if ($declaration.size()>0&&$declaration::isTypedef) {
            // add ID to list of types for current scope
            $Symbols::types.add($ID.text);
            System.out.println("define type "+$ID.text);
        }
    }
    ;
```

This example illustrated how prior statements can affect future statements in C. The next section provides an example where a phrase in the future affects the interpretation of the current phrase.

C++ Typecast vs. Method Call

In C++, the proper interpretation of an expression might depend on *future* constructs. For example, T(i) can be either a constructor-style typecast or a method call depending on whether T is a type name or a method. Because T might be defined below in a class definition file, prior context is insufficient to properly interpret T(i). The recognizer needs future context in a sense.

You can solve this dilemma in two ways. The first solution involves using a parser generator based upon GLR [Tom87] that allows all context-tree grammars including ambiguous grammars such as this one for the typecast vs. method call ambiguity. The parser returns a *parse forest*, rather than a single parse tree, that contains all possible interpretations of the input. You must make a pass over the trees to define methods and types and then make a second pass to choose which interpretation is appropriate for each ambiguous construct.

Using ANTLR, you can implement a similar strategy. Build a single tree for both constructs with a subtree root that represents both cases:

```
primary
    :   ID '(' exprList ')' // ctor-style typecast or method call
        -> ^(TYPECAST_OR_CALL ID exprList)
    |   ID
    |   INT
    ...
    ;
```

Then, similar to the GLR solution, walk the tree, and flip the type of the node once you have the complete symbol table information. The solution does not always work because some constructs need a completely different tree. You must parse the input twice no matter how you want to think about this problem because of forward references.

The second solution, using ANTLR, is not particularly satisfying either. You can parse a file twice, once to find the definitions and then a second time to distinguish between syntactically ambiguous constructs. You might even be able to do a quick initial "fuzzy" pass over the input file just looking for method and type definitions to fill up your symbol table and then parse the code again for real. Because lexing is expensive, tokenize the input only once—pass the token buffer to the second pass to avoid relexing the input characters.

No matter how you approach this problem, there is no escaping multiple passes. This example illustrates again that you can draw the line between syntax and semantics in different places.

Once you have complete symbol table information, the second pass can use semantic predicates to distinguish between typecasts and method calls where isType() looks up its token argument to see whether it is defined as a type in the symbol table:

```
primary
    :   {isType(input.LT(1))}? ID '(' expr ')' // ctor-style typecast
        -> ^(TYPECAST ID expr)
    |   ID '(' exprList ')'                     // method call
        -> ^(CALL ID exprList)
    |   ID
    |   INT
    ...
    ;
```

It is because of this ambiguity and many others that language implementers loathe C++.

Semantic predicates resolve context-sensitivity problems in grammars but are sometimes used to examine the token stream ahead of the current position in order to make parsing decisions. In a sense, such semantic predicates are like manually specified lookahead DFA. Although ultimately powerful because semantic predicates are unrestricted actions in the target language, it is better to use a formal method to describe arbitrary lookahead.

In the next section, we'll look at formal solutions to a number of non-*LL(*)* problems from Java, C, and C++ that require arbitrary lookahead.

12.2 Resolving Ambiguities and Nondeterminisms with Syntactic Predicates

ANTLR supports arbitrary lookahead in the form of *syntactic predicates* that are similar to semantic predicates except that they specify the syntactic validity of applying an alternative rather than the semantic validity. Both kinds of predicates alter the parse based upon information available at runtime. The difference is that syntactic predicates automatically examine future input symbols, whereas semantic predicates test arbitrary programmer-specified expressions.

You can view syntactic predicates as a special case of semantic predicates. Indeed, ANTLR implements syntactic predicates as special semantic predicates that invoke parser backtracking methods. The backtracking methods compare the grammar fragments found in syntactic predicates against the input stream. If a fragment matches, the syntactic predicate is true, and the associated alternative is considered valid.

Syntactic predicates and normal *LL(*)* lookahead are similar in that both support arbitrary lookahead. The difference lies in how much syntactic, structural awareness the two methods have of the input. *LL(*)* uses a DFA to examine the future input symbols, whereas syntactic predicates use a pushdown machine, a full context-free language parser (see Section 2.4, *Enforcing Sentence Tree Structure*, on page 23). In Section 2.2, *The Requirements for Generating Complex Language*, on page 21, you learned that DFAs are equivalent to regular expressions, and therefore, DFAs are too weak to recognize many common language constructs such as matched parentheses. For that, you need a recognizer capable of matching nested, tree-structured constructs (see Section 2.3, *The Tree Structure of Sentences*, on page 22). Syntactic predicates contain context-free grammars, which were designed specifically to deal with the tree-structured nature of sentences. The result of all this is that syntactic predicates can recognize more complicated sentential structures in the lookahead than DFAs. Consequently, syntactic predicates dramatically increase the recognition strength of *LL(*)* parsers. Better yet, backtracking is a simple and well-understood mechanism.

Syntactic predicates are useful in two situations:

- When *LL(*)* cannot handle the grammar the way you would like to write it

- When you must specify the precedence between two ambiguous alternatives; ambiguous alternatives can both match the same input sequence

This section shows three examples whose natural grammar is non-*LL(*)* and then provides an example from C++ where a syntactic predicate resolves an ambiguity between declarations and expression statements by specifying the precedence.

How to Resolve Non-*LL(*)* Constructs with Syntactic Predicates

Let's start with a simple non-*LL(*)* example that we can easily resolve with a syntactic predicate. Consider the following natural grammar for matching expressions followed by two different operators: percent and factorial:

```
grammar x;

s : e '%'
  | e '!'
  ;

e : '(' e ')'
  | INT
  ;

INT : '0'..'9'+ ;
```

Rule **s** is non-*LL(*)* because the left prefix **e** is common to both alternatives. Rule **e** is recursive, rendering a decision in **s** non-*LL(*)*. Prediction DFAs do not have stacks and, therefore, cannot match recursive constructs such as nested parentheses. ANTLR reports this:

```
$ java org.antlr.Tool x.g
ANTLR Parser Generator  Version 3.0  1989-2007
x.g:3:5: [fatal] rule s has non-LL(*) decision due to recursive rule
invocations reachable from alts 1,2.  Resolve by left-factoring or
using syntactic predicates or using backtrack=true option.
warning(200): x.g:3:5: Decision can match input such as "'(' '('"
using multiple alternatives: 1, 2
As a result, alternative(s) 2 were disabled for that input
```

and builds a DFA:

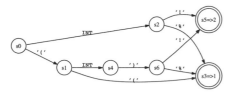

DFAs vs. Backtracking in the Maze

The DFAs of *LL(*)* and the backtracking of syntactic predicates both provide arbitrary lookahead. In the maze, the difference lies in who is doing the lookahead. A DFA is analogous to a trained monkey who can race ahead of you, looking for a few symbols or simple sequences. When a trained monkey isn't smart enough, you must walk the alternative paths emanating from a fork yourself to figure out exactly what is down each path. You are smarter, but slower, than the agile trained monkey.

The recognizer can't match input such as ((x))!. ANTLR resolves nondeterministic input ((by choosing alternative one (via accepts state s3). Notice that the DFA knows how to handle one invocation of rule **e**, (INT), but cannot figure out what to do when **e** invokes itself.

Rather than left-factor the grammar, making it less readable, like this:

```
s : e ('%'|'!')
  ;
```

we can use a syntactic predicate that explicitly tells ANTLR when to match alternative one:

```
s : (e '%')=> e '%'
  | e '!'
  ;
```

This says, "If e '%' matches next on the input stream, then alternative one will succeed; if not, try the next conflicting alternative." ANTLR generates the following prediction DFA:

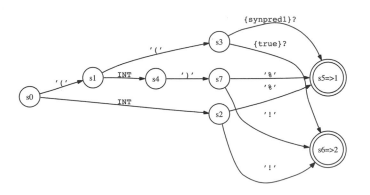

Notice that now, upon ((, the DFA evaluates synpred1, which asks the parser to evaluate the syntactic predicate. You can think of the syntactic predicates as forking another parser that tries to match the grammar fragment in the predicate: e '%'.

We do not need to put a predicate on the second alternative because the parser always attempts the last conflicting alternative like an **else** clause. In the DFA, the **else** clause is represented by the {true}? predicate.

ANTLR also supports an auto-backtracking feature whereby ANTLR inserts syntactic predicates on the left edge of every alternative (see Section 14.4, *Auto-backtracking*, on page 332). The auto-backtracking does not cost anything extra because the *LL(*)* algorithm incorporates these predicates only when normal *LL(*)* grammar analysis fails to produce a deterministic prediction DFA. Using the auto-backtracking feature, we avoid cluttering the grammar with syntactic predicates:

```
grammar x;
options {backtrack=true;}
s : e '%'
  | e '!'
  ;
...
```

The example in this section epitomizes a common situation in real grammars where recursion renders a grammar non-*LL(*)*. The following sections provide more realistic examples from Java and C.

Java 1.5 For-Loop Specification

LL(*) cannot handle alternatives that reference recursive rules. For example, the following rules describe the enhanced "foreach" **for-loops** in Java 1.5:

```
// E.g., enhanced: "for (String n : names) {...}"
//      old style: "for (int i; i<10; i++) {...}"
stat: 'for' '(' forControl ')' statement
    ...
  ;

// E.g., "String n : names" or "int i; i<10; i++"
// non-LL(*) because both alternatives can start by matching rule type
forControl
    :   forVarControl
    |   forInit? ';' expression? ';' forUpdate?
    ;
```

```
forInit
    :   'final'? type variableDeclarators
    |   expressionList
    ;

forVarControl // new java 1.5 "foreach"
    :   'final'? annotation? type Identifier ':' expression
    ;

forUpdate
    :   expressionList
    ;
```

Rule **forControl** is non-*LL(*)* because rule **type** is reachable at the start of both **forVarControl** and **forInit**. This would not be a problem except that **type** is self-recursive because of generics, which can have nested type specifications such as List<List<int>>. For example, an *LL(*)* parser cannot decide which alternative to match after seeing this input:

```
for (List<List<int>> data = ...
```

LL(*)'s DFAs cannot see past the recursive type structure.

Rewriting this grammar to be *LL(*)* might be possible, but it would mean extra work and a less readable grammar. Inserting a single syntactic predicate resolves the issue quickly and easily:

```
forControl
    :   (forVarControl)=> forVarControl
    |   forInit? ';' expression? ';' forUpdate?
    ;
```

To be clear, the alternatives have no valid sentence in common—it is just that *LL(*)* by itself is too weak to distinguish between the two alternatives as written. ANTLR scales back the analysis to *LL(1)* from *LL(*)* because it knows *LL(*)* will fail to yield a valid DFA. *LL(1)* plus a syntactic predicate is sufficient, however.

The DFA looks like this:

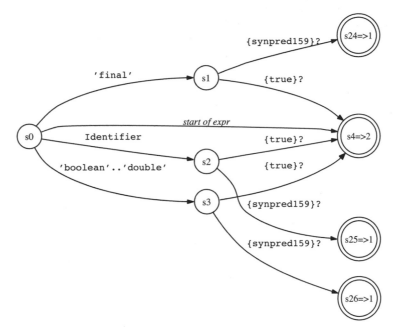

The DFA is not minimized, as you can see—a future version of ANTLR will optimize the generated DFA.

The DFA forces backtracking unless it is clear that the lookahead represents an expression. In that case, the parser knows that only the second alternative would match. Although pure *LL(*)* fails, you can turn on auto-backtracking mode and increase the fixed lookahead to *LL(3)* in order to help ANTLR optimize the decision:

```
forControl
options {k=3; backtracking=true;}
    :    forVarControl
    |    forInit? ';' expression? ';' forUpdate?
    ;
```

Now, the DFA will not backtrack upon input such as Color c : colors because it can see the ':' with three symbols of lookahead (the DFA is too large to effectively show here). The functionality is the same, but this particular decision is much faster for the common case. The increased fixed lookahead prevents backtracking. Manually specified syntactic predicates are always evaluated, but those implicitly added by auto-backtracking mode are not. Auto-backtracking syntactic predicates are evaluated only if *LL(*)* fails to predict an alternative.

The following section provides a similar situation from C where recursive constructs stymie *LL(*)*.

C Function Definition vs. Declaration

Section 11.2, *Why You Need LL(*)*, on page 255 motivated the need for *LL(*)* by showing a rule matching both abstract and concrete methods:

```
method
    : type ID '(' args ')' ';'            // E.g., "int f(int x,int y);"
    | type ID '(' args ')' '{' body '}' // E.g., "int f() {...}"
    ;
```

The prediction DFA easily saw past the left common prefix to the ';' or the '{' because neither **type** nor **args** is recursive. In C, however, arguments are recursive constructs and can be arbitrarily long because of nested parentheses. Here is a sample C function definition whose single argument, p, is a pointer to a function returning **int** that has a **float** argument:[2]

```
void f(int ((*p))(float)) { «body» }
```

The argument declarator can be arbitrarily nested, making it impossible for a DFA to recognize the argument list in order to see past it properly:

```
external_declaration
    : function_definition
    | declaration
    ;
```

Although you could simply turn on the auto-backtracking feature, that is unnecessarily inefficient because the parser will backtrack over the entire function body:

```
external_declaration
options {backtrack=true;}
    : function_definition // uses (function_definition)=> predicate
    | declaration
    ;
```

The implicitly created syntactic predicate for the first alternative references **function_definition**, which tells ANTLR to try to match the entire function. A more efficient approach is to use a manually specified syntactic predicate that provides the minimum necessary lookahead to distinguish the first alternative from the second:

```
external_declaration
    : ( declaration_specifiers? declarator declaration* '{' )=>
          function_definition
    | declaration
    ;
```

---

2. See http://www.cs.usfca.edu/~parrt/course/652/lectures/cdecls.html for a complete description of how to easily read any C declaration.

With this predicate, the backtracking mechanism stops after seeing the '{' instead of parsing the entire function body. Another way to make the decision efficient, without the manually specified syntactic predicate, is to simply reorder the alternatives:

```
external_declaration
options {backtrack=true;}
    : declaration
    | function_definition
    ;
```

Now, even with the auto-backtracking, the parser will stop backtracking much sooner. The backtracking stops at the ';' in **declaration** (resulting in success) or the '{' in **function_definition** (resulting in failure). This reordering works because the two alternatives do not have any valid sentences in common.

In practice, ANTLR generates a very large (nonoptimized) DFA for this decision even with the backtracking; turning on $k=1$ is a good idea to reduce its size:

```
external_declaration
options {backtrack=true; k=1;}
    : declaration
    | function_definition
    ;
```

The previous three examples illustrated how to use syntactic predicates to resolve grammar nondeterminisms arising from weaknesses in $LL(*)$'s DFA-based lookahead. The next sections examine the second use of syntactic predicates: resolving ambiguous alternatives. The examples show constructs that result in grammars where two alternatives can match the same input. The solutions use syntactic predicates to order the ambiguous alternatives, giving precedence to the alternative with the proper interpretation.

Resolving the If-Then-Else Ambiguity

Recall from Section 11.5, *Nondeterministic Decisions*, on page 272 that all grammar ambiguities lead to parser nondeterminisms, meaning that ambiguous decisions are not $LL(*)$ and result in ANTLR warnings. Sometimes, however, the syntax of the language makes a single sentence consistent with two different interpretations. The language reference manual specifies which interpretation to use, but pure context-free grammars have no way to encode the precedence. The most famous example is the **if-then-else** ambiguity:

```
stat:    'if' expr 'then' stat ('else' stat)?
    |    ID '=' expr ';'
    ;
```

ANTLR reports that the grammar has two paths that match the **else** clause. The parser can enter the ('else' stat)? subrule or bypassing the subrule to match the **else** clause to a previous **if** statement. ANTLR resolves the conflict correctly by choosing to match the **else** clause immediately, but you still get an analysis warning. To hush the warning, you can specify a syntactic predicate or turn on auto-backtracking. The warning goes away because syntactic predicates specify the precedence of the two alternatives. Simply put, the alternative that matches first wins. The following rewrite of rule **stat** is not ambiguous because it indicates that the parser should match the **else** clause immediately if present:

```
stat
options {backtrack=true;}
    :    'if' expr 'then' stat 'else' stat
    |    'if' expr 'then' stat
    |    ID '=' expr ';'
    ;
```

The only problem is that the decision is now much less efficient because of the backtracking. This example merely demonstrates how syntactic predicates resolve true ambiguities by imposing order on alternatives. For this situation, do not use syntactic predicates; let ANTLR resolve the nondeterminism because it does the right thing with the $k=1$ lookahead. The next section provides an example from C++ whose solution absolutely requires a syntactic predicate.

Distinguishing C++ Declarations from Expressions

Some C++ expressions are valid statements such as x; or f();. Unfortunately, some expressions require arbitrary lookahead to distinguish from declarations. Quoting from Ellis and Stroustrup's *The Annotated C++ Reference Manual* [ES90], "There is an ambiguity in the grammar involving expression-statements and declarations...The general cases cannot be resolved without backtracking... In particular, the lookahead needed to disambiguate this case is not limited." The authors use the following examples to make their point, where T represents a type:

```
T(*a)->m=7; // expression statement with type cast to T
T(*a)(int); // a is a pointer to function returning T with int argument
```

These statements illustrate that expression statements are not distinguishable from declarations without seeing all or most of the statement. For example, in the previous expression statement, the '->' symbol is the first indication that it is a statement. Syntactic predicates resolve this nondeterminism by simply backtracking until the parser finds a match.

It turns out that the situation in C++ gets much worse. Some sentences can be both expressions and declarations, a true language syntactic ambiguity. For example, in the following C++ code, I(x) is both a declaration (x is an integer as in I x;) and an expression (cast x to type I as in (I)x):[3]

```
typedef int I;
char x = 'a';
void foo() {
    I(x); // read as "I x;" not "(I)x;" (hides global char x)
}
```

The C++ language definition resolves the ambiguity by saying you should choose declaration over expression when a sentence is consistent with both. To paraphrase Ellis and Stroustrup further, in a parser with backtracking, the disambiguating rule can be stated simply as follows:

1. If it looks like a declaration, it is.

2. Otherwise, if it looks like an expression, it is.

3. Otherwise, it is a syntax error.

There is no way to encode these rules in a context-free grammar because there is no notion of order between alternatives. Syntactic predicates, on the other hand, implicitly order alternatives. They provide an exact formal means of encoding the precedence dictated by the C++ language reference:

```
stat: (declaration)=> declaration // if looks like declaration, it is
    | expression                  // else its expression
    ;
```

The beauty of this solution is that a syntactic predicates handles both cases: when the parser needs arbitrary lookahead to distinguish declarations from expressions and when it needs to disambiguate sentences that are both declarations and expressions.

---

3. $T(x)$ for type T can be a constructor-style typecast in C++.

In general, semantic and syntactic predicates overcome the weaknesses of pure context-free grammars. Predicates allow you to formally encode the constraints and rules described in English in a language reference manual using an ANTLR grammar. Parser generators without predicates force the use of *ad hoc* hacks, tweaks, and tricks. For example, a common trick is to insert a smart token filter between the lexer and parser that flips token types when necessary.

This chapter informally defined syntactic predicates, showed how to use them, and demonstrated their power. This information will get you started building predicated grammars, but ultimately you will need to understand how ANTLR implements these predicates more precisely. The next two chapters explain the important details about semantic and syntactic predicates.

Chapter 13

Semantic Predicates

Translators map input sentences to output sentences, which means that the translator must establish a unique interpretation for each input sentence. Some languages, unfortunately, have ambiguous phrases whose syntax allows more than a single interpretation (Section 2.5, *Ambiguous Languages*, on page 26). The proper interpretation depends on the phrase's context. In C++, for example, T(i); syntactically looks like a function call and a constructor-style typecast. The proper interpretation depends on what kind of thing T is, which in turn depends on how the input defines T elsewhere. Pure context-free grammars are unable to impose such conditions on rules in order to uniquely interpret that phrase. ANTLR gets around this problem by augmenting context-free grammars with *semantic predicates* that can alter the parse based upon context.

Semantic predicates are boolean expressions you can use to specify the semantic validity of an alternative. The term *predicate* simply means conditional, and the term *semantic* implies you are talking about arbitrary boolean expressions rather than a syntactic condition. In practice, the rule is pretty simple: if a predicate's expression is false, the associated alternative is invalid. Because predicates can ask questions about other input phrases, you can encode the context in which alternatives apply. For example, in Section 12.1, *C++ Typecast vs. Method Call*, on page 295, you saw how to use semantic predicates to distinguish between C++ method calls and constructor-style typecasts.

Semantic predicates have been in the literature since the 1970s, but Russell Quong and I extended the functionality to include hoisting, whereby you can incorporate a predicate in one rule into the prediction decision of another rule.

Semantic predicates are available to any ANTLR grammar and have three variations:

- Disambiguating semantic predicates, which disambiguate syntactically identical statements

- Gated semantic predicates, which dynamically turn on and off portions of a grammar
- Validating semantic predicates, which throw a recognition exception if the predicate fails

This chapter describes the functional details and limitations of semantic predicates, whereas the previous chapter illustrated how to use semantic predicates. Let's begin with the most important kind of semantic predicate: disambiguating semantic predicates that can resolve nondeterministic $LL(*)$ decisions.

13.1 Resolving Non-$LL(*)$ Conflicts with Disambiguating Semantic Predicates

Upon finding an $LL(*)$ nondeterminism, ANTLR typically emits a grammar analysis warning. In the presence of semantic predicates, however, ANTLR tries to *hoist* them into the alternative prediction for that decision to resolve the conflict. More specifically, ANTLR hoists only those semantic predicates that are reachable from the left edge without consuming an input symbol. When a prediction DFA evaluates a semantic predicate, that predicate is called a *disambiguating semantic predicate*. For efficiency reasons, ANTLR hoists predicates into DFAs only when $LL(*)$ lookahead alone is insufficient to distinguish alternatives.

For semantic predicates to fully resolve a nondeterminism, you must *cover* all alternatives that contribute to the nondeterminism, as shown in the following grammar:

```
a : {p}? A
  | {q}? A
  ;
```

Predicates implicitly specify the precedence of the conflicting alternatives. Those predicated alternatives specified earlier have precedence over predicated alternatives specified later. Generally speaking, parsers evaluate semantic predicates in the order specified among the alternatives. For this grammar, ANTLR generates the following DFA:

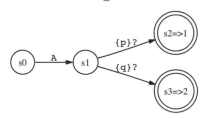

If **A** is the next symbol of lookahead and p evaluates to true, the DFA predicts alternative one; otherwise, if **A** and q, the DFA predicts alternative two. The following Java implementation clarifies the functionality:

```
int alt1=2;
int LA1_0 = input.LA(1);
if ( (LA1_0==A) ) {
    if ( (p) ) { alt1=1; }
    else if ( (q) ) { alt1=2; }
    else {
        NoViableAltException nvae =
            new NoViableAltException(
            "2:1: a : ({...}? A | {...}? A );", 1, 1, input);
        throw nvae;
    }
}
```

ANTLR can also hoist a predicate out of its original rule into the prediction decision for another rule. The following grammar is equivalent to the previous version in that ANTLR generates the same prediction DFA for rule **a**:

```
// ANTLR hoists {p}? and {q}? into a's prediction decision
a : b
  | c
  ;
b : {p}? A ;
c : {q}? A ;
```

This nonlocal hoisting allows you to specify the semantics and syntax for language constructs together in the same place. Here is a commonly used rule that indicates when an identifier is a type name:

```
// typename when lookahead token is ID and isType says text is a type
typename : {isType(input.LT(1))}? ID ;
```

The next section explains what happens if you leave off one of the predicates.

Alternatives That ANTLR Implicitly Covers

As a convenience, you can cover just $n-1$ alternatives with predicates for n conflicting alternatives. The following rule is perfectly fine even though it has two alternatives and just one predicate:

```
a : {p}? A
  | A
  ;
```

ANTLR implicitly covers this special case of an uncovered final conflicting alternative with {true}? as sort of an **else** clause. ANTLR computes a DFA with one real predicate, p, and one implied predicate, true:

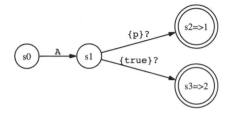

lThis feature also automatically covers the exit branch of a looping subrule, as shown in the following rule:

```
loop: ( {p1}? A )+ A
    ;
```

Upon lookahead **A** and p, the rule stays in the loop. Because of the implied order between conflicting alternatives, ANTLR cannot add {true}? unless the uncovered alternatives is last. In general, ANTLR must assume that the nth predicate is the complement of the union of the other n-1 predicates. Consider the same grammar as before, but with the predicate on the second alternative instead of the first:

```
a : A
  | {q}? A
  ;
```

ANTLR generates the following DFA:

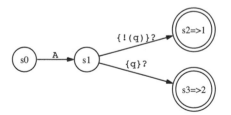

If ANTLR assumed predicate true implicitly covered the first alternative, the second alternative covered with q would be unreachable because the first predicate would always win.

If you fail to cover all nondeterministic alternatives implicitly or explicitly, ANTLR will give you a nondeterminism warning. This rule:

```
a : {p}? A
  | A
  | A
  ;
```

results in the following warning:

```
warning(200): t.g:2:5: Decision can match input such as "A"
using multiple alternatives: 1, 2, 3
As a result, alternative(s) 3,2 were disabled for that input
warning(201): t.g:2:5: The following alternatives are unreachable: 2,3
```

Supplying a semantic predicate for all conflicting alternatives is not always sufficient to resolve nondeterminisms because ANTLR can hoist predicates out of their original rules. The next section illustrates a situation where a single predicate does not sufficiently cover a nondeterministic lookahead sequence.

Insufficiently Covered Nondeterministic Lookahead Sequences

ANTLR assumes you know what you're doing when you specify semantic predicates that disambiguate alternatives, but it does its best to identify situations where you have not given a complete solution. ANTLR will warn you if you have insufficiently covered an alternative rather than simply forgotten to add one.[1] In the following grammar, lookahead token **A** predicts both alternatives of rule **a**:

```
grammar T;
a : b
  | A          // implicitly covered with !predicates from first alternative
  ;
b : {q}? A
  | A          // alternative not covered
  ;
```

The pure *LL(*)* prediction DFA for **a** is, therefore, nondeterministic because **A** labels multiple transitions (predicts more than one alternative). ANTLR looks for semantic predicates to resolve the conflict. It hoists {q}? from **b** into the prediction DFA for **a**, but a problem still exists. ANTLR warns the following:

```
warning(203): t.g:3:5: The following alternatives are insufficiently
covered with predicates: 2
warning(200): t.g:3:5: Decision can match input such as "A"
using multiple alternatives: 1, 2
As a result, alternative(s) 2 were disabled for that input
warning(201): t.g:3:5: The following alternatives are unreachable: 2
```

---

1. Paul Lucas brought the issue of insufficiently covered alternatives to my attention at the ANTLR2004 workshop at the University of San Francisco.

ANTLR notices that not every path to an **A** token reachable from the first alternative of **a** is covered by a predicate—only the first alternative of **b** has a predicate. As a result, ANTLR warns you about the uncovered nondeterministic lookahead sequence. Note that the lookahead decision for rule **b** is OK because it has one predicate for two **A** alternatives. Without this "flow analysis," subtle and difficult-to-find bugs would appear in your grammars. The next section shows how ANTLR combines predicates when it does find sufficient predicates to cover a lookahead sequence.

Combining Multiple Predicates

When ANTLR finds more than one predicate reachable from a decision left edge, it combines them with the && and || operators to preserve the semantics. For example, in the following grammar, ANTLR can see two predicates for the first alternative, p1 and p2:

```
a : {p1}? {p2}? A
  | {q}? A
  ;
```

The grammar results in the following prediction DFA:

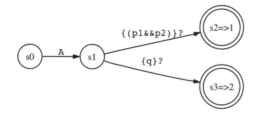

ANTLR combines sequences of predicates with the && operator. Looking at the grammar, it is clear that the semantic validity of applying the first alternative is p1&&p2. Both predicates must be true for the alternative to be semantically valid.

When combining multiple predicates taken from different alternatives, however, ANTLR combines the alternative predicates with the || operator. Consider the following grammar where rule **a**'s decision is nondeterministic upon token **A**:

```
a : b
  | {p}? A
  ;
b : {q1}? A
  | {q2}? A
  ;
```

ANTLR creates the following DFA:

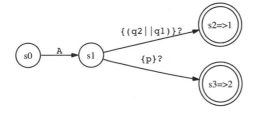

Rule **b** can match token **A** in either of two semantic contexts: q1 or q2; hence, those predicates must be ||'d together to specify the semantic applicability of the first alternative of rule **a**.

Naturally, combinations also work:

```
a : {r}? b
  | {p}? A
  ;
b : {q1}? A
  | {q2}? A
  ;
```

This results in the following DFA:

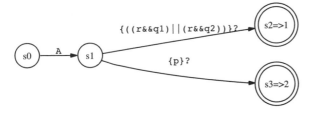

The DFA says that rule **a** can match an **A** via the first alternative if r and q1 are true or r and q2 are true. Otherwise, rule **a** can match **A** via the second alternative if p.

Decisions with Both Deterministic and Nondeterministic Alternatives

ANTLR properly handles the case where a subset of the alternatives are nondeterministic and when there are multiple conflicting alternatives. The following grammar has three alternatives that match **A**, but there are sufficient predicates to resolve the conflict:

```
a : {p}? A
  | B
  | A
  | {q}? A
  ;
```

ANTLR generates the following prediction DFA:

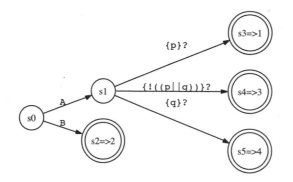

The important observation is that, upon input **B**, the DFA immediately predicts the second alternative without evaluating a semantic predicate. Upon token **A**, however, the DFA must evaluate the semantic predicates in the order specified in the grammar. The second alternative is semantically valid when the other **A** alternatives are invalid: !p and !q or equivalently !(p||q).

The final issue related to disambiguating semantic predicates is that DFAs must evaluate predicates within their syntactic context.

Evaluating Predicates in the Proper Syntactic Context

When ANTLR hoists semantic predicates into prediction DFAs, it must carry along the syntactic context in which it found the predicates. Consider the following grammar. ANTLR resolves rule **a**'s nondeterministic prediction DFA with the predicates p1 and p2.

```
a : b
  | {p2}? ID
  ;
b : {p1}? ID // evaluate only upon ID not INT
  | INT
  ;
```

A predicate covers every path reaching an **ID** reference. But what about **INT**? Both **INT** and **ID** syntactically predict the first alternative of rule **a**. It turns out that it is important for the DFA to avoid evaluating p1 upon **INT**. For example, p1 might look up the token in the symbol table, which makes no sense for **INT**; worse, looking it up might cause an exception.

ANTLR generates the following DFA:

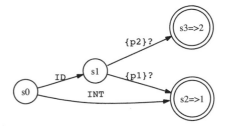

Token **INT** immediately predicts alternative one without using a predicate. It is only after seeing **ID** in s1 that the DFA evaluates the predicates.

As you have seen, ANTLR hoists disambiguating semantic predicates only when the *LL(*)* lookahead is insufficient to distinguish between alternatives. Sometimes, however, you always want ANTLR to hoist a predicate into the decision DFA, as explained in the next section.

13.2 Turning Rules On and Off Dynamically with Gated Semantic Predicates

Sometimes you want to distinguish between alternatives that are not syntactically ambiguous. For example, you might want to turn off some language features dynamically such as the Java **assert** keyword or GCC C extensions. This requires a semantic predicate to turn off an alternative even though the enclosing decision is deterministic. But, disambiguating semantic predicates are not hoisted into deterministic decisions. ANTLR introduces a new kind of predicate called a *gated semantic predicate* that is always hoisted into the decision. Gated semantic predicates use the syntax {*pred*}?=>, as the following grammar demonstrates:

```
stat: 'if' ...
    | {allowAssert}?=> 'assert' expr
    ...
    ;
```

To see the difference between disambiguating semantic predicates and gated semantic predicates, contrast the following grammar:

```
a : A
  | {p}? B
  ;
```

with the following grammar:

```
a : A
  | {p}?=> B
  ;
```

In the first version, with the disambiguating semantic predicate, ANTLR ignores the predicate because syntax alone is sufficient to predict alternatives. In the second version, however, the gated semantic predicate is included in rule **a**'s decision:

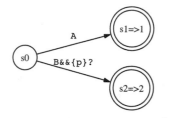

The DFA predicts alternative two only when p is true. The transition from s0 to s2 effectively disappears when p is false; the only viable alternative would be the first one.

In general, gated predicates appear along the transitions along all paths leading to the accept state predicting the associated gated alternative. For example, the following grammar can match input .. either by matching the first alternative of rule **a** once or by matching the second alternative twice:

```
a : {p}?=> ('.'|'-')+
  | '.'
  ;
```

The grammar distinguishes between the two cases using the p gated semantic predicate. The following DFA does the appropriate prediction:

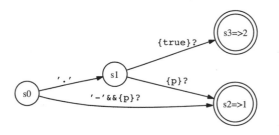

The DFA guards access to accept state s2, predicting alternative one, with gated predicate p. But, notice that the DFA doesn't test p on the transition from states s0 to s1. That transition is common to both alternatives one and two. When p is false, the DFA must still be able to match . to alternative two.

Remember that ANTLR hoists predicates out of one rule to use in the decision for another rule. In this respect, gated predicates behave just like disambiguating semantic predicates. In the following grammar, the predicate is hoisted from rule **b** into the prediction decision for rule **a**:

```
a : A
  | b // as if you had used {p}?=> here too
  ;
b : {p}?=> B
  ;
```

ANTLR generates the following DFA:

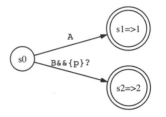

Even though syntax alone yields a deterministic prediction decision, rule **a**'s DFA uses the gated semantic predicates hoisted from **b**.

The next section describes the third and final predicate variation.

13.3 Verifying Semantic Conditions with Validating Semantic Predicates

Although most semantic analysis occurs in a separate phase for complicated language applications, sometimes it is convenient to place semantic checks within a grammar that throw an exception upon failure like syntax errors do. For example, in the following grammar, the recognizer throws a FailedPredicateException if the input program references a variable without a prior definition where the highlighted region is the code generated for the validating semantic predicate:

```
grammar t;
expr:   INT
    |   ID {isDefined($ID.text)}?
    ;
```

Such a predicate is called a *validating semantic predicate*, and ANTLR generates the following code for rule **expr**:

```
public void expr() throws RecognitionException {
    Token ID1=null;
    try {
        «alternative-prediction-code»
        switch (alt1) {
            case 1 :
            // t.g:2:9: INT
            match(input,INT,FOLLOW_INT_in_expr10);
            break;
            case 2 :
            // t.g:3:7: ID {...}?
            ID1=(Token)input.LT(1);
            match(input,ID,FOLLOW_ID_in_expr18);
            if ( !(isDefined(ID1.getText())) ) {
                throw new FailedPredicateException(input,
                            "expr", "isDefined($ID.text)");
            }
            break;
        }
    }
    catch (RecognitionException re) {
    reportError(re);
    recover(input,re);
    }
}
```

All semantic predicates result in such predicate validation code regardless of how else ANTLR uses the predicates.

Validating semantic predicates do not alter the decision-making process—they throw exceptions after the recognizer sees an erroneous statement. The true power of semantic predicates, however, is their ability to alter the parse upon runtime information. The next section examines such disambiguating semantic predicates in detail.

At this point, you have all the details about how ANTLR uses semantic predicates, but you need to know about some limitations imposed on predicate expressions.

13.4 Limitations on Semantic Predicate Expressions

Semantic predicates must be free of side effects in that repeated evaluations must return the same result and not affect other predicates. Further, the order in which DFAs evaluate predicates must not matter within the same decision. Alternatives specified first still have priority over subsequent alternatives, but the DFA must be able to evaluate predicates in any order. Here is an example grammar where the predicate is not free of side effects:

```
a
@init {int i=0;}
  : {i++==0}? A  // BAD! side effects in predicate
  | A
  ;
```

ANTLR generates the following code:

```
if ( (LA1_0==A) ) {
►     if ( (i++==0) ) {  // increments i here
►         alt1=1;
►     }
►     // i is now 1
      else if ( (true) ) { alt1=2; }
      else «error»;
}
else «error»;
switch (alt1) {
    case 1 :
        // t.g:5:4: {...}? A
►       // i is not 0 anymore so exception will be thrown
►       if ( !(i++==0) ) { // tests i (and increments) again here
►           throw new FailedPredicateException(input, "a", "i++==0");
►       }
        match(input,A,FOLLOW_A_in_a18);
        break;
    «alternative-two»
}
```

The highlighted lines derive from the predicate. The first time the DFA evaluates the predicate i is 0, so it predicts alternative one. Upon reaching the code for the first alternative, the recognizer evaluates the predicate again as if it were a simple validating predicate. But i is 1, and the validating predicate fails.

Another limitation on semantic predicates is that they should not reference local variables or parameters. In general, predicates should not reference anything not visible to all rules just in case they are hoisted out of one rule into another's prediction DFA. If you are positive that the predicate will not be hoisted out of the rule, you can use a parameter.

For example, here is a rule that alters prediction as a function of its parameter:

```
/** Do not allow concrete methods (methods with bodies) unless
 *  parameter allowConcrete is true.
 */
method[boolean allowConcrete]
    :    {allowConcrete}?=> methodHead body
    |    methodHead ';'
    ;
```

If ANTLR hoists that predicate out of rule **method**, however, the target compiler will complain about undefined references. Technically, this is a limitation of the target language, not a limitation of semantic predicates or ANTLR. For example, you can usually use attributes or dynamic scopes to overcome limitations related to using parameters and semantic predicates.

Semantic predicates are a powerful means of recognizing context-sensitive language structures by allowing runtime information to drive recognition. But, they are also useful as an implementation vehicle for syntactic predicates, the subject of the next chapter. As we'll see, the fact that ANTLR hoists semantic predicates into decisions only when *LL(*)* fails automatically minimizes how often the recognizer needs to backtrack.

Chapter 14

Syntactic Predicates

A *syntactic predicate* specifies the syntactic validity of applying an alternative just like a semantic predicate specifies the semantic validity of applying an alternative. Syntactic predicates, as we've seen, are parenthesized grammar fragments followed by the => operator. If a syntactic predicate matches, the associated alternative is valid. Syntactic predicates are a simple way to dramatically improve the recognition strength of any *LL*-based recognizer by providing arbitrary lookahead. In practice, this means syntactic predicates let you use write grammars that ANTLR would otherwise reject. For example, Section 12.2, *Resolving Ambiguities and Nondeterminisms*, on page 297 illustrated difficult-to-parse language constructs from Java, C, and C++ that resolve nicely with syntactic predicates.

Syntactic predicates have been available since ANTLR v1.0 (since the early 1990s) and are certainly one of the big reasons why ANTLR became popular. Russell Quong and I invented the term and mechanism.

Syntactic predicates also let you specify the precedence between two or more ambiguous alternatives. If two alternatives can match the same input, ANTLR ordinarily emits a grammar analysis warning. By adding a syntactic predicate, you force the generated recognizer to try the alternatives in order. ANTLR resolves the ambiguity in favor of the first alternative whose predicate matches. Such precedence resolves the ambiguity, and ANTLR does not emit a warning. For example, Section 12.2, *Resolving the If-Then-Else Ambiguity*, on page 304 illustrated how to hush the warning from ANTLR stemming from the classic **if-then-else** ambiguity.

Chapter 12, *Using Semantic and Syntactic Predicates*, on page 283 delineated a number of examples that illustrated how to use syntactic predicates and demonstrated their power. This chapter focuses on the details of their implementation and other information necessary to fully understand syntactic predicates. In particular, we'll see the following:

- ANTLR implements syntactic predicates using semantic predicates.
- Syntactic predicates force the parser to backtrack.
- ANTLRWorks has a number of visualizations that can help you understand backtracking parsers.
- Parsers do not execute actions during the evaluation of syntactic predicates to avoid having to undo them during backtracking.
- Auto-backtracking is a great rapid prototyping mode that automatically inserts a syntactic predicate on the left edge of every alternative.
- Memoization is a form of dynamic programming that squirrels away partial parsing results and guarantees linear parsing complexity.
- Syntactic predicates can hide true ambiguities in grammars.
- Backtracking does not generally affect the use of embedded grammar actions.

Let's begin with a discussion of how ANTLR incorporates syntactic predicates into the parsing decision-making process.

14.1 How ANTLR Implements Syntactic Predicates

For each syntactic predicate, ANTLR defines a special method[1] that returns true or false depending on whether the predicate's grammar fragment matches the next input symbols. In this way, ANTLR can implement syntactic predicates as semantic predicates that invoke special boolean recognition methods. Consider the following simple non-*LL(*)* grammar that requires backtracking because of the two ambiguous alternatives. As with semantic predicates, you do not have to predicate the final nondeterministic alternative.

```
a : (A)=>A {System.out.println("ok");}
  | A       {System.out.println("this can never be printed");}
  ;
```

ANTLR rephrases the problem in terms of gated semantic predicates by translating the grammar to the following equivalent grammar:

```
a : {input.LA(1)==A}?=> A {System.out.println("ok");}
  | A {System.out.println("this can never be printed");}
  ;
```

---

1. Unfortunately, because of a limitation in Java, the bookkeeping machinery cannot be generalized with any kind of efficiency, resulting in code bloat.

The "this can never be printed" Error

The "this can never be printed" error message (in the first grammar example of Section 14.1, *How ANTLR Implements Syntactic Predicates*, on the preceding page) came out of some Unix program I was using 20 years ago, but I can't remember which one. It cracked me up.

My favorite compiler of all time was the Apple MPW C compiler. If I remember correctly, it gave error messages such as the following:

"Don't you want a ')' to go with that '('?"

When it got really confused, it would say this:

"That ';' came as a complete surprise to me at this point your program."

Pure genius.

To be precise, manually specified syntactic predicates become gated semantic predicates. These syntactic predicates are always evaluated just like gated semantic predicates.

On the other hand, syntactic predicates implicitly added by auto-backtracking mode become regular semantic predicates. Such predicates are evaluated only when *LL(*)* fails to predict an alternative.

The prediction DFA for rule **a** with the gated semantic predicate is as follows:

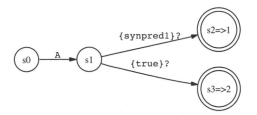

where synpred1() is the method that ANTLR generates to evaluate the syntactic predicate. The DFA indicates that, after seeing **A**, the syntactic predicate chooses between alternative one (s2) and two (s3).

The following straightforward Java code implements the DFA:

```
int alt1=2;
int LA1_0 = input.LA(1); // get first symbol of lookahead
if ( (LA1_0==A) ) {
    if ( (synpred1()) ) { alt1=1; } // test syntactic predicate
    else if ( (true) ) { alt1=2; }  // default to alternative 2
    else {
        if (backtracking>0) {failed=true; return ;}
        «throw-NoViableAltException» // throw only if not backtracking
    }
}
else {
    // no A found; error
    if (backtracking>0) {failed=true; return ;}
    «throw-NoViableAltException» // throw only if not backtracking
}
```

The highlighted sections specify what to do if the prediction code does not find a match. The code indicates that the recognizer should throw an exception unless it is backtracking. If backtracking, the recognizer *Improved in v3.* sets a failed instance variable and returns, which is much faster than throwing an exception in all target languages.[2] ANTLR incorporates that prediction decision code into the method that it generates for rule **a**:

```
public void a() throws RecognitionException {
    «prediction-code»
    try {
        switch (alt1) {
            case 1 :
                match(input,A,FOLLOW_A_in_a14); if (failed) return ;
                if ( backtracking==0 ) {
                    System.out.println("ok");
                }
                break;
            case 2 :
                match(input,A,FOLLOW_A_in_a22); if (failed) return ;
                if ( backtracking==0 ) {
                    System.out.println("this can never be printed");
                }
                break;
        }
    }
    catch (RecognitionException re) {
        reportError(re);
        recover(input,re);
    }
}
```

---

2. According to the NetBeans C/C++ Development Pack team (http://www.netbeans.org), removing exceptions from backtracking in ANTLR v2 sped up recognition rates by about 2.5 times.

The highlighted chunks illustrate how ANTLR generates code for the actions embedded in a grammar. Actions are not executed if the recognizer is backtracking because there is no general mechanism to undo actions (for example, how would you undo a print statement?).

If a syntactic predicate matches for an alternative, the recognizer rewinds the input and matches the alternative again "with feeling." The recognizer rewinds and reparses so that it can execute any actions embedded in the alternative. In this way, you do not really have to worry about how backtracking affects your actions at the cost of some time efficiency.

To avoid using exceptions during backtracking, ANTLR generates extra code to test for recognition failure. For example, you will see code such as the following after every call to a rule's method and after every token match:

```
if (failed) return;
```

In terms of the predicate, ANTLR generates a method that matches the predicate grammar fragment:

```
public void synpred1_fragment() throws RecognitionException {
    match(input,A,FOLLOW_A_in_synpred111); if (failed) return ;
}
```

It also generates method synpred1(), which the semantic predicate invokes. Method synpred1() increases the backtracking level, tests the predicate, rewinds the input, and decreases the backtracking level. backtracking is 0 upon entry to synpred1() unless the recognizer is already backtracking when it enters rule a.

```
public boolean synpred1() {
    backtracking++;
    int start = input.mark();
    try {
        synpred1_fragment(); // can never throw exception
    } catch (RecognitionException re) {
        System.err.println("impossible: "+re);
    }
    boolean success = !failed;
    input.rewind(start);
    backtracking--;
    failed=false;
    return success;
}
```

By examining the code ANTLR generates, you'll understand precisely how ANTLR implements syntactic predicates. In the next section, you'll see how ANTLRWorks makes syntactic predicates easier to understand by visualizing parse trees and prediction DFAs.

14.2 Using ANTLRWorks to Understand Syntactic Predicates

ANTLRWorks provides an excellent means to become familiar with the backtracking process. For example, in the following grammar, rule **backtrack** is non-*LL(*)*. It has three alternatives, each requiring arbitrary lookahead to see past the recursive structure in rules **e** and **cast** to the symbols beyond.

`synpred/b.g`

```
grammar b;
backtrack
    :   (cast ';')=> cast ';'
    |   (e ';')=>    e ';'
    |                e '.'
    ;

cast:   '(' ID ')' ;

e   :   '(' e ')'
    |   ID
        ;

ID  :   'a'..'z'+ ;
```

Rule **backtrack** matches input ((a)); with the second alternative; hence, ANTLRWorks shows the parse tree[3] for both the syntactic predicate and the actual match for the alternative:

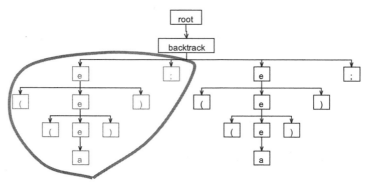

---

3. The lassos look like a four-year-old drew them on purpose—mainly I like the way they look, but also their roundness makes it easy for you to distinguish them from the rigid, automatically drawn diagrams.

The first two subtrees of rule **backtrack** (the lassoed region) represent the successful parse of ((a)); by the syntactic predicate (e ';')=> in the second alternative. Note that the syntactic predicate in the first alternative is avoided altogether because ((at the start of the input cannot begin a **cast**. The prediction DFA shown in Figure 14.1, on the following page, illustrates this. The only input that routes through the DFA to the syntactic predicate for alternative one (at s8) is (a);.

For input ((a))., however, the syntactic predicate in the second alternative fails. The trailing period does not match, and the recognizer matches the third alternative instead. The successful parse yields a parse tree with one (failed) predicate evaluation, followed by the actual parse tree built from matching alternative three of rule **backtrack**:

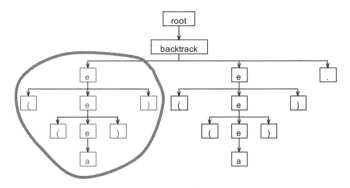

The parser does not need to backtrack in order to choose between alternatives two and three once the first predicate fails (input ((does not match predicate cast ';'. State s4 in the prediction DFA shown in Figure 14.1, on the next page illustrates that if the second syntactic predicates fails, the DFA can immediately predict alternative three by traversing s2 to s6.

Using ANTLRWorks to visualize decision DFAs and parse trees helps even more when your recognizer needs to start backtracking when it is already backtracking, the subject of the next section.

14.3 Nested Backtracking

While attempting one syntactic predicate, the recognizer might encounter another decision that requires it to backtrack. In this case, the recognizer enters a nested backtracking situation. There are no implementation problems, but nested backtracking can be the source of some confusion (and is the source of the worst-case exponential time

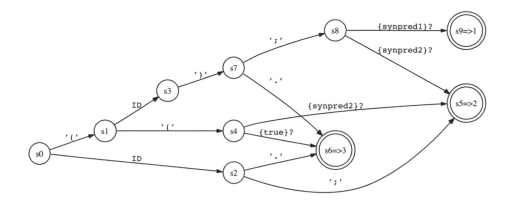

Figure 14.1: THE PREDICTION DFA FOR RULE **BACKTRACK** ILLUSTRATING WHEN THE RECOGNIZER MUST EVALUATE SYNTACTIC PREDICATES

complexity). The current nesting level is stored in instance variable backtracking. Consider the following grammar that matches an expression followed by either ';' or '.'. An expression, in turn, is either a type-cast, a conventional nested expression, or a simple identifier.

synpred/nested.g

```
grammar nested;

a : (e ';')=> e ';'
  | e '.'
  ;

e : ('(' e ')' e)=> '(' e ')' e  // type cast
  | '(' e ')'                    // nested expression
  | ID
  ;

ID      :       'a'..'z'+ ;
```

Input ((x))y; forces the recognizer to backtrack. Let's examine how ANTLRWorks visualizes the backtracking. When the recognizer completes the predicate in the first alternative of rule **a** and is about to match the first alternative for real, ANTLRWorks shows the partial parse tree, as shown in Figure 14.2, on the facing page. The outer lasso shows all the nodes associated with matching the predicate in rule **a**, and the inner lasso shows the nodes associated with matching the predicate in the first

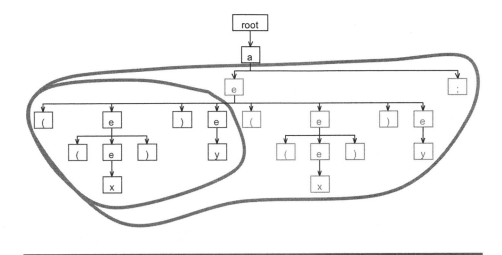

Figure 14.2: PARTIAL PARSE TREE FOR ((X))Y; SHOWING SPECULATION OF SYNTACTIC PREDICATES IN RULES **A** AND **E**

alternative of rule **e**. At the outer level, rule **a**'s predicate matches rule **e** followed by ';', which is what you see as the two children of **a**'s parse tree node. The predicate in rule **e** matches '(' e ')' e, which is what you see as the first four children of the topmost **e** node. That topmost node shows the speculative match for the predicate and then the real match for the first alternative of rule **e**.

Because ANTLR-generated recognizers parse each alternative predicted by successful syntactic predicates twice, the full parse tree for input ((x))y; repeats the nodes in the outer lasso, making the tree twice as wide, as shown in Figure 14.3, on the next page. Figure 14.3, on the following page is the right half of the full parse tree, and Figure 14.2, is the left half.

The recognizer does a lot of extra work during nested backtracks. For example, the recognizer matches ((x))y against the predicate in the first alternative of rule **e** twice. It also matches the inside of the typecast, (x), multiple times. See Section 14.5, *Memoization*, on page 335 to learn how ANTLR can save partial parsing results to avoid repeated parsing at the cost of some memory.

Now consider input ((x)); that also matches alternative one in rule **a**. While evaluating the outermost **e** invocation, the second alternative of **e** matches input ((x)). This means the syntactic predicates in the first

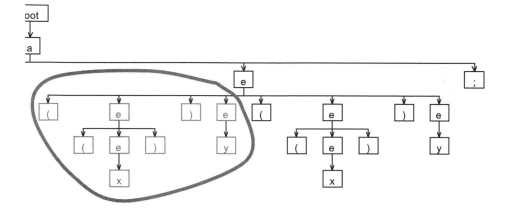

Figure 14.3: PARTIAL PARSE TREE FOR ((X))Y; SHOWING REEVALUATION OF SYNTACTIC PREDICATE IN RULE **e**

alternative of **e** fails. Figure 14.4, on the next page, shows the partial parse tree for this input. The inner lasso (in red in the PDF version) shows the nodes matched until the predicate failed. The outer lasso shows that, nonetheless, the syntactic predicate in the first alternative of rule **a** succeeded.

Specifying lots of predicates to resolve non-*LL(*)* decisions can be a hassle and can make your grammar less readable. The next section describes how you can simply turn on automatic backtracking, which automatically engages backtracking for non-*LL(*)* decisions.

14.4 Auto-backtracking

Altering your grammar to suit the needs of the underlying *LL(*)* parsing algorithm can be a hassle, but so can adding syntactic predicates all over the place. Instead, you have the option to leave the grammar as is and turn on the **backtrack** option:

```
grammar Cpp;
options {backtrack=true;}
...
```

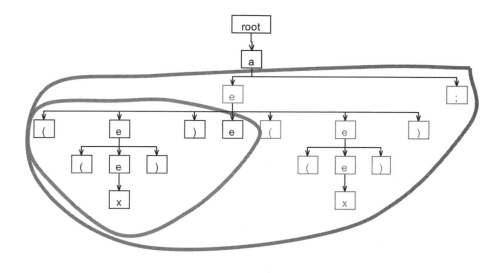

Figure 14.4: PARTIAL PARSE TREE FOR ((X)); SHOWING SPECULATION OF SYNTACTIC PREDICATES IN RULES A AND E WHERE THE SYNTACTIC PREDICATE IN THE FIRST ALTERNATIVE OF E FAILS

The idea is that, when *LL(*)* analysis fails, the recognizers should automatically backtrack at runtime to figure it out. This feature provides a "newbie," or rapid prototyping, mode that makes it fast to build a grammar. After you have created a correct and readable grammar, you can optimize the grammar a little to reduce the amount of backtracking by tweaking rules to make them *LL(*)*.

ANTLR implements the auto-backtracking mode by adding a syntactic predicate to the left edge of every alternative. These implicit syntactic predicates become regular (nongated) semantic predicates. *LL(*)* analysis uses such semantic predicates only in non-*LL(*)* decisions; that is, recognizers evaluate the predicates only when *LL(*)* fails.

In contrast, manually specified syntactic predicates become gated semantic predicates; they are always evaluated when predicting the associated alternative. By converting implicit syntactic predicates to nongated semantic predicates, you get clarity, power, and efficiency.

To illustrate this, here is a version of the **nested** grammar from earlier rewritten to use auto-backtracking mode; it is much easier to read:

```
grammar nested;
options {backtrack=true;}
a : e ';'
  | e '.'
  ;

e : '(' e ')' e // type cast
  | '(' e ')'    // nested expression
  | ID
  ;

ID: 'a'..'z'+ ;
```

You still need manually specified syntactic predicates in some cases, however. To illustrate how manually specified predicates differ from auto-backtracking syntactic predicates, consider the following grammar. It reflects a situation where you want to treat identifiers s and sx differently depending on whether they followed by an integer. The syntactic predicates examine more of the input than the associated alternatives match (consume).

synpred/P.g

```
lexer grammar T;
/** For input s followed by INT, match only s; must exec action1.
 *  For sx followed by INT, match only sx; exec action2.
 */
ID : ('s' INT)=> 's'                      {action1;}
   | ('sx' INT)=> 'sx'                    {action2;}
   | 'a'..'z' ('a'..'z'|'0'..'9')*  {action3;}
   ;
INT : '0'..'9'+ ;
```

Input s must trigger action3 unless followed by an integer. In that case, s must trigger action1 but still consume only the s. The same is true for input sx. Without the syntactic predicates, ANTLR emits a warning about the same input predicting multiple alternatives. ANTLR resolves the ambiguity by forcing s to always predict alternative one. sx would always predict alternative two. Using auto-backtracking mode won't work in this case as a replacement for manually specified syntactic predicates. Auto-backtracking adds predicates to each alternative, but they would not have the **INT** reference in them. Clearly, you would not get the desired functionality.

When using auto-backtracking mode, ANTLR grammars behave like Bryan Ford's *parser expression grammars* (PEGs) [For04]. Several interesting PEG-based parser generators are available, including Ford's original implementation [For02] and Robert Grimm's Rats! [Gri06]. I also want to mention James Cordy's TXL [Cor06] that has ordered alternatives but without syntactic predicates and without partial result memoization, the topic of the next section.

Although auto-backtracking is useful, it can be very expensive in time. The next section describes how recognizers can record partial parsing results to guarantee linear time at the cost of memory.

14.5 Memoization

New in v3.

Backtracking is an exponentially complex algorithm in the worst case. The recognizer might have to try multiple alternatives in a decision, which, in turn, might invoke rules that also must try their alternatives, and so on. This nested backtracking yields a combinatorial explosion of speculative parsing. For any given input position, a backtracking parser might attempt the same rule many times, resulting in a lot of wasted effort. In contrast, a parser without backtracking examines the same input position at most once for a given rule, resulting in linear time complexity.

If, on the other hand, the recognizer remembers the result of attempting rules at the various input positions, it can avoid all the wasted effort. Saving partial results achieves linear complexity at the cost of potentially large amounts of memory.

This process of remembering partial recognition results is a form of dynamic programming called *memoization* or, more specifically in the parsing arena, as *packrat parsing* [For02]. Bryan Ford introduced the technology and coined the term.[4] Because ANTLR uses packrat parsing only when *LL(*)* fails, it often generates parsers that are substantially more efficient in time and space than pure packrat parsers such as Grimm's Rats!

The easiest way to demonstrate the benefit of memoization is to examine the vivid differences in the parse trees for the same input with and without memoization.

---

4. See http://pdos.csail.mit.edu/~baford/packrat for more information about packrat parsing.

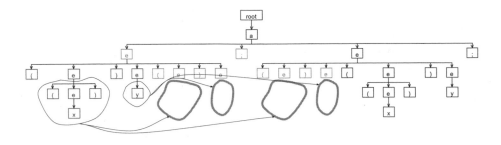

Figure 14.5: PARSE TREE FOR ((X))Y; SHOWING REDUNDANT PARSE SUB-TREE ELIMINATION FOR TWO SUCCESSFUL INVOCATIONS OF RULE E DURING EVALUATION OF E'S SYNTACTIC PREDICATE

Let's revisit the nested syntactic predicate grammar from Section 14.3, *Nested Backtracking*, on page 329 but with the addition of the **memoize** option:

synpred/memoize.g

```
grammar memoize;
options {memoize=true;}

a : (e ';')=> e ';'
  | e '.'
  ;

e : ('(' e ')' e)=> '(' e ')' e  // type cast
  | '(' e ')'                    // nested expression
  | ID
  ;

ID: 'a'..'z'+ ;
```

Reexamine Figure 14.2, on page 331, and Figure 14.3, on page 332. Again with input ((x))y;, compare those figures to Figure 14.5. Focus on the overall shape of the parse trees here rather than the individual nodes. Notice that the memoized version is missing redundant subtrees. The lassos indicate portions of the parse that the parser avoids because of memoization. The thin lassos and arrows indicate which partial results the parser reused. The nested syntactic predicate in rule **e** succeeds, as does the outer syntactic predicates in the first alternative of rule **a**. When that outer predicate succeeds, rule **a** reenters **e** during the actual parse of the first alternative of rule **a**. Rule **e** again enters the ('(' e ')' e)=> syntactic predicate. Thanks to memoization, the

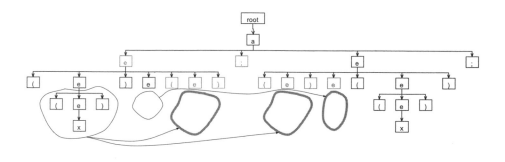

Figure 14.6: PARSE TREE FOR ((X)); SHOWING REDUNDANT PARSE SUB-
TREE ELIMINATION FOR ONE SUCCESSFUL AND ONE FAILED INVOCATION
OF RULE e DURING EVALUATION OF e'S SYNTACTIC PREDICATE

parser does not have to enter the two e references for that predicate. It already knows they will succeed.

Memoization also records failures to avoid reparsing rules that it knows won't succeed. Compare Figure 14.4, on page 333, to Figure 14.6, again with input ((x));. The syntactic predicate in rule a's first alternative invokes rule e. Rule e then evaluates the syntactic predicate in its first alternative. That syntactic predicate recursively invokes rule e and records success for (x) (the '(' e ')' portion of the predicate). Because no identifier comes after the parentheses and before the ';', the parser records failure for the second invocation of rule e in the '(' e ')' e predicate. Failing the predicate, rule e matches its second alternative instead. This allows the outer syntactic predicate in the first alternative of rule a to succeed. During the subsequent real parse of a's first alternative, the parser invokes e immediately and reencounters e's syntactic predicate in its first alternative. Memoization tells the parser that the first e reference in the syntactic predicate will succeed, but the second will fail. The parser fails just as it did before while evaluating a's predicate, but this time, the parser skips the redundant parse thanks to memoization. The lassos in Figure 14.6, show redundant parse subtree elimination and the original subtree computation.

To implement memoization, ANTLR inserts code at the beginning of each rule recognition method to check for prior attempts. Naturally, the parser can avoid parsing a rule only when backtracking:

```
if ( backtracking>0 && alreadyParsedRule(input,rule-number) ) {return;}
```

If the recognizer has already attempted this rule and at the same input position, the recognizer seeks ahead to where the rule finished parsing last time. Then the rule returns immediately, effectively skipping all the previously done parsing work. Moreover, the parser has effectively handled the rule in constant time. If the rule failed during the previous attempt, the rule also returns immediately but sets an error flag indicating failure.

To do the actual memoization, ANTLR inserts code at the end of a rule. This code records whether the rule completed successfully at this input position:

```
if ( backtracking>0 ) {
    memoize(input, rule-number, rule-starting-input-position);
}
```

In other words, the **memoize** option alters code generation from this:

```
public void r() throws RecognitionException {
    try {
        «r-prediction»
        «r-matching»
    }
    catch (RecognitionException re) {
        reportError(re);
        recover(input,re);
    }
}
```

to the following:

```
public void r() throws RecognitionException {
    int r_StartIndex = input.index();
    try {
        if ( backtracking>0 && alreadyParsedRule(input,r-index) ) {
            return;
        }
        «r-prediction»
        «r-matching»
    }
    catch (RecognitionException re) {
        reportError(re);
        recover(input,re);
    }
    finally {
        if ( backtracking>0 ) { memoize(input,r-index,r_StartIndex); }
    }
}
```

The «r-prediction» and «r-matching» code blocks are the same as is the usual **try/catch** surrounding them to handle error recovery. The difference is that, when backtracking, the rule immediately returns if it has already parsed the input starting from the current input position. If there is no memoized result for this rule, the method memoizes success or failure after it finishes parsing.

A word about memoization efficiency: thanks to *LL(*)* prediction DFA, recognizers often avoid backtracking even in the presence of multiple syntactic predicates. This has the side effect of requiring much less storage space than a pure packrat parser because ANTLR-generated parsers are not always backtracking. This does not mean, however, that ANTLR optimizes away all unnecessary memoization.

In the future, ANTLR will have a "redundant reevaluation hotspot analysis" feature that you can turn on at runtime to figure out which rules are invoked repeatedly at the same input position.

Recording the result of each rule invocation during backtracking is expensive in memory and time, often actually slowing your recognizer down instead of speeding it up. The general rule is that you should use memoization on a rule-by-rule basis. Determining which rules to memoize can be difficult just by looking at the grammar. In general, look for sequences of syntactic predicates within the same decision that invoke the same rule directly or indirectly, as shown in the following grammar:

```
/** This rule must backtrack because of the common left prefix
 *  that is not only arbitrarily long but has nested structure;
 *  hence non-LL(*).
 */
s
options {backtrack=true;}
  : e ';' // invoke e once
  | e '.' // invoke e twice at same position
  | e '!' // default, invoke e "with feeling"
  ;

/** This rule should memoize parsing results because it is invoked
 *  repeatedly by rule s at the same input position.
 */
e
options {memoize=true;}
  : '(' e ')'
  | ID
  ;
```

You want to turn on memoization for the repeatedly invoked rule **e**, not the invoking rule. In this grammar, input ((x))! causes the parser to enter rule **e** from the implicit syntactic predicate in the first alternative of rule **s**. At the end of that invocation, the recognizer records the successful parse of **e**. The second invocation of **e** from the second alternative of **s** can use that result to avoid reparsing **e**. The implicit syntactic predicates for rule **s**'s first two alternatives fail because the input ends with '!', not ';' or ':'. After the syntactic predicate for alternative two of **s** fails, the parser begins nonspeculative matching of **s**'s third alternative. At this point, the recognizer is no longer speculating because the third alternative is clearly the final choice. Even though the recognizer knows that rule **e** will succeed, it must enter rule **e** to execute any potential embedded actions (none in this case).

In the previous sections, you saw that ANTLR can automatically backtrack to handle just about any grammar, and you saw how that can be done in linear time. Unfortunately, automatic backtracking comes at the cost of some potential pitfalls when you build grammars—automatic backtracking can hide grammar ambiguities.

14.6 Grammar Hazards with Syntactic Predicates

If you turn on the **backtrack** option at the grammar level, you will not get any static grammar analysis warnings because the generated recognizer can resolve any non-$LL(*)$ decisions at runtime by backtracking. Although this is a good way to rapidly prototype a language, the lack of static analysis can hide a number of serious problems with your grammar. Ultimately, your best bet is to selectively turn on backtracking at the rule level to resolve non-$LL(*)$ decisions (assuming you don't want to alter the grammar instead).

This section describes a number of situations where you will not get what you want despite the lack of warnings from ANTLR. These hazards are inherent to the backtracking strategy, not a limitation of ANTLR.

The simplest way to explain the problem is with the following example grammar where the **k** option artificially constrains grammar analysis to a single symbol of lookahead:

```
parser grammar t;
s
options {k=1;}  // can't see past ID
  : ID
  | ID ';'
  ;
```

ANTLR reports this:

```
warning(200): t.g:4:5: Decision can match input such as
"ID" using multiple alternatives: 1, 2
As a result, alternative(s) 2 were disabled for that input
warning(201): t.g:4:5: The following alternatives are
unreachable: 2
```

With only a single symbol of lookahead, the recognizer cannot see past the **ID** in order to properly predict an alternative. Now, turn on auto-backtracking to allow ANTLR to resolve the conflict at runtime with backtracking:

```
parser grammar t;
options {backtracking=true;}
s
options {k=1;}  // force backtracking
  : ID
  | ID ';'        // unreachable
  ;
```

ANTLR issues no warnings, but the grammar can't ever match input x; even though that is clearly the intention. Syntactic predicates remove ambiguity by ordering alternatives, but just because a decision is un-ambiguous doesn't mean you get what you expect. The second alternative of rule **s** is unreachable because the first alternative will always win when **ID** is the next input symbol. The implied predicate on the first alternative is (ID)=>, which says "match this alternative if the first symbol of lookahead is an ID." The way to fix this is simply to reorder the alternatives:

```
parser grammar t;
options {backtracking=true;}
s
options {k=1;}  // force backtracking
  : ID ';'
  | ID
  ;
```

These hazards typically emerge only after extensive unit testing. To illustrate a less obvious hazard, recall the Java grammar from Section 11.5, *Nondeterministic Decisions*, on page 272 that matched a code block in rule **decl** as well as rule **stat**. Rule **slist** is ambiguous because both alternatives can match the same input construct, {...}:

```
options {backtrack=true;}
...
slist:  decl // can match {...} as default ctor
    |   stat // code block {...} is UNREACHABLE!
    ;
```

Turning on auto-backtracking mode will hush any ANTLR grammar warnings because ANTLR can then silently choose **decl** over **stat** for input that matches both alternatives. Clearly, though, turning on auto-backtracking is not the solution. You should refactor the grammar, as shown in Section 11.5, *Nondeterministic Decisions*, on page 272. Most grammars are unambiguous, and therefore, you do not want to hide improperly resolved *LL(*)* nondeterminisms by choosing alternatives in the order presented.

The next kind of grammar hazard involves optional rules and alternatives, which are commonly used in grammars. Sometimes an optional alternative renders further alternatives in that decision unreachable, as illustrated in the following grammar that ANTLR processes without warning:

synpred/unreachable.g

```
grammar unreachable;

slist
    : (var)=>var ';' {System.out.println("slist alt 1");}
    |            ';' {System.out.println("slist alt 2");}
    ;

var
    : 'int' ID      {System.out.println("match var");}
    |               {System.out.println("bypass var");}
    ;

ID: 'a'..'z'+ ;
WS: (' '|'\n'|'\r')+ {skip();} ;
```

Because the first alternative invokes an optional rule, **var**, the recognizer will not know what to do upon lookahead symbol ';' because both alternatives match the simple ';'. Because of the syntactic predicates, ANTLR assumes you know what you're doing and does not warn you about the nondeterminism. The syntactic predicates assumes that you mean to order the alternatives in terms of precedence. Without the syntactic predicate, however, ANTLR does warn you:

```
$ java org.antlr.Tool unreachable.g
ANTLR Parser Generator  Version 3.0  1989-2007
warning(200): unreachable.g:4:5: Decision can match input such as
"';'" using multiple alternatives: 1, 2
As a result, alternative(s) 2 were disabled for that input
warning(201): unreachable.g:4:5: The following alternatives are unreachable: 2
```

This highlights that you should use syntactic predicates as sparingly as possible to avoid hiding grammar conflicts.

Take a look at the prediction DFA for the decision in rule **slist**:

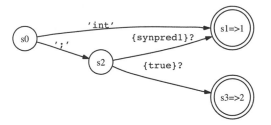

The DFA transitions from s0 to s2 upon input ; and then uses the syntactic predicate synpred1() to distinguish between alternatives one and two (predicted by s1 and s3, respectively). The syntactic predicate will always return true because even if the first alternative of rule **var** fails, the second alternative will always succeed because it does not have to match anything. Consequently, rule **slist**'s alternative two is unreachable. Input ; will always force the recognizer to match the second alternative of **var** and the first alternative of **slist**. You can use the following test harness to verify this behavior:

synpred/TestUnreachable.java

```
import java.io.*;
import org.antlr.runtime.*;

public class TestUnreachable {
    public static void main(String[] args) throws Exception {
        unreachableLexer lex =
            new unreachableLexer(new ANTLRInputStream(System.in));
        CommonTokenStream tokens = new CommonTokenStream(lex);
        unreachableParser p = new unreachableParser(tokens);
        p.slist();
    }
}
```

Sending in a valid variable declaration behaves as you would expect, but sending in ; does not execute the action in the second alternative of **slist**. Most likely, given that the grammar designer specifically provided an alternative matching purely a semicolon, this behavior would be unwelcome.

The worst-case scenario for the optional rule hazard results in an infinite loop. Imagine that an EBNF looping construct must backtrack to distinguish between an optional alternative and the implicit exit branch.

This loop will never terminate because you will always choose the optional alternative rather than the exit. The optional alternative matches any symbol; hence, the syntactic predicate's speculative parse will always succeed. Since syntactic predicates tell the recognizer to choose the first alternative that matches, the "stay in the loop" alternative always wins. The following grammar matches an optional list of variable definitions and illustrates exactly such an infinite loop situation:

synpred/infloop.g

```
grammar infloop;

slist
   : ( (var)=> var {System.out.println("in loop");} )+
   ;

var
   : 'int' ID ';' {System.out.println("match var");}
   |              {System.out.println("bypass var");}
   ;

ID: 'a'..'z'+ ;
WS: (' '|'\n'|'\r')+ {skip();} ;
```

It is worth looking at the prediction DFA:

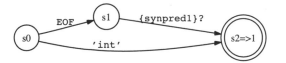

Clearly, the DFA can predict only alternative one, but the syntactic predicate hushes the warning about alternative two being unreachable. Here are the warnings ANTLR emits if the subrule were var+ (without the syntactic predicates):

```
$ java org.antlr.Tool infloop.g
ANTLR Parser Generator  Version 3.0  1989-2007
warning(200): infloop.g:4:44: Decision can match input such as
"{EOF, 'int'}" using multiple alternatives: 1, 2
As a result, alternative(s) 2 were disabled for that input
warning(201): infloop.g:4:44: The following alternatives are
unreachable: 2
$
```

> ### Backtracking and Action Execution in the Maze
>
> While backtracking in the maze, you do not want to record anything in your notebook as you speculatively explore the various paths emanating from a fork. It is difficult to remember what you need to erase after each speculative walk. Worse, some actions are impossible to undo such as print statements or annoying your spouse from your cell phone as you walk the maze. It is easier to ignore actions until you are sure which alternative path you will take. Then, you can write in your notebook (execute actions) as you move down the correct path for the second time.

Using the following test harness, you can verify that this program will not terminate either on a valid variable definition or on an empty input stream.

synpred/TestInfLoop.java

```java
import java.io.*;
import org.antlr.runtime.*;

public class TestInfLoop {
    public static void main(String[] args) throws Exception {
        infloopLexer lex =
            new infloopLexer(new ANTLRInputStream(System.in));
        CommonTokenStream tokens = new CommonTokenStream(lex);
        infloopParser p = new infloopParser(tokens);
        p.slist();
    }
}
```

Fortunately, these grammar hazards are not huge problems as long as you are aware of them. As a general rule, use auto-backtracking mode to resolve non-*LL(*)* conflicts and use manually specified syntactic predicates to explicitly resolve grammar ambiguities. The next section discusses one final potential difficulty when using syntactic predicates.

14.7 Issues with Actions and Syntactic Predicates

ANTLR allows you to embed arbitrary actions (written in the target language) in your grammar, which is a really nice feature unavailable in a lot of recent parser generators. The reason other tools do not support arbitrary actions is because actions often conflict with the parsing strategy. As you saw earlier, ANTLR recognizers always match success-ful alternatives twice—once during backtracking and once "with feeling" to execute any actions.

To avoid executing actions while backtracking, ANTLR generates an **if** statement around all embedded actions that turns the action off unless the backtracking level is 0:

```
if (backtracking==0) { «action» }
```

This implies that you should not define local variables in actions other than the **init** action because the scope of a variable is limited to the **if** statement. ANTLR does not gate **init** actions in and out because they typically include variable declarations. If you need to, you can define your own special action gate expression with a global action:

```
@synpredgate { «my-expr-to-turn-on-actions» }
```

There is another important limitation that ANTLR must impose upon your grammar actions and rules because of backtracking. Consider the following grammar with non-*LL(*)* rule **a** that needs backtracking:

```
grammar t;
a
@init {int y=34;}
  : (b[y] '.')=> b[y] '.'
  |            b[y] ':'
  ;

b[int i]
  : '(' b[i] ')' {System.out.println(i);}
  | 'z'
  ;
```

For syntactic predicate (b[y] '.')=> in the first alternative, ANTLR gener-ates this:

```
public void synpred1_fragment() throws RecognitionException {
    // t.g:5:5: b[y] '.'
    b(y); // TROUBLE! local variable y undefined!
    if (failed) return ;
    // match '.'
    match(input,4,FOLLOW_4_in_synpred144); if (failed) return ;
}
```

Unfortunately, this code will not compile because argument y passed to rule **b** does not exist in synpred1_fragment()'s scope. That argument is essentially an action, albeit a single expression, and ANTLR has taken it out of its original context. ANTLR cannot simply leave it out because the method for rule **b** requires a parameter. Without a parameter on b(), synpred1_fragment() would still not compile.

Fortunately, this problem is not a limitation of the fundamental parsing strategy, and there is a way out using dynamic scoping (Section 6.5, *Dynamic Attribute Scopes for Interrule Communication*, on page 135). We need a solution that does not require the use of method parameters so that syntactic predicates, taken out of context, will compile. But, at the same time, we must still be able to pass information from one rule to another. ANTLR's dynamic scopes are a perfect solution. Here is the equivalent grammar using a dynamic scope in rule **a**:

```
grammar t;
a
scope {
  int i;
}
@init {$a::i=34;}
  : (b '.')=> b '.'
  |          b ':'
  ;

b : '(' b ')' {System.out.println($a::i);}
  | 'z'
  ;
```

This version is not as explicit and is less conventional, but it does yield a functionally equivalent recognizer that compiles.

Rule return values do not have the same problem because ANTLR can simply avoid generating code that stores a return value. In the regular code, ANTLR generates x=b();. For syntactic predicate fragments, however, ANTLR generates just b();.

In a nutshell, if you use backtracking and parameter passing a lot, you might run into a situation where method arguments result in noncompilable code. In such a situation, recode the arguments as dynamically scoped variables.

Syntactic predicates, introduced more than 15 years ago, have become a well-entrenched bit of parsing technology. Thanks to Bryan Ford, we now have a formal language treatment in the form of PEGs and, most important, the packrat parsing strategy that guarantees linear parse time at the cost of nonlinear memory. ANTLR's implementation of packrat parsing is particularly efficient because it avoids backtracking whenever classical *LL(k)* lookahead or the new *LL(*)* lookahead is capable of distinguishing between alternatives. Moreover, static *LL(*)* grammar analysis provides useful ambiguity warnings that help avoid grammar hazards; this analysis is not available to pure PEG parser generators.

This chapter concludes a long (four-chapter) sequence representing a complete course of study in predicated-*LL(*)* parsing. If you have read and grokked most of this, you are well on your way to becoming a practical parsing and grammar expert. The discussion is short on theory but long on annotated examples because those are more valuable to programmers trying to get their jobs done. At the same time, each chapter contains sufficient details for someone to reimplement the technology in another parser generator. In the interest of friendly competition, I hope that the authors of other parser generators will incorporate hoisted semantic predicates and something akin to *LL(*)* static grammar analysis.

Appendix A

Bibliography

[Cor06]   James R. Cordy. The txl source transformation language. *Sci. Comput. Program.*, 61(3):190–210, 2006.

[ES90]   Margaret A. Ellis and Bjarne Stroustrup. *The annotated C++ reference manual*. Addison-Wesley Longman Publishing Co., Inc., Boston, MA, USA, 1990.

[FHP92]   Christopher W. Fraser, Robert R. Henry, and Todd A. Proebsting. Burg: fast optimal instruction selection and tree parsing. *SIGPLAN Not.*, 27(4):68–76, 1992.

[For02]   Bryan Ford. Packrat parsing:: simple, powerful, lazy, linear time, functional pearl. In *ICFP '02: Proceedings of the seventh ACM SIGPLAN international conference on Functional programming*, pages 36–47, New York, NY, USA, 2002. ACM Press.

[For04]   Bryan Ford. Parsing expression grammars: a recognition-based syntactic foundation. In *POPL '04: Proceedings of the 31st ACM SIGPLAN-SIGACT symposium on Principles of programming languages*, pages 111–122, New York, NY, USA, 2004. ACM Press.

[Gri06]   Robert Grimm. Better extensibility through modular syntax. In *PLDI '06: Proceedings of the 2006 ACM SIGPLAN conference on Programming language design and implementation*, pages 38–51, New York, NY, USA, 2006. ACM Press.

[Gro90]   Josef Grosch. Efficient and comfortable error recovery in recursive descent parsers. *Structured Programming*, 11(3):129–140, 1990.

[Joh79]   Steven C. Johnson. Yacc: Yet another compiler compiler. In *UNIX Programmer's Manual*, volume 2, pages 353–387. Holt, Rinehart, and Winston, New York, NY, USA, 1979.

[Les75]   M.E. Lesk. Lex - a lexical analyzer generator. Technical Report Computing Science Technical Report No.39, Bell Telephone Laboratories, 1975.

[Pin94]   S. Pinker. *The Language Instinct: How the Mind Creates Language*. HarperCollins, New York, 1994.

[Tom87]   Masaru Tomita. An efficient augmented-context-free parsing algorithm. *Comput. Linguist.*, 13(1-2):31–46, 1987.

[Top82]   Rodney W. Topor. A note on error recovery in recursive descent parsers. *SIGPLAN Not.*, 17(2):37–40, 1982.

[TTG94]   J. C. Trueswell, M. K. Tanenhaus, and S. M. Garnsey. Semantic influences on parsing: Use of thematic role information in syntactic ambiguity resolution. *Journal of Memory and Language*, 33(3):285–318, June 1994.

[Wir78]   Niklaus Wirth. *Algorithms + Data Structures = Programs*. Prentice Hall PTR, Upper Saddle River, NJ, USA, 1978.

Index

Pragmatic Projects

Your application is feature complete, but is it ready for the real world? See how to design and deploy production-ready software and *Release It!*.

Have you ever noticed that project retrospectives feel too little, too late? What you need to do is start having *Agile Retrospectives*.

Release It!

Whether it's in Java, .NET, or Ruby on Rails, getting your application ready to ship is only half the battle. Did you design your system to survive a sudden rush of visitors from Digg or Slashdot? Or an influx of real world customers from 100 different countries? Are you ready for a world filled with flakey networks, tangled databases, and impatient users?

If you're a developer and don't want to be on call at 3AM for the rest of your life, this book will help.

Design and Deploy Production-Ready Software
Michael T. Nygard
(368 pages) ISBN: 0-9787392-1-3. $34.95
http://pragmaticprogrammer.com/titles/mnee

Agile Retrospectives

Mine the experience of your software development team continually throughout the life of the project. Rather than waiting until the end of the project—as with a traditional retrospective, when it's too late to help—agile retrospectives help you adjust to change *today*.

The tools and recipes in this book will help you uncover and solve hidden (and not-so-hidden) problems with your technology, your methodology, and those difficult "people issues" on your team.

Agile Retrospectives: Making Good Teams Great
Esther Derby and Diana Larsen
(170 pages) ISBN: 0-9776166-4-9. $29.95
http://pragmaticprogrammer.com/titles/dlret

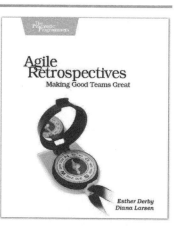

Rails and More

If you know Java, and are curious about Ruby on Rails, you don't have to start from scratch. Read *Rails for Java Developers* and get a head start on this exciting new technology.

And whatever language you use, you'll need a good text editor, too. On the Mac, we recommend TextMate.

Rails for Java Developers

Enterprise Java developers already have most of the skills needed to create Rails applications. They just need a guide which shows how their Java knowledge maps to the Rails world. That's what this book does. It covers: • The Ruby language • Building MVC Applications • Unit and Functional Testing • Security • Project Automation • Configuration • Web Services This book is the fast track for Java programmers who are learning or evaluating Ruby on Rails.

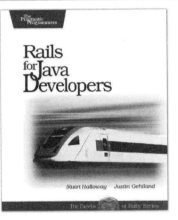

Rails for Java Developers
Stuart Halloway and Justin Gehtland
(300 pages) ISBN: 0-9776166-9-X. $34.95
http://pragmaticprogrammer.com/titles/fr_r4j

TextMate

If you're coding Ruby or Rails on a Mac, then you owe it to yourself to get the TextMate editor. And, once you're using TextMate, you owe it to yourself to pick up this book. It's packed with information which will help you automate all your editing tasks, saving you time to concentrate on the important stuff. Use snippets to insert boilerplate code and refactorings to move stuff around. Learn how to write your own extensions to customize it to the way you work.

TextMate: Power Editing for the Mac
James Edward Gray II
(200 pages) ISBN: 0-9787392-3-X. $29.95
http://pragmaticprogrammer.com/titles/textmate

The Pragmatic Bookshelf

The Pragmatic Bookshelf features books written by developers for developers. The titles continue the well-known Pragmatic Programmer style, and continue to garner awards and rave reviews. As development gets more and more difficult, the Pragmatic Programmers will be there with more titles and products to help you stay on top of your game.

Visit Us Online

The Definitive ANTLR Reference
http://pragmaticprogrammer.com/titles/tpantlr
Source code from this book, errata, and other resources. Come give us feedback, too!

Register for Updates
http://pragmaticprogrammer.com/updates
Be notified when updates and new books become available.

Join the Community
http://pragmaticprogrammer.com/community
Read our weblogs, join our online discussions, participate in our mailing list, interact with our wiki, and benefit from the experience of other Pragmatic Programmers.

New and Noteworthy
http://pragmaticprogrammer.com/news
Check out the latest pragmatic developments in the news.

Save on the PDF

Save on the PDF version of this book. Owning the paper version of this book entitles you to purchase the PDF version at a terrific discount. The PDF is great for carrying around on your laptop. It's hyperlinked, has color, and is fully searchable.

Buy it now at pragmaticprogrammer.com/coupon.

Contact Us

Phone Orders:	1-800-699-PROG (+1 919 847 3884)
Online Orders:	www.pragmaticprogrammer.com/catalog
Customer Service:	orders@pragmaticprogrammer.com
Non-English Versions:	translations@pragmaticprogrammer.com
Pragmatic Teaching:	academic@pragmaticprogrammer.com
Author Proposals:	proposals@pragmaticprogrammer.com